JEWISH SIGHTS
OF BOHEMIA
AND MORAVIA

GUIDE BOOK

JEWISH SIGHTS
OF BOHEMIA
AND MORAVIA

Jiří Fiedler

Introduction by
Arno Pařík

S E F E R
PRAGUE
1991

Print Svoboda, a.s. Prague Czechoslovakia 1991

ISBN 80-900895-0-X

This book was published with the generous assistance of the Doron Foundation
for Education and Welfare.

FROM THE HISTORY OF THE JEWISH COMMUNITIES IN BOHEMIA AND MORAVIA

The history of the Jewish religious communities of Bohemia and Moravia goes back to the early Middle Ages. According to the Raffelstetten customs and navigation regulations from the years 903-06, Jewish merchants appeared in the crownlands towards the end of the 9th century. The records mention Jewish merchants passing through the customs-house on the Danube river, the frontier between the Frankish Empire and the neighbouring Slavic countries. Prague was most likely to be their first stop, lying in the heart of the country and being the seat of the prince and an ancient crossroad of important trade routes. The presence of Jewish merchants in Prague is mentioned in the report of the Arab-Jewish merchant and diplomat Ibrahim ibn Jacob dating from 965-66, when a Jewish settlement grew most probably close to the marketplace beyond Prague Castle. Jewish merchants in Prague in the late 10th century are also mentioned in the biographies of the Prague Bishop St. Adalbert. In the second half of the 11th century King Vratislav transferred his seat to Vyšehrad where another Jewish settlement was recorded in 1091. This settlement is said to have vanished during a period of anti-Jewish riots related to the first crusade in 1096-98. The existence of a Jewish settlement is mentioned again in the first half of the 12th century on the left bank of the Vltava river in Malá Strana, below Prague Castle. Apart from the two above mentioned

Jewish settlements another one grew up not later than the second half of the 12th century. It was situated on the right bank of the Vltava river, near an international marketplace and along the road connecting the oldest Prague fords. Other foreign merchants had settled in this region and their settlements played an important role during the reign of Wenceslas I (1230-53) when this agglomeration changed into the Old Town of Prague. Within the walls of the Old Town were the newly founded settlement of St. Havel, two early marketplaces near the Old Town Square, the settlements of foreign merchants surrounding the square and the Jewish settlement lying north-west of the square. In the following centuries this Jewish settlement grew and became an independent Jewish Town, gradually separated from the rest of the town by a wall and six gates and enjoying autonomy in its social, political and legal affairs. The extraordinary importance of the Prague Jewish community rested not only in its size and cultural and material wealth but above all in the fact that up to the mid-17th century the Prague Jewish community represented all the Jewish communities in Bohemia in relation to the sovereign and the government.

Jews formed a fairly independent entity in the Middle Ages, according to records referring to the changes in location of early Jewish settlements in the territory of Prague. In those days Jews enjoyed the same legally guaranteed rights and princes' privileges as Roman and German merchants. The earliest regulation of the legal status of foreign merchants is included in the charters granted by Prince Soběslav II from 1174-78 which reaffirmed an earlier charter from 1092. Jews were granted permission to settle freely in walled homesteads along trade routes or near marketplaces, the communities enjoyed absolute interior autonomy and were free to trade and practise crafts. Jews in Bohemia traded mainly in furs, corn, wool, wax, tin and cloth but also in cattle, horses and slaves. Jewish merchants imported exotic goods, luxury fabrics, jewels, arms, salt, wine and oriental herbs. Some Jews were active as physicians or as officials at the royal court, such as Jacob Apella during the reign of Vladislav I (1120-25) or Žid Podiva (the Jew Podiva), founder of the Moravian castle Podivín.

The Jewish community in Prague represented a significant cultural centre as early as the turn of 12th and 13th centuries. The earliest preserved Hebrew manuscript in Prague is the 12th-century commentary on the Talmudic tractate by Isaac ben Jacob, also known as ha-Lavan. His disciple Abraham ben Azriel, known as Chládek, became one of the leading personalities of the Prague Jewish community and is known as the author of the analysis of the synagogical liturgy "Aruchat ha-bosem"(Flower-bed of Balsam) from the early 13th century. Chládek's disciple was most probably Isaac ben Moses, known after his principal work also as Isaac Or Zaru'a, who having spent several years in communities in Rhineland returned to Prague and died about 1250 in Vienna. His extensive work "Or Zaru'a" (Light Diffused), a commentary on Talmudic ritual laws, has been quoted and imitated in Germany, Poland and Italy and the shortened version written by his son became extremely popular with Jews throughout the whole of Europe. Both Abraham Chládek and his disciple Isaac Or Zaru'a used Old Czech to explain difficult Hebrew terms. Both scholars must have spoken the language well and Or Zaru'a referred to Old Czech as "our language" or "the language we speak" which proves that Jews in Bohemia during the reign of the Přemyslid dynasty used the language to make themselves understood.

The situation of the formerly almost free Jews considerably worsened in the late 11th century after a number of anti-Jewish riots which swept the country in connection with the first crusade in Rhineland in 1096-99 and affected Prague in 1096. When the Jews of Prague were getting ready to leave the country for fear of further pogroms and settle in neighbouring Hungary or Poland, Prince Břetislav II (1092-1100) had their property forcibly confiscated. The persecution of Jews was repeated during all the following crusades of the 12th century. The burden of discriminatory legislation worsened in 1215 following the Fourth Lateran Council, which prohibited Jews from holding land, dealing in agriculture and practising crafts and reduced their activities to money lending while limiting the rates of interest Jews could charge on loans, since Christians had been prohibited to practise usury by the Church. Other laws enacted by the Council strongly restricted relations between Jews and Christians, ordered Jews to settle in enclosed quarters and mandated distinctive Jewish dress or other defamatory indications of Jewishness. The Church solved the position of Jews within Christian society by means of the so-called theory of "the testimonial people" to acknowledge the truth of the events in biblical history. The inferior status of Jews was supposed to demonstrate repudiation as a consequence of their crucifixion of Jesus Christ. These church regulations resulted in the almost entire economic and social segregation of Jews and encouraged the rise of numerous anti-Jewish stories, such as the belief that Jews are to blame for the death of Jesus Christ and accusations concerning the desecration of the Host. Rumours about ritual murders also resulted in a number of pogroms and anti-Jewish outrages in the period of the mid and late Middle Ages. Deprived of all rights and forced to exist on the margin of society, Jews became completely dependent on the will of the nobility who regarded them as their property and servants. The nobility granted the Jews permission to settle in the country and promised temporary and often only formal legal protection in exchange for high taxes and special monetary payments which often represented the lordship's steadiest source of income.

Repeated persecution for religious reasons on the one hand and the increasing demands on their financial means imposed by the nobility in the 13th century on the other brought forth an urgent need for an improvement in the legal status. In view of this situation Friedrich II granted special privileges to Austrian Jews in 1244, Pope Innocent IV issued a bull for the protection of Jews in 1247 and 1253 and Bella IV granted Hungarian Jewry privileges in 1251. Consequently, King Přemysl Ota-

Jews with period Jewish hats
(Passional of Abbess Kunhuta, 1320)

7

kar II (1253-78) issued on March 29, 1254 substantial amendments regarding the legal position of Jews in the Bohemian Crownlands. For the first time in history the legal position of Jews in society was determined - Jews were subject to the king who became responsible for their protection and granted them permission to trade and practise money-lending and pawnbroking. Any kind of violence against Jews or their property was prohibited, accusations of Jews using human blood for ritual purposes were denounced, baptism of Jews by force was prohibited and so were any forms of disturbances of Jewish

Statuta Judaeorum, privileges granted
by Přemysl Otakar II, reaffirmed by Charles IV
(manuscript from 1357)

8

holidays and desecration of their cemeteries and synagogues. Violence against Jews was to be regarded as damage of royal property and was therefore to be punished. Jewish communities were promised freedom to practise their religion, were to be granted substantial independence in running their internal affairs and were to be allowed to establish their own self-government and judiciary. A royal "Jewish-judge" was appointed for lawsuits between Jews and Christians. In exchange for the promised protection and privileges Jewish communities were obliged to pay the king high annual taxes and if necessary to provide special monetary payments and loans. Přemysl Otakar II reaffirmed and extended the privileges in 1268 for the Jewish community in Brno.

The Royal Charter of Přemysl Otakar II legalized the status of Jews in Bohemia and Moravia for a long period of time and was reaffirmed in principle by the following sovereigns. However, the following facts show how the rights of Jews were ignored even by the sovereign himself. In 1296 Wenceslas II (1278-1305), successor to Přemysl Otakar II, seized the Jews of Prague and rural Jews under the pretext of their protection and released them only after they had paid a ransom. Similarly, in 1336 John Luxembourg (1310-46) had the Jews of Prague imprisoned and seized a considerable part of Jewish property in the ghetto. When Charles IV (1347-78) ascended the throne as the first Bohemian king he made the Jews servants of the Royal Chamber (servi camerae) and in 1356 reaffirmed the privileges which Jews had been granted by Přemysl Otakar II. However, during his reign Charles IV often settled his debts at the expense of Jews by cancelling their bonds or by putting them in pawn of imperial towns which often meant exposing them to immediate danger and usually resulted in pogroms. Wenceslas IV (1378-1419) implemented this practice to an even larger extent by cancelling Jewish bonds in a number of royal cities in 1385 and by having Bohemian Jews imprisoned and consequently confiscating their property. In 1390 Wenceslas IV exempted Christian debtors throughout the whole empire from compound interest payment. Similarly, in Moravia margrave Jošt had all the wealthy Jews imprisoned in 1394 and demanded ransom. In 1411 all Jewish bonds older than 10 years were cancelled in Moravia. Fourteenth century Germany witnessed numerous anti-Jewish riots which also spread to the Bohemian Crownlands. Pogroms broke out in Čáslav and Jindřichův Hradec in 1337 and also in Kouřim, Jemnice, Třebíč and Znojmo in 1338 as result of alleged desecration of the Host. The most serious persecution of Jews in German towns came in 1348-49 when Jews were accused of having caused a plague epidemic. At the time many Jews fled from Germany to Bohemia and Moravia, where only two major pogroms occurred - one in Vratislav in 1349 and one a year later in Cheb. The worst medieval pogrom in Bohemia broke out in Prague in 1389 during Easter which fell on the last two days of Passover that year. Members of the Prague clergy had spread stories of Jewish blasphemy and desecration of the Host and thus encouraged numerous angry mobs to ransack and loot the Jewish quarter. About three thousand Jews, including children, women and old people, were murdered. Among the few who survived the massacre was the poet and later Rabbi Avigdor Kara, who witnessed the massacre and captured the anguish of the Jewish community in an elegy which is recited every year by the Jews of Prague in the Altneuschul on Yom Kippur, the Day of Atonement. In his effort to revive the Prague Jewish community Wenceslas IV reaffirmed in 1393 the charter granted by Přemysl Otakar II and ordered that all disputed questions between Jews and their debtors be henceforward settled before the Royal Court.

The government policy that rendered the Jews servants of the royal chamber did not go unchallenged for long. A considerable decline in royal authority and loss of control over Jewish matters occurred during the Hussite wars 1419-1437 which resulted in a new political balance favouring the nobility in the countryside and the burgher estate in the independent towns and weakening the power of the Catholic church and the king. The Catholics declared the Hussites a Judaizing sect and Hussites themselves, namely the radical wing in Tábor, identified themselves to a considerable extent with Biblical Israel. Jews sympathized with the Hussites in their fight against the Catholic church and German crusaders, e.g. in 1420 they helped them to build fortifications against Vyšehrad and supported them financially, including the imports of arms. Rabbis also expressed their sympathy with the Hussite movement and the Prague Rabbi Avigdor Kara (died in 1439) is said to have had a certain influence on the movement itself, which seemed to correspond with the messianic hopes of Judaism. The Hussite revolution also loosened feudal social bonds and for a certain period freed Jews from some restrictions on occupations, enabling them to practise various crafts. The Hussite theologian Jakoubek of Stříbro (about 1379-1429) believed that Jews turned to money lending as a result of the social discrimination directed against them and he suggested they should be allowed to practise various crafts and to engage in agriculture. Despite the above mentioned facts concerning from support of the Hussites, anti-Jewish riots occurred in Prague again in 1421 and 1422 and after the Hussites had besieged the town of Chomutov in 1421 they inflicted heavy casualties on both the Jews and Catholics. On the other hand, for having collaborated with the Hussites many Jews were expelled from Austria (1421), Bavaria (1422), Jihlava (1426), Cheb (1430) and Most (1456).

The independence of towns was increasing and the burgher population began to assume many banking and commercial functions that previously

Burning of Jews to death alive,
woodcut from Schedel's Chronicle of the World
(Nuremberg, 1493)

*Kiddush - the prayer over wine and a loaf of bread
that sanctifies the Sabbath and Jewish holy days (Seder Zemiroth u-Birkath ha-Mazon,
the second oldest Hebrew print in Prague, 1514)*

had been performed almost exclusively by Jews. As a consequence of the growing competition in the mid-15th century many German and Austrian towns rose up to expel their Jewish populations. The Minorite priest Jan Kapistrán encouraged a wave of violence against the Jewish population in Silesia which was followed by the expulsion of Jews from Wroclaw, Swidnice, Strzegom and Jawor in 1453. After several earlier attempts the Jewish population of Opava was expelled from the town in 1522. In 1454 Jews were expelled from the Moravian royal cities - Brno, Olomouc, Znojmo and Uničov; in Uherské Hradiště Jews were assigned to the town and expelled only in 1514. The expelled groups of Jews settled where possible in small towns throughout the countryside or were concentrated on estates where they found relative safety and freedom to practise trade and crafts. The period of the weak reign of Vladislav Jagellon (1471-1516) was marked by constant disputes between the sovereign, nobility and burghers over the control of Jewish affairs. Many Jews still remained under the admini-stration of the nobility or burghers, however, they often had to pay both the aldermen and the nobility as well as the king for their protection. In 1499 the king again reserved the right of controlling Jewish affairs and in 1501 the Bohemian Landtag reaffirmed the ancient privileges of Jews and granted them permission to settle in the countries of the Bohemian Crownlands forever, stating that no one had the right to expel them from the countries. Nevertheless, in the following years burghers of many royal towns, often after repeated requests, received consent to expel their Jewish inhabitants. Consequently, the Jews were expelled from Cheb (1497), Karlovy Vary (1499), from Pilsen and the small town of Hostouň (1504), from Jihlava again in 1506, the Jews were expelled under tragic circumstances from České Budějovice in 1505-6, from Louny (1508), Chomutov (1517) and also from Kadaň, Loket, Strakonice and Český Krumlov. Although the Jews of Prague paid great sums of money to the city's treasury the Old Town aldermen repeatedly in 1507 and 1509 demanded their expulsion from the whole country. However, in 1510, the king issued an edict in Olomouc reaffirming the right of Jews to stay in the country.

When Ferdinand I (1526-64) ascended the throne the Czech lands became part of the Habsburg domains and it seemed that royal power would be strengthened and thus also the hitherto insecure position of Jews. As soon as Ferdinand I ascended the throne he reaffirmed all the Jewish privileges and promised he would protect their rights. In 1527 he established in Prague the so-called Bohemian Chamber which was in charge of all financial matters throughout the whole kingdom and which also aimed at maintaining a regular flow of Jewish income-taxes. Ferdinand I endeavoured to regain control of Jewish affairs and thus entered into a controversy with the nobility and burghers who had repeatedly demanded the expulsion of Jews. Jews were accused of smuggling silver out of the country, of collaborating with the - Turks during the war as spies, of starting fires and of encouraging the foundation of Judaistic sects in Bohemia. Finally, all the above mentioned accusations resulted in Ferdinand I's decision to a expel the Jews from the kingdom in 1541. The expulsion order gave rise to a wave of violent looting and pogroms in a number of towns, e.g.

in Litoměřice, Nymburk, Roudnice, Žatec. The emperor postponed the deadline of the expulsion order twice, however, in 1543 most Jews had to leave the Bohemian royal cities. The majority of Jews decided to move to Poland but despite royal protection they were often held up and robbed on their way. Only a few Jewish families were granted permission to stay in Prague to settle the remaining affairs of the community. Only in 1545 was a safe-conduct issued temporarily cancelling the expulsion order. In 1551 Ferdinand I ordered the Jews to wear a yellow circle on their clothes and in 1557 demanded a new expulsion order. The deadline of their departure was again postponed under the pressure of different intercessions and new safe-conducts were issued, however, the Jews were being robbed again and killed at the frontiers. This time the expulsion order was cancelled in 1563 only after Pope Pius IV had released the emperor from his promise to expel the Jews from the country.

After the death of Ferdinand I in 1564 and after a long period of hardship and insecurity Jewish communities in Bohemia and, especially in Prague, began to witness their greatest period of economic and cultural prosperity. Maxmillian II (1564-76) reaffirmed the Jewish privileges in 1567 and issued an

Jewish oath at the municipal court
(Prague, 16th cent.)

12

*Emperor and King Rudolph II
(1576-1612)*

Imperial Charter granting liberty of trade and business to the Jews and promising they would not be ordered to leave the kingdom in future. However, Jews were not allowed to enter or settle in any of the mining-towns which caused hardship to several communities. In 1571 Emperor Maxmillian visited the Prague Jewish Town with his wife and courtiers and received the rabbi's blessing. Rudolph II (1576 -1611) transferred his seat to Prague and soon a number of outstanding scientists, diplomats, artists as well as astrologers and alchemists concentrated at the court of this eccentric but tolerant and art-loving emperor. In 1577, Rudolph II also reaffirmed the Jewish privileges, which had been granted by his predecessors, and assured the Jews that they would not be expelled from Prague or the Bohemian Crownlands. During his discord with the burghers of the Old Town Rudolph II confirmed that the Jews came under the authority of the imperial judge. The emperor also took the Jewish community under his protection in 1593 and 1602 after complaints voiced by the guilds of the Old Town of Prague. In 1599 he freed the Jewish community from paying cus-

tom-duty and toll in all parts of Prague. Under the rule of Rudolph II the Prague Jewish community gained its autonomy again, life in the ghetto began to change rapidly with the development of trade, money-lending and crafts, while one sign of vitality was the quick growth in population. Rudolph's successor Matthias (1611-19) also favoured the Jewish community and also reaffirmed all the ancient privileges in 1611.

Life in the Prague Jewish Town benefitted during the Renaissance from the presence of many outstanding personalities - prominent thinkers and scholars as well as wealthy bankers and sponsors of the ghetto. In the early 16th century one of the most influential families in the Prague Jewish community was the Horowitz family. Jesaia Halevi Horowitz (died in 1519) was well-known as a Maecenas of the earliest Hebrew prints published in Prague and his son Aaron Mesullam Horowitz (died in 1545) was the builder of the magnificent Pinkas synagogue in Prague. The first Hebrew press north of the Alps was established in Prague in 1512 and its earliest prints established a reputation for excellent typography and ornamentation. The Hebrew press in Prague operated until the early 17th century and had a strong influence on the foundation of Hebrew presses in other towns in Central Europe. The first burial society, which became an important social organization in the ghetto, was formed in Prague by Rabbi Eleazar Ashkenazi (died in 1586) in 1564. The representative of the Jewish Town in the period of Renaissance was its mayor Marcus Mordecai Maisel (1528-1601), financier of emperor Rudolph II, who was responsible for the building of the Jewish Town Hall, the High and Maisel synagogues and the foundation of the Prague yeshivah and hospital. However, the most outstanding personality of the community's spiritual life was Judah ben Bezalel (1512-1609), better known in Jewish tradition as Rabbi Loew or Maharal, who officiated as Landesrabbiner of Moravia in Mikulov (Nikolsburg) in 1553-73 but devoted most of the remaining years of his life to serving the Jewish community in Prague where he became rector at the Talmudic academy which gained prominence during his time. Šelomo Efraim of Lenczyce (died in 1619) became Chief Rabbi of Prague after Rabbi Loew and was followed later by Rabbi Yom Tov Lipmann Heller Wallerstein (died in 1654) who is regarded as one of the most significant followers of Rabbi Loew and became famous for his excellent commentary on the Mishnah. The person who loomed largest over the scientific activities of Prague Jewry was the mathematician, astronomer and first modern Jewish chronicler David Gans (1541-1613), who was also in contact with the prominent scholars at the court of Rudolph II. Another interesting personality was the physician, philosopher and astronomer Joseph Delmedigo (1591-1655), disciple of Galileo Galilei at the university of Padua, who spent the last years of his life in Prague.

At the beginning of the revolt of the Protestant Czech Estates in 1618 the urban poor attacked the Jewish Town of Prague and the following year the inhabitants of the Old Town rose up to demand the expulsion of the Jews. The Jewish community did not take part in the revolt and after the Battle of the White Mountain in 1620 the Jews were exempted from persecution by the Imperial forces. However, Ferdinand II (1620-37) made them pledge themselves to support his military campaign with a loan of 240,000 ducats and shortly afterwards came an extraordinary increase of annual taxation. The representative of the Prague Jewish community in those days was the financier Jacob Bassewi (1580-1634), originally an Italian, who was he first Jew to be ennobled (in 1622) and was given the title of Treuenberg in return for having supported the emperor financially. In the following years he became a member of the coiners' association, headed by Prince Charles of Lichtenstein, that was in charge of the devaluation of currency so as to gain means to purchase the confiscated property of those who had participated in the revolt of the Czech estates. Despite the protest of the Old Town burghers, the Jewish community with the help of Jacob Bassewi and Charles Lichtenstein managed to purchase 39 adjacent buildings which represented the greatest enlargement of the ghetto up to that time. Since the imperial government was in desperate need of Jewish financial support, Ferdinand II renewed and extended the privileges of the Jews in Bohemia in 1623, including their rights to practise trade freely and sell their goods throughout the whole country. They were also exempted from paying custom-duty and tolls in all parts of Prague and were given permission to strengthen the legal force of the Jewish Elders and the Royal Jewish Judge to the detriment of the municipal court's jurisdiction. At the beginning of the Thirty Years' War Jewish taxes fluctuated and were supplemented by demands for large loans. Therefore the Council of Jewish Elders and the Bohemian Chamber agreed to increase the annual contributions to 40,000 ducats in Bohemia and 12,000 ducats in Moravia. On account of this agreement Ferdinand II further extended the privileges of Jews in the field of economy. They were allowed to attend all the markets throughout the whole country having equal rights as Christian merchants and they were free to learn and practise almost all crafts. The financial situation of Bohemian Jewry fluctuated during the war as Jews were obliged to pay higher taxes and extraordinary monetary payments to support the military campaign and, finally, the plague that broke out in the Jewish Town in 1639 together with the negative effects of the war on trade brought the Jewish community to the verge of financial exhaustion. Ferdinand III (1637-57) issued a decree in 1642 whereby Jews were not to be expelled from the country without his consent. In 1648 the Jews of Prague participated in the defense of the city against the Swedes who had besieged Hradčany and Malá Strana. In recognition of their bravery and help in the construction of fortification walls and the extinguishing of fires, Ferdinand III granted the Jews permission to build a small belfry onto the Jewish Town Hall and presented the Jewish community with a flag with a Swedish cap in the middle of the Star of David, which became the official emblem of the Prague community. After the conclusion of peace in Westphalia in 1648 the emperor granted the Jewish community, in recognition of their financial support, a privilege which constituted for a long period the legal status of Jews in the Bohemian Crownlands. According to this Imperial Charter the Jews were permitted to stay wherever they had settled and were not to be expelled without the emperor's consent. They were allowed to practise all trades and crafts (with the exception of manufacturing arms) and were free to set up their own shops and stalls on squares and marketplaces. Several other laws were also changed to the benefit of Jewry.

The hardship caused by the Thirty Years' War and the impact of high taxation resulted also in a considerable decrease in the Jewish populations both in Bohemia and Moravia. However, after the war the number of Jews increased since Bohemia had absorbed many refugees from Poland and the Ukraine in the aftermath of the Chmielnicki massacres of 1648-49, the Cossak-led assault on hundreds of Jewish communities over the course of the Ukraine's uprising against Polish overlordship. Contrary to the privileges spe lled out in the Imperial Charter, the Bohemian Diet decided in 1650 to curtail the number of Jews permitted to reside in Bohemia and restricted their residence to places where Jews had been allowed to live before 1618 or where they had settled according to special Imperial permission. Despite the fact that the emperor opposed this decision by issuing a rescript in 1652, many towns demanded the expulsion of Jews with reference to the decision of the Bohemian Diet. Thus Jews were expelled e.g. from Kadaň (1650), Hradec Králové (1652), Tábor (1662),

Pardubice (1663), Teplice (1667), Týn nad Vltavou (1684), Planá (1686) and Česká Skalice (1705). Despite the efforts to curtail the size of the Jewish population, new refugees came to the country in the following years. When the war against the Turks broke out in 1663 the Jewish community again had to bear the burden of increased taxation and extraordinary monetary payments while new refugees were pouring into the country from Hungary and Poland. Moreover, after the expulsion of Jews from Vienna in 1670 a large number of refugees found shelter in Jewish rural communities in Bohemia and Moravia. The awful plague epidemic of 1680 which claimed 3,500 lives in the Prague ghetto alone put an end to the measures to limit the growth of the Jewish population in the country. Another disaster came on June 21, 1689 when a great fire broke out in the Old Town destroying much of the ghetto - 318 houses and 11 synagogues burnt down and 150 people perished in the flames. After the fire the authorities aimed at limiting the area of the Jewish Town and suggestions were put forward that the Jews of Prague should reside beyond the city in Libeň or Štvanice. However the support of the Bohemian Chamber and the financial aid that had come from Jewish communities abroad enabled a rapid reconstruction of the ghetto. In 1694 shortly after the fire, the Jewish community of Prague was shaken by the propagandist show-trial of the alleged murderers of a twelve-year-old convert Simon Abeles, which represented the culmination of the efforts of the Jesuits to Christianize the Jews.

Despite the above-mentioned hardships and disasters which had inflicted heavy casualties, the population of the Prague Jewish Town grew from 6,000 in the early 17th century to about 11,500 by the end of the century, making the Prague Jewish community most probably the largest Jewish community in the world. Although it is somewhat more difficult to ascertain the precise Jewish population in the countryside at this time there is no doubt that there

Story of Simon Abeles
(leaflet from 1694)

was a similar rapid growth in population and by the mid-17th century the number must have surpassed the number of Jews in the Prague ghetto. Towards the end of the century the number of Jews living outside Prague formed over two thirds of the total number of Jews in the countries of the Bohemian Crownlands. In consequence of the shift in the demographic balance between the city and the countryside the rural Jewry demanded independent representation from the Prague community. Subsequently, in 1659 the Böhmische Landesjudenschaft achieved formal recognition as an independent entity with the right of independent representation and the right of collecting and distributing Jewish tax revenue. The Böhmische Landesjudenschaft had the right to take action in legal matters and questions concerning religion and marriage. Aaron Spira Wedeles (1600-1679) became the first Landesrabbiner and also represented the Jewish community of Prague. He was followed by Abraham Broda (1640-1717). In 1691 the realms of the Landesrabbiner were divided in two, one remaining under Broda's jurisdiction and the other given to the chief justice of the Prague Rabbinical Court, Wolf Spiro Wedeles (1640-1715). The two rabbinical posts were united in the early 18th century under the leadership of Rabbi David Oppenheim (1664-1736), who had officiated as Landesrabbiner of Moravia in Mikulov since 1689 before being named Chief Rabbi of Prague in 1702. He assumed the two provincial rabbinical posts in 1713 and 1715. Already during Oppenheim's lifetime district rabbis were appointed, eventually making the function of the Landesrabbiner obsolete - the position was abolished in 1749. David Oppenheim became also famous as an enthusiastic collector of old Hebrew manuscripts and prints. His collection comprised about 7,000 volumes and in 1829 they became a part of the Bodleian Library in Oxford.

In Moravia, where Jews had been expelled from royal cities as early as the mid-15th century and had settled in small towns, there originated no centre of Jewish autonomy similar to Prague in Bohemia. Perhaps this is the reason why at the end of the 15th century individual Jewish communities united to create their own autonomous representative body, whose main function was to collect and distribute tax monies, to represent Jewish interests to the government and to engage in the legislation of Jewish communities. The Landesrabbiner, whose seat was in Mikulov, had the right of jurisdiction on both religious and secular affairs. He was in charge of the Small Council, consisting of six members, with two members representing each of the three Moravian provinces, who used to meet once a year and the Great Legislative Council, whose members used to meet every three years in a different community. The last meeting took place in 1748 and 61 representatives elected by 367 house owners took part in it. The preserved collection of laws of the Moravian Jewish Council from the years 1650-1748 represents one of the most significant documents showing

the self-government of Jewish communities in Central Europe at that time. Many outstanding personalities held the position of Landesrabbiner of Moravia - let us mention, e.g. Judah Loew ben Bezalel (1553-73), Rabbi Tov Lippman Heller Wallerstein (1625-26), Rabbi Menachem Krochmal (1648-61), who officiated as rabbi in Kroměříž from 1636 and from 1648 in Prostějov, author of the significant work "Tzemech Zedek". Then came Rabbi David Oppenheim (1690-1702) and at the same time Rabbi Gabriel ben Jehuda Löb Eskeles (1690-1718) was appointed. After his death his son Issachar Berusch Eskeles (1718-53) officiated as Landesrabbiner of Moravia and gained recognition for having the expulsion order in 1744 cancelled. The well-known mystic and cabalist Rabbi Samuel Schmelke Horowitz also officiated as Landesrabbiner in Mikulov from 1772 to 1778. One of the most famous rabbis in Moravia was Shabtai ben Meir Kohen, called Shach, who came from Poland and officiated as rabbi in Holešov from 1648 to 1663. Besides Mikulov (Nikolsburg) important centers of education were to be found in Boskovice, Kroměříž, Prostějov, Uherský Brod and Lipník nad Bečvou.

Under the rule of Charles VI (1711-40) the efforts to control and curtail the number of Jews continued. For this reason the first detailed census of the Jewish population was taken in 1724. In Bohemia the number of Jews living outside Prague reached 30,000 in 168 towns and small towns and in 672 villages while in Moravia the number was 20,000. In Prague the census was not taken until 1729 and indicated that there were 2,335 Jewish families in Prague and a total of 10,507 Jews. Of the 2,335 "gainfully employed" Jews in Prague, more than 700 were listed as artisans - these included 158 tailors, 100 shoemakers, 39 hatmakers, 20 goldsmiths, 37 butchers, 28 barbers and bath attendants and 15 musicians. Similarly, in provincial Bohemia 19% of the Jewish families practised trades and crafts and an additional 13% worked as

*Primus of the Jewish Town of Prague Israel Frankl Spira
in a ceremonial parade commemorating the birth of
Prince Joseph in 1741*

leasers of distilleries, tanneries, carriages or as innkeepers. After the census had been taken, in 1726 a fixed number of Jewish families was set - 8,541 in Bohemia and 5,106 in Moravia. In order to maintain this numerus clausus in the countryside the so-called "family law" was issued in 1727 according to which only the eldest son of every family was permitted to marry. For a long period of time this law hindered the growth of the Jewish population in the country. Families which had only daughters were regarded as predetermined to die out and second sons who wanted to get married had to leave the country. In those days many younger Jews moved to Poland and to western Slovakia. In 1789 Joseph II granted permission to slightly increase the number of Jewish families allowed to reside in the country - 8,600 families in Bohemia and 5,400 in Moravia. In addition, Jews working in agriculture or as artisans were given an opportunity to apply for special permission to start a family irrespective of the fixed number. The law that limited the number of Jewish families in the country remained in effect right up until 1849. The life of Jewish communities was also strongly affected by the so-called Translocation Rescript of 1727 by which Jews in all towns and villages were to be concentrated again in enclosed quarters far from churches, squares and places where Christian religious festivals took place.

The Silesian wars, which broke out after the accession of Maria Theresa (1740-80) to the throne, entailed tragic consequences for all Jewish communities in the Bohemian Crownlands, especially Prague. On December 18, 1744 Maria Theresa issued a decree stating that the presence of Jews in the kingdom should no longer be tolerated since Jews had allegedly supported the Prussian army in their attempt to besiege Prague in September 1744. All the Jews of Prague were supposed to leave the city by January 1745 and the whole territory of Bohemia by the end of June. On January 2, 1745 Jews were expelled from Moravia and Silesia. Despite all the interpellation of the Bohemian governorship, court-office and the estates as well as all the pro-

Expulsion of Jews from Prague in 1745

19

tests of ambassadors of England, the Netherlands, Denmark and Turkey, the empress did not cancel her decision but only postponed the deadline of the expulsion order to the end of February because of the severe winter that year and, finally, to the end of March. All Jews, with the exception of the seriously sick, were ordered to leave Prague by March 31, 1745. Some of the Jews settled in Libeň, at Židovské pece near Olšany, in Holešovice, Košíře, Brandýs and Čelákovice or they dispersed throughout the country and settled wherever they got the chance. In May Maria Theresa issued temporary permission for Jews to stay in the country and allowed them to return to the ghetto over the winter. However, in Spring 1746 she reaffirmed the expulsion order for the Jews of Prague and its vicinity and Jews were given 6 years to move out of the country completely, being allowed in the meantime to reside in the countryside only. The absence of Jewish merchants and craftsmen in Prague had a strong impact which was reflected in the market and lack of raw material and consequently in an increase of prices and a drop in taxation revenue. In September 1747 representatives of all the guilds of Prague demanded to be heard as most guilds began to feel the loss of Jewish customers and suppliers. Meanwhile, the Jewish Town, which had been left without protection, was being devastated and wrecked by the urban poor. Eventually, in July 1748, the situation brought Maria Theresa to prolong the residence permission for another 10 years and she allowed the Jews to return to Prague in August. A total of 6,061 Jews (1,418 Jewish families) re-settled in Prague by October 1749. However, in return for the residence permit the empress imposed upon the Jewry of the Bohemian Crownlands the so-called toleration tax amounting to 204,000 ducats a year, which was more than ten times the taxes from the year 1723. Every five years the taxes were increased and finally reached the sum of 300,000 ducats. Constantly increasing taxation and another devastating fire which swept through the ghetto in

Fire of the Prague ghetto in 1754
(an anti-Semitic leaflet)

1754, destroying 190 houses and 6 synagogues, resulted in the ghetto going deeply into debt and being incapable of regaining its former economic prosperity.

Although Jewish society was influenced in many ways in the past by the outside world, the Jewish communities represented autonomous administrative and social entities right up until the late 18th century. Communal life was subject to special territorial laws and rules, however, inside the community the Jews enjoyed judicial autonomy and the community operated within the confines of the languages spoken by the Jews, maintaining for centuries unchanged traditional attitudes and beliefs. The Enlightenment and Joseph II's (1780-90) accession to the throne in 1780 produced crucial changes in the structure of the entire society. Developments in trade, new forms of production together with legal and social reforms began to create conditions which encouraged Jews to participate in the economic and cultural life of society in general. The Edict of Toleration, issued on October 13, 1781, not only affirmed the principle of religious toleration for Protestants and Orthodox Christians as well for Jews, but also cancelled the obligation for the Jewish people to wear distinctive dress and, especially, enabled Jews to engage fully in all forms of trade and commerce, artisanal production and agriculture and encouraged them to establish factories. The most far-reaching changes occasioned by the Edict of Toleration took place in the educational sphere with the doors of all types of local schools and institutes of higher education being opened for Jewish enrollment. The government invited all of the Jewish communities to set up schools of their own to instruct students in mathematics, German language, geography and morality. Five years after the project was begun a report claimed that 559 children were attending 25 newly established rural Jewish schools and another 278 Jewish children had enrolled in Christian schools in over fifty different localities. The aim of the

"On the Uselessness and Harmfulness of Jews" - front page of a pamphlet against the Edict of Toleration (Prague, 1782)

government to introduce the German language into all the spheres of administration brought forth an order according to which communal and business records were to be kept in German only and in 1787 Jews were ordered to change their first names and surnames, being offered a choice of 109 permitted German male names and 35 female names. The new laws encouraged the assimilation of Jews on the one hand but restricted considerably the traditional autonomy of Jewish communities on the other. In 1783 all Jews were subject to general public justice and the judicial autonomy of the Jewish community was abolished in 1784. Rabbinical courts were free to engage only in religious affairs and marital law. The numerus clausus concerning the number of Jewish families permitted to reside in the country as well as the demographic restrictions and demands for special Jewish taxation

seph II's reforms were summed up and supplemented by the Jewish Systemic Decree, issued on August 3, 1797: the decree restricted their residence to places where Jews had been allowed to live before 1725; Jews were free to learn and practise all kinds of trades and crafts with the exception of working as leasers of distilleries and mills or as innkeepers; Jews were free to ask for special permission to build synagogues and prayer halls. Compulsory attendance of German elementary school was required and became one of the preconditions for marriage. Only men who had graduated from a local university having studied philosophy, law and ethics were qualified to become rabbis. In 1799 Jewish taxation in Bohemia was fixed at 216,000 ducats.

Despite the growing influence of Enlightenment in the Czech lands Judaism remained until the early 19th century under the influence of traditional rabbinical Orthodoxy. The Chief Rabbi of Prague and rosh yeshiva Ezekiel Landau (1713-1793), author of a famous collection of halakhist responses "Noda bi-yehudah" and his successor and disciple Eleazar Fleckeles (1754-1826) provided decidedly conservative leadership to the Prague community. One of the leading adherents of Orthodox Judaism in Moravia was Samuel Kolin (died in 1806), rosh yeshivah at the Talmudic academy in Boskovice and author of the famous collection of commentaries "Machazit ha-Schekel" and also Chatam Moses Sepher (1762-1839), an opponent of the Enlightenment movement, who was influenced by Hasidism and had worked in Prostějov and Strážnice before establishing his career as rosh yeshivah of the famous Talmudic academy in Bratislava. Supporters of Orthodox Judaism often clashed with adherents of Joseph II's reforms and the Enlightenment movement, who aimed at introducing universal education and religious reforms as means of achieving the cultural, economic and social emancipation of Jews. The two leading personalities supporting the Enlightenment

movement in Prague were Herz Homberg (1749-1841), whose main aim was to establish Jewish elementary schools in Bohemia and Peter Beer (1758-1838), the author of works on history and ethics and teacher at the Prague Jewish school. The brothers Baruch (1762-1813) and Judah (1773-1838) Jaiteles belonged among the conservative supporters of the Enlightenment and emancipation. Reform services were held for the first time in the Altschul in Prague in the 1830s. Also Moses Landau (1788-1852) gained recognition for supporting the Englightenment movement among the Jews by publishing a number of educational and popular books. A central figure of the Englightenment was the Chief Rabbi of Prague Solomon Judah Rapoport (1790-1867), founding father of the new science of Judaism who elaborated a collection of biographies of prominent rabbis and engaged in the historical-critical research of lesser-known periods in the history of Jewry. The Landesrabbiner of Moravia Mordecai Benet (1793-1829), who officiated in Mikulov for 40 years, was also partly influenced by the Enlightenment movement.

It was only in 1848 thanks to the first Austrian constitution that Jews were granted equality with the other population in the Czech lands under the law. Consequently, there occurred anti-Jewish incidents in Prague and many other places. However, a year later Jews were permitted to reside in all areas of Bohemia and Moravia, restrictions on marriage were removed and they were made equal with Christians under the law. In 1852 the government also confirmed the right of Jews to purchase houses and in 1859 the right to own land, and thus the last barriers to free economic activity were torn down. Finally, with the creation of the Dual Monarchy in 1867, the full civic and political emancipation of the Jews was proclaimed officially. The abolition of ghettos and the so-called "family law" brought forth considerable demographic changes in the structure of Jewish population in Bohemia and Moravia. After 1852 Jewish families left the crammed ghettos and settled in the near-by villages and small towns where many new Jewish communities originated. In 1872, 327 Jewish religious congregations and 47 religious societies were recorded. The Jewish population considerably increased in the middle of the century and reached its peak in 1890 when Jewish population stood at 94,599 Jews in Bohemia and 45,324 in Moravia. Soon large numbers of rural Jews began to migrate to larger towns and industrial or commercial centres of Bohemia and Moravia. Consequently, this migration resulted in a gradual decline and extinction of many important historical Jewish settlements in the countryside and the foundation of new communities in cities, in which Jews had not been allowed to settle right up until the mid-19th century. Only 197 Jewish religious congregations are recorded in Bohemia in 1890 and 50 in Moravia (of which 13 became extinct and 11 were newly founded). Besides Prague the largest Jewish population concentrated in the following Bohemian towns - Plzeň, Teplice, Karlovy Vary, České Budějovice, Ústí nad Labem and Liberec.

In Moravia the largest Jewish populations were in Brno, Olomouc, Moravská Ostrava, Prostějov and Jihlava. The migration of Jews from rural areas into cities and later on abroad, especially to Vienna but also to other European cities, caused a constant decline of Jewish population in Bohemia and Moravia.

However, the hitherto successful process of Jewish emancipation in the Austro-Hungarian empire was to face serious problems. At the precise moment that the Jews of the Czech lands were adopting the German language and assimilating German cultural patterns, an increasingly vociferous group in Czech society, influenced by the growing movement of the Czech national revival, was challenging the very position of the German minority in the balance of economic and political power in the country. As early as the 1840s a group of Jewish intellectuals associated with the Young Bohemia literary movement - Siegfried Kapper, L. A. Frankl, M. Hartmann, David Kuh, A. Meissner, I. Kuranda and others - advocated a program of cultural and political rapprochement between the Slavs and the Jews. By and large their efforts at a Czech-Jewish alignment went unappreciated in the forties as the Jews felt no compulsion to alter the course of their cultural and political assimilation and Czech nationalism had not yet fully matured and did not put a very high value on the prospects of Jewish cooperation. Further reforms instituted by the Viennese government after 1848 had the overall effect of strengthening the German-Jewish cultural synthesis. During the 1870s, when more and more Jews were streaming from the countryside to settle in large cultural centres, an extensive network of Jewish institutions and associations emerged which were dedicated in one way or another to the achievement of a genuine Czech-Jewish acculturation. In 1876 the "Association of Czech-Jewish University Graduates" was founded in Prague which started to publish the popular annual "Kalendář Česko-Židovský" (Czech-Jewish Calendar) in 1881, the religious association "Or Tomid" for the promotion of worship in Czech and Hebrew languages was founded in 1884, and in 1894 a political movement "National Union of Czech Jews" came into existence, publishing a bi-weekly "Czech-Jewish Letters". In 1907 the "Union of Progressive Czech Jews" was founded and many similar unions and associations sprang up in smaller towns. By the end of the 19th century over fifty per cent of Jews in Prague and over fifty per cent of Jews in Bohemia declared their language of daily use to be Czech and their number continued to increase rapidly. The Czech-Jewish movement began to flourish under the new Czechoslovak Republic which was founded in 1918.

In reaction to a wave of nationalistically motivated anti-Jewish sentiment, which arose towards the end of the 19th century (the work of the Catholic theologian A. Rohling, the

Cartoon from the time of the Hilsner trial
(Humoristické listy, Prague, 1900)

infamous Hilsner blood-libel case in Polná in 1899) a small but active organization of university students called "Maccabi" was founded in Prague in 1893 (from 1896 "Association of Jewish University Graduates in Prague" and from 1899 "Bar Kochba"). Members of this organization doubted the possibility of a complete Czech or German orientated assimilation, insisted on abstaining from the national conflict and wished to remain neutral on the question of the use of the German or the Czech language, and sought to create independent modern Jewish culture drawing on the Jewish cultural tradition. Most members of this movement came from a Czech-Jewish background and consciously drew inspiration from the Czech national awakening movement of the past century.

However, in the first decades of the 20th century the German language maintained a privileged position in culture, especially in literature and remained the common language of communication in the multinational Austrian empire. These were the years when the phenomenon known as Prager Deutscher Literatur emerged as one of the truly great archievements in world literature with most of the writers being Jewish - let us mention, e.g. Franz Kafka, Max Brod, Franz Werfel, Oskar Baum, Leo Winder, Johannes Urzidil and others. Within the broad spectrum of the two national and linguistic spheres in the first half of the

20th century Jewish writers played an extremely important role as translators and cultural mediators - e.g. Otokar Fischer, Arnošt Kraus, Otto Pick, Rudolf Fuchs, Max Brod and many others. The Jewish contribution in this period, whether in the form of participation in the Czech national movement, modern German literature or in their endeavour to revive the Jewish cultural tradition was marked by remarkable efforts to create broad areas of understanding and mutual cooperation while preserving the ethnic, religious and linguistic diversity so characteristic of the Central European cultural tradition.

Under the Czechoslovak Republic, which was founded on October 28, 1918, members of all Jewish movements and representatives of modern culture contributed to the development of the new state and the fashioning of its new cultural orientation. The auspicious progress of Masaryk's humanistic democracy, offering favourable conditions for the cultural adaptation of Czech Jewry, was tragically cut short after only twenty years. Following the Munich Pact on September 30, 1938 Czechoslovakia was forced to cede its frontier regions to Nazi Germany. As many as 25,000 Jews from Sudetenland fled together with an overwhelming majority of Czech inhabitants of the frontier region to the truncated Czechoslovakia. During the so-called Kristallnacht pogroms on November 9-10, 1938 about 35 synagogues and a number of Jewish cemeteries were burnt down and demolished in the occupied frontier regions of Bohemia and Moravia. Parts of south Slovakia and Subcarpathian Ruthenia with a Jewish population of about 80,000 were ceded to Hungary on November 2, 1938. Immediately before the German troops occupied the country Slovakia declared its independence on March 14, 1939 and proceeded to sign a Treaty of Protection with Nazi Germany. At that time the Jewish population of Slovakia numbered 135,918. Simultaneously Subcarpathian Ruthenia, whose Jewish population stood at 102,542 in 1930, was occupied by Hungarian troops. On March 15, 1939 Germany sealed the fate of the Czech lands as Nazi troops occupied the country and declared the so-called Protectorate of Bohemia and Moravia.

The Jewish population of Bohemia and Moravia had dropped to 117,551 in 1930 which was a combined result of emigration, low birth rate and rapid assimilation. The movement of refugees from Nazi Germany and later from Austria into the Czech lands temporarily reversed the pattern of decline and in 1938 the Jewish population stood at 122,000. Over 118,000 Jews remained in the Czech lands on the eve of the Nazi occupation in March 1939. After the occupation an order was issued under which the Germans became the exclusive administrators of Jewish property thus enabling the Nazis to control the most important economic positions in the Protectorate. Jews were ordered to hand in lists of all their property and deposit their valuables in banks and their bank accounts were closed. At first Jews were excluded from practising as lawyers and physicians and from all spheres of public administration, later on they were excluded from most professions, their membership in different organizations was terminated and Jewish children were gradually forbidden to attend any kind of school. Their identity cards were marked with the letter "J" and from September 1, 1940 all Jews were ordered to wear the yellow Star of David with the inscription "Jude" on their clothes. Further regulations required Jews to stay indoors after 8 p.m., forbade them to move house and travel, to use public transport, enter restaurants and cafés, go to theatres, cinemas, markets, swimming pools and other public places. They were not allowed to enter parks and gardens, woods, embankments and some squares. Jews were ordered to hand in their radios, they were not allowed to buy newspapers and use telephones, drycleaners and laundries, they were able to do their shopping in certain shops at given hours only. They were excluded from rations of fruit, cheese, sugar, fish, poultry, game, eggs, milk, bread, legumes, meat, sweets, wine and spirits, onions and garlic, coffee and tobacco, shaving soap and they were not allowed to buy clothes, hats, suitcases etc. By October 1941 over 26,000 Jews managed to escape more or less empty-handed and emigrated mostly to Palestine, the United States, South America and Western Europe. Approximately 92,000 citizens subjects to the Nuremberg law remained in the Protectorate. The vast majority of these people - some 89,000 - were deported during the period from October 1941 to March 1945 to the concentration camp at Terezín or to the extermination camps in Poland, in which about 78,000 Jews of Bohemia and Moravia perished. Many others were arrested before the deportation to concentration camps, others committed suicide or died while trying to cross the frontier illegally. Many Jews who managed to leave the country in time perished fighting the Nazis on the eastern or western fronts or during battles in Africa and the Near East.

Given the enormity of the loss of life and property during the Holocaust, it would have been inconceivable for the post-war Jewish community in Czechoslovakia to have revived its pre-war strength and vitality. The size of the Jewish population increased with the arrival of refugees from Subcarpathian Ruthenia which was incorporated into the Soviet Union in 1945. In Bohemia and Moravia 52 Jewish religious congregations were re-established for a short period of time with which about 20,000 people registered in 1948 and Slovakia at the time showed a Jewish population of 24,500. Within the following two years nearly 19,000 Jews emigrated to Israel and more than 7,000 to other countries. In 1950 the Jewish population stood at around 18,000. A second wave of post-war emigration took place in 1968 and in 1969 - that year approximately 15,000 people registered with Czechoslovakia's Jewish congregations. Today some 6,000 people are registered with the remaining five Jewish congregations in Bohemia and Moravia in the towns of Prague, Plzeň, Ústí nad Labem, Brno and Ostrava and with the few in Slovakia. There is regular public worship in the larger towns and kosher restaurants exist in Prague, Bratislava and Košice. Prague is the seat of the Federation of Jewish Congregations in the Czech Republic, while Bratislava is the seat of the Central Union of the Jewish Religious Congregations in the Slovak Republic. The Federation of Jewish Congregations in Prague publishes a monthly bulletin "Roš Chodeš" and a literary yearbook.

Arno Pařík

GHETTOS, SYNAGOGUES AND CEMETERIES

Former ghettos, synagogues and cemeteries, scattered throughout the whole country, are remains of both ancient and modern Jewish communities. Many such remains have vanished in the past: they were destroyed either by anti-semites during the crusades in the 11th and 12th cent. or after the expulsion of Jews from individual towns; many buildings in villages which the Jews had abandoned in the 19th cent. were pulled down to be used as building material. Many Jewish structures were devastated by the Nazis, and even nowadays disused synagogues and dilapidated cemeteries are gradually vanishing from the face of the earth. Nevertheless, a considerable number of Jewish historical monuments has survived until the present day throughout the country.

GHETTOS

In many places in the period of feudalism Jewish families lived in houses **scattered** among Christian inhabitants (especially in places where the number of Jewish inhabitants was small but also in places where a sizeable Jewish community existed - e.g. Benešov, Dobříš, Neveklov). However, in the course of historical development in most places Jewish inhabitants were concentrated in special settlement precincts. Two small Jewish settlements allegedly existed as early as in the 11th cent. on the territory of what later became Pra-

gue; a Jewish settlement is recorded on the territory of Brno in the 13th cent. and "Jewish streets" are mentioned in different towns throughout the country in the 14th century.

The reasons for this concentration were legal, economic and religious. Jewish inhabitants, forming a tolerated minority, lived under the protection of the sovereign or the landlord (having to pay rather high "safeguard fees" in return), who guaranteed (or at least was supposed to guarantee) their safety and that of their property. This enabled the Jews to perform their professions or trade and ensured their freedom to practise their religion. Not only did the concentration of Jewish houses in special streets and quarters secure the Jews better against anti-Jewish outrages and pogroms but it also enabled them to lead an undisturbed religious life, ensured social welfare and promoted trades and crafts. In some places Jewish families were able to live in houses owned by their feudal superior or landlord who either offered their "protégés Jews" the opportunity to take up residence in some of their older houses or had houses or even whole streets (the so-called Židovny) built at their own expense so as to let them to Jewish families (e.g. Blatná, Česká Skalice, Koloděje nad Lužnicí, Rábí, Radenín, Velká Bukovina and other places).

Such a concentration of Jewish houses in separate streets or neighbourhoods - **ghettos** - was obligatory in

27

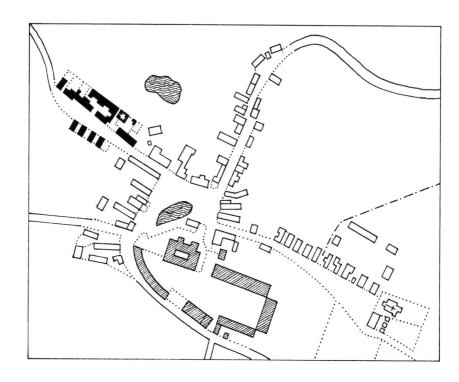

most places as early as in the Middle Ages. A more consistent segregation of Jews from the general population was launched by Emperor Charles VI in 1727; under the so-called translocation rescript ghettos were to be set up in all towns and villages where segregation had not previously existed. In most places this was realised by a forced exchange of houses between Jewish and Christian inhabitants. The reasons were primarily religious, and the decree restricted Jewish residence to places remote from Catholic churches and routes of religious processions.

The ghettos varied in size. In some places there were only small **clusters of cottages or houses** (mainly in villages), whereas in others there were rows of adjacent houses either on one or both sides of **the so-called "Jewish street"** (this was the most common type of a ghetto).

In places with larger Jewish communities there originated entire **Jewish quarters with a network of narrow streets** (e.g. Bezdružice, Bílence, Dambořice, Dolní Kounice, Doudleby nad Orlicí, Golčův Jeníkov, Heřmanův

Example of a village Jewish street (Dub, 1st half of the 19th cent.)

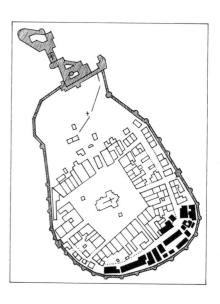

Example of a Jewish street in a walled town (Náchod, 1st half of the 19th cent.)

Městec, Humpolec, Ivanovice na H., Luže, Miroslav, Mladá Boleslav, Nový Bydžov, Pohořelice, Prostějov, Rousínov, Slavkov u Brna, Strážnice, Šafov, Teplice, Třešť, Údlice). Among our **greatest Jewish quarters** (apart from the Jewish Town in Prague) were the Moravian ghettos in Boskovice, Mikulov, Třebíč and Uherský Brod.

In several places there existed **two ghettos** in one town, occasionally situated on the opposite sides of the city centre (Blovice, Lázně Kynžvart, Mašťov, Podivín, Prostějov).

In fortified towns the ghetto was usually situated **inside the walled city,** -

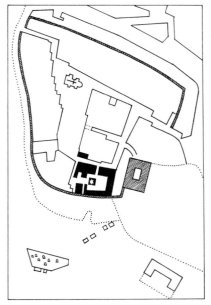

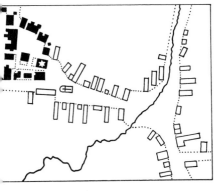

Example of a Jewish quarter in a walled town, a Jewish cemetery beyond the town walls (Jemnice, 1st half of the 19th cent.)

Example of a village Jewish quarter with its village green (Hořenice, 1st half of the 19th cent.)

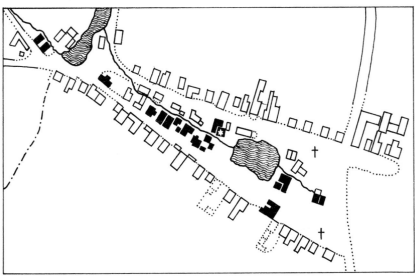

Example of a cluster of Jewish houses with a synagogue in the centre of the village (Drmoul, 1st half of the 19th cent.)

chiefly on its edge and adjacent to the wall. There were only a few towns where the Jewish quarter was **outside the walled city**, usually in the suburb (Budyně nad Ohří, Česká Lípa, Mikulov, Polná, Rožmberk nad Vltavou, Třebíč, Uherský Brod until the Thirty Years' War, Velké Meziříčí).

From a town-planning standpoint, it is interesting to note the places where the Jewish quarter or the group of Jewish houses is situated **in the centre of the town or village**, as if additionally built in the middle of the village green or square (e.g. Barchůvek, Dambořice, Dešenice, Drmoul, Hroubovice, Kamýk nad Vltavou, Lesná, Nové Sedliště, Ošelín, Pňovany, Terešov).

The boundaries of compact ghettos were always clearly marked. Some Jewish quarters were isolated from the rest of the town and separated by **gates or wickets** (e.g. Březnice, Prague, Roudnice nad Labem), **a barrier** or **a chain or wire** put up across the street. Thus, the ghetto used to be closed, at least symbolically, on Saturdays (so as to prevent non-Jews from disturbing the Sabbath) and also on Sundays (so that the ghetto's inhabitants did not disturb the rest of the town on Sunday), and also during various religious holidays of both faiths. The borders of some ghettos were marked by wires permanently fixed across the street at a height of about the first floor.

The synagogue or prayer room was the religious centre of the Jewish street or quarter. Every Jewish community maintained **a school** (sometimes even only with one classroom). In larger communities there would be **a community house**, often called **the Jewish town-hall**, which included a meeting room, an office, a record office and sometimes the rabbi's living quarters, a classroom and a winter prayer room. In many ghettos **the rabbi's house** used to be an important building owned by the community (e.g. Batelov, Mikulov, Polná). **The ritual bath** or **mikva** with a pool of water or a large bath was usually built on the lowest floor of the synagogue or special small bathhouses may be found in some places (e.g.

Velká Bukovina, Všeruby in the Domažlice district). Jewish communities also used to set up important social welfare institutions - **the hospital** was often combined with an old people's home, the care of the sick, aged and lonely Jews. Larger communities used to run **butchers' shops** often together with **a slaughterhouse**, since Jews observe special dietary laws concerning the ritual slaughtering of animals and the preparation of meat. Some larger ghettos also maintained their own night-watchmen and built special **watch-houses** for them (e.g. Šafov, Třešť).

(In Slovak towns and sometimes even in villages the most important community buildings used to be concentrated in several buildings around a communal courtyard. Such **Jewish districts** with a synagogue now abolished, a former Beth ha-Midrash, a school, a ritual bathhouse, a slaughterhouse, a matzah bakery and former living quarters of the rabbi, the shammash and the teacher can still be found in Slovakia today. Such a purposeful concentration of community buildings did not exist in the Czech lands.)

After the Jews had been made equal before the law, i. e. after the mid-19th century, most of the former ghettos, Jewish quarters and streets either underwent a radical rebuilding and modernization programme or, in some cases, became extinct. Nevertheless, several significant pieces of architecture have survived in Bohemia and Moravia. Among the most remarkable from a town-planning standpoint are those which show a planned foundation: e.g. **urban ghettos with a central square** (Batelov, Kasejovice, Kosova Hora, Lomnice) or, even with two squares (Březnice, Polná), and **village ghettos**, e.g. in Hořenice (with a large village green), in Radenín or in Široké Třebčice. A rare example of a well-preserved Jewish street with timber framed houses is to be found in Velká Bukovina. The architecture of the formerly mostly Jewish village of Neznašov is also worthy of attention. The remarkable urban ghettos in Boskovice and Velké Meziříčí have hitherto been little disturbed as has, above all, the unique Jewish quarter in Třebíč, which represents the most probably best preserved Jewish quarter in Europe.

SYNAGOGUES

The synagogue or the prayer hall was the spiritual centre of every Jewish community. We cannot draw a precise distinction between the two terms and therefore both could be used to describe many buildings or places serving as Jewish houses of worship.

In fact, we may say that **a prayer room** is a room for worship (or a complex of several rooms: for men and for women), which forms a part of a multipurpose, mostly residential building. The principal architectural character of the entire building was not influenced by its designation for worship. Smaller and less prosperous Jewish religious congregations and religious groups usually maintained a prayer hall, sometimes however, even larger Jewish religious congregations used to maintain a prayer room only - as was the case of the Jewish religious congregation in the Prague district of Žižkov, where a spacious prayer room occupied an entire floor of a multi-storey residential building. **Temporary prayer rooms** were set up in many places either before the building of an independent synagogue or after a fire had destroyed the original synagogue. In large cities (e.g. in Prague) so-called **auxiliary prayer rooms** were set up to be used during the main festivals, when the synagogues could not hold the large number of worshippers. **Seasonal prayer rooms** were to be found in some spas during the summer season (e.g. Jeseník, Luhačovice, Rožnov pod Radhoštěm). The majority of present Jewish religious congregations and synagogue groups in Bohemia and Moravia mostly maintain only prayer rooms converted from flats in ordinary residential buildings (Karlovy Vary, Liberec, Olomouc, Ostrava, Plzeň, Ústí n. L.).

We speak of **a synagogue** in cases when a spacious room of Jewish congregational worship forms the principal, dominant space in the building and its function of a place of worship sets the architectural character of the entire building.

The earliest preserved record mentions a synagogue in Prague which was destroyed in the first half of the 12th century but synagogues had presumably existed in the Czech lands even before that time. The earliest synagogues were most probably simple, timber buildings - the tradition of building **wooden** synagogues was kept alive for a long time, especially by less prosperous communities. Several timber framed synagogues were to be found in the Czech lands right up until the early 20th century, however, at present there is only one surviving synagogue of this type, which has been converted into a dwelling house (in Vlachovo Březí). The last two wooden synagogues in Slovakia vanished after World War II (Brezovica, Veličná).

Since the Middle Ages larger Jewish communities have built **masonry** synagogues. The construction and appearance of these structures basically correspond with the building techniques and styles of the period. However, the authorities issued a number of laws restricting synagogue builders so that synagogues could not compete with Christian churches: e.g. the authorities could dictate the size and seating capacity of a synagogue, a synagogue had to have a modest exterior, undecorated walls and no tower. It was only after the mid-19th century, when Jews had been made equal before the law, that - depending on the wealth of the community - ostentatious synagogues following the contemporary styles in architecture could be built. Occasionally even a synagogue with a tower was built (e.g. in Český Krumlov, Liberec) or a twin tower (e.g. in České Budějovice, Krnov, the Ostrava synagogues, Prague-Vinohrady). Some synagogues were built not only outside the territory of the former ghettos, but even on the town's main street (e.g. Kdyně, Město Touškov, Plzeň) or, exceptionally, on the main square (e.g. Vyškov).

*Portal of the main hall of
the Old New Synagogue in Prague
(last third of the 13th cent.)*

Prague (the Pinkas and the High synagogues) and Velké Meziříčí.

Among the many synagogues built in the **Baroque and Rococo** periods those in Kasejovice, Lomnice, Luže, Prague (the Klaus synagogue), Radnice, Třebíč and in Úsov have best preserved the original character of the architecture.

An even greater number of preserved synagogues reflect both the simplicity and ornamental character of the **Classicist style** (with occasional **Empire style** features): e.g. Batelov, Březnice, Čkyně, Divišov, Doudleby nad Ohří, Ivančice, Nečtiny, Prague-Uhříněves, Prostějov, Třešť, Volyně, Všeradice, Zalužany.

There is an abundance of synagogues built in the so-called **pseudo-historical styles** throughout the whole country, especially neo-Romanesque and neo-Gothic synagogues, which were built from the mid-19th century to the early 20th century. Neo-Gothic style elements were even added to earlier synagogues during rebuilding (e.g. Boskovice, Polná, Prague - the Maisel synagogue, Třebíč).

The early Gothic Old New Synagogue in Prague, built in the last third of the 13th century, represents the earliest surviving synagogue in our country. **The late Gothic and Renaissance** are represented among others by remarkable synagogues in Dolní Kounice, Holešov, Kojetín, Kolín, Lipník nad Bečvou,

*Types of synagogue windows (from left to right):
Renaissance (16th cent.),
Baroque (18th cent.),
from the period of the so-called Oriental styles
(2nd half of the 19th cent.)*

Example of a village Classicist style synagogue from about 1800 (Kolinec)

Functionalist synagogue from the 1930's (Velvary)

The so-called **Moorish** (or **Oriental, Byzantine-Oriental**) **style**, which, with its unusual, maily decorative elements, was in vogue in the 2nd half of the 19th century and the early 20th century, had a strong influence on the architecture of our synagogues. This somewhat heterogeneous and often very colourful architectural style was here applied almost solely to synagogues (e.g. Golčův Jeníkov, Jablonec nad Nisou, Písek, Prague - the Spanish and Jubilee synagogues, Uhlířské Janovice, Znojmo). "Oriental" elements were also combined with neo-Romanesque elements (e.g. Děčín, Louny, Nová Cerekev) or with Art Nouveau features (e.g. Čáslav).

Art Nouveau ornamentation was added to several earlier synagogues at the beginning of our century (e.g. Jevíčko, Nový Bydžov, Uherské Hradiště). The synagogue in Hradec Králové represents a fine example of Art Nouveau architecture. Two other Art Nouveau buildings (Klobouky and Prostějov) were later rebuilt and completely modernized.

Also modern **styles of the 20's and 30's**, above all Functionalism, influenced the architecture of several synagogues: both newly built (e.g. Brno, Český Těšín, Velvary) and rebuilt (Prague - Smíchov). The synagogue in Milevsko (completed in 1919) represents a unique piece of architecture, combining Empire and Cubist style elements. The last synagogue was built in Czechoslovakia in 1937-38 (in Kamenice nad Lipou).

In accordance with the time-honoured tradition the synagogue was, as far as possible, built near **running water** - a river, a stream, a mill-race or the like. There is custom (tashlich) whereby Jews, on the first day of Rosh Hashanah, walk out of the synagogue and proceed to a nearby body of water and throw small pieces of bread into it, symbolizing the casting off of their sins.

The synagogue vestibule was a typical feature - its floor often lay a few steps above that of the prayer hall, sometimes even one step was enough between the entrance and the prayer hall. This was done to allow prayers to rise "out of the depth", the tradition of the symbolic **deeper setting of the prayer hall** originates from Psalm 130: "out of the depths have I cried unto thee, O LORD".

The interior decoration has always been very modest. Human images are never to be found in the decoration of synagogues. Neither are animals (with the exception of symbolic lions and birds). The stucco decoration and paintings on walls, vaults and ceilings are mostly restricted to geometrical and plant ornaments, fruits mentioned in the Bible, various drapery motifs. Walls may be inscribed with quotations from the Old Testament. The original interior decoration has survived in some synagogues until today (e.g. in Boskovice, Březnice, Holešov, Kasejovice, Kdyně, Kojetín, Kolín, Plzeň, Prague, Úštěk, in Všeruby - in the Plzeň region).

A typical feature of Jewish services is **the separation of women from men.** Men always pray in the main prayer hall which has the lowest floor level. In older synagogues women attend prayers in the women's area, which is usually placed in the aisle or in an annex added to the side of the synagogue (e.g. Dolní Kounice, Kojetín, Kolín, Lipník nad Bečvou, Mikulov, Prague - the Pinkas synagogue). The Old New Synagogue in Prague has two ground floor annexes used as women's areas, connected with the main prayer hall by windows.

A women's gallery, resembling a balcony supported by columns, was built in many later synagogues. In smaller synagogues the women's gallery used to be along the side, usually at the rear of the synagogue or along the western wall. In some places the women's gallery used to be along two or three walls of the main prayer hall and exceptionally along all four as was the case of the synagogue in Terešov. A double, or two storey women's gallery may be found in several synagogues (e.g. Brandýs nad Labem).

In very small and simple synagogues as well as in most prayer rooms there were no women's galleries and women attended prayers in the main prayer hall separated from the men's space by a screen, a grille, a curtain or the like.

In synagogues of the older type the women's gallery was often accessible from a flight of stairs attached to the building from the outside (e.g. Jičín, Kojetín, Kolín, Plzeň - the old synagogues, Stráž nad Nežárkou, Vojkovice). This is also the case in the modern synagogue in Milevsko. There are rare cases where women could enter the women's gallery from an adjacent building connected with the synagogue by a bridge (in Heřmanův Městec).

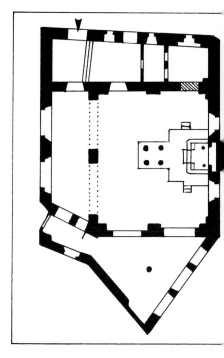

Plan of the ground floor of the Old Synagogue in Mikulov, the last surviving synagogue of the so-called Lvov (Polish) type in Bohemia and Moravia. The bimah is situated in the central space between the four central piers, a polygonal women's section adjacent to the main hall at the south side of the synagogue.

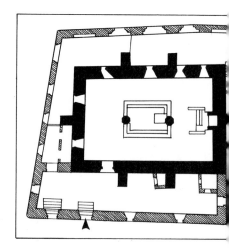

Groundplan of the Altneuschul (the Old New Synagogue) in Prague (the main hall is divided into two naves, with the bimah between two main piers and women's annexes along two sides)

34

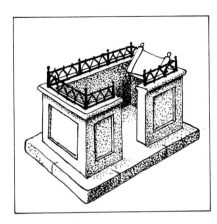

Bimah or almemar - a raised platform in the centre of the synagogue of the traditional rite where the Torah scrolls are read

Until the first half of the 19th century the men's **seats** ran along the walls of the prayer hall so that the worshippers were facing the centre or **the bimah** also known as **the almemar** (a raised platform enclosed with a railing or grille), from where the officiant reads from the Torah scrolls. This original interior design has survived mostly only in the Orthodox and tradi-

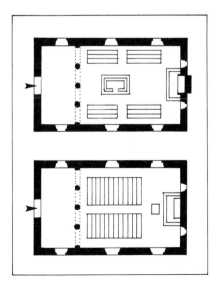

Interior of a synagogue of the traditional rite (with the bimah in the centre and benches facing the bimah) and a synagogue of the Reform rite

tional rite synagogues (e.g. Holešov, Luže, Prague - the Old New Synagogue and the Pinkas Synagogue). Around the mid-19th century (and elsewhere much later) the place for the reading of the Torah scrolls moved farther toward the eastern wall (eventually becoming a pulpit), while the seats were arranged in parallel rows (as in Christian churches) with the worshippers facing the eastern wall and the ark.

The aron ha-kodesh (the shrine or closet in which the Torah scrolls are kept) represents the most significant point in the synagogue. It is generally a niche in the wall, which was usually strenghtened from the outside, with a decorated cabinet, in which the Torah scrolls are kept, i.e. a Hebrew hand-written parchment transcript of the Pentateuch. Every synagogue has several Torah scrolls, kept in a cabinet with a decorated curtain (parochet) which hangs before the holy ark. The aron ha-kodesh is always a conspicious architectural feature: sometimes it is elevated with steps in front of it, framed by carved masonry or wooden columns, crowned by a tympanum or canopy, framed by stucco ornaments etc. The decoration of the aron ha-kodesh best reflects the different styles in architecture - ranging from the Gothic (the Old New Synagogue) to Classicism, which is the most common style of our surviving synagogues, including its later immitations.

The aron ha-kodesh is, in our country, placed on the eastern wall of all the synagogues: we say that the synagogue or prayer room is orientated toward the east. Only a few modern synagogues, built in this century, do not follow this tradition and are orientated toward the south (e.g. the synagogue in Prostějov) or the north (e.g. the synagogue in Dobříš).

A synagogue lavabo for washing of hands before prayer is to be found in the vestibule. Ancient lavaboes have survived e.g. in Holešov, Kojetín, Luže and Prague.

The synagogue façade or portal was usually inscribed with a Hebrew inscription. These are generally **verses of**

psalms referring to the "house of prayer" (mostly Psalms 100,4-84,2-68,5). Some of the inscriptions are still well-preserved.

A stone **Decalogue** was a typical feature of a synagogue, placed on the façade or decorating the gable above the main entrance and visible from a distance. The Decalogue has been preserved on a number of former synagogues, despite the building being at present used for different purposes.

Synagogues or their annexes have sometimes housed **the rabbi's living quarters** (e.g. Humpolec, Kdyně, Kralupy nad Vltavou, Prague - Michle, Rakovník, Stádlec, Světlá nad Sázavou), children's **classrooms** (e.g. Březnice, Humpolec, Rakovník, Slatina) or so-called **winter prayer rooms** (a smaller room with a stove, used for prayer in the winter season), occasionally a **matzah bakery** (e.g. Bezdružice, Luka, Poutnov) or a **ritual bath** in the basement (e.g. Malín, Poběžovice).

The vanishing of Jewish communities in many places resulted in **the abolition of synagogues**. Deserted and disused synagogues were converted into Christian chapels in the Middle Ages (e.g. following the expulsion of Jews from Brno, České Budějovice, Cheb, Jihlava, Olomouc, Znojmo) or into dwelling houses or other secular buildings. Occasionally the former synagogues was pulled down and used as a source of building material. At the end of the 19th century a similar fate befell a great number of rural synagogues in villages, where the members of the Jewish community had moved to large towns. The Nazi occupation represents the third and the most tragic period of synagogue abolition and destruction. Not only did the Nazis destroy at least 35 synagogues in the occupied frontier regions during the so-called Kristallnacht pogroms on November 9-10, 1938 but in the course of the following six years and during the final battles of World War II at least another 25 synagogues were destroyed.

Only a few Jewish religious congregations could be revived after World War II (the majority of the Jewish population having been killed by the Nazis) and nearly 300 synagogues in the Czech lands fell into disuse. Some of the synagogues had to be demolished owing to their poor static condition or bad state of repair, others gave way to modern urban renewal (e.g. Benešov, Brtnice, Bučovice, Dašice, Horní Cerekev, Náchod, Pardubice, Postoloprty, Přeštice, Strakonice, Švihov, Teplice), new communications (e.g. Dvůr Králové n. L., Koloděje, Krásno n. B., Malín) or to the construction of a dam (Dolní Kralovice).

In Bohemia and Moravia more than 200 synagogues have survived until the present day. Three are still used as synagogues (in Brno and Prague - the Old New Synagogue and the Jubilee Synagogue), 39 have been reverently converted into Christian churches, 12 have been converted into museums and another 15 house different cultural centres (concert halls, exhibition halls, cinemas, clubs, libraries), 46 synagogues have been converted into flats and 38 have been used as temporary storehouses. The remaining synagogues have been converted mostly into schools, offices, health centres, gymnasiums, workshops or trade establishments. A similar fate befell the surviving synagogues in other European countries, which had been afflicted by the Nazi genocide.

The State Jewish Museum in Prague is a repository of a unique heritage of the vanished synagogues, treasuring various ceremonial objects and Torah scrolls, which were shipped to Prague during the Nazi occupation. In 1964 a further 1564 Torah scrolls were reverently transported to the Westminster Synagogue in London, where they are gradually being restored, and then sent on permanent loan to Jewish communities all over the world as a symbolic reminder of their massacred Czech coreligionists.

CEMETERIES

Most Jewish communities maintained their own **cemetery**. Today, there are still 334 preserved independent Jewish cemeteries (including minor remains) in Bohemia and Moravia and 20 Jewish sections preserved in communal cemeteries in different towns. There are still many other local cemeteries where we may find groups of or individual Jewish tombstones from more recent times.

The principal difference between Jewish and Christian cemeteries arises from the traditional Jewish principle concerning **the sanctity of graves**: the remains of a body must forever remain in the place where the body was buried (exhumation was prohibited by Jewish law and has always been very exceptional). Whereas in Christian cemeteries graves may be opened after several decades and another deceased may be buried in the grave, those in Jewish cemeteries are never disturbed. In places therefore where a full Jewish cemetery could not be extended the existing graves were covered by a thick layer of earth creating a layer for new graves above the former ones. Tombstones from the former graves were set again in the new layer of earth. For this reason in some old cemeteries there are **several layers of graves** (e.g. Mikulov, Pacov, Rabštejn n. St.). In cemeteries with a good many strata of burials we may find clusters of tombstones of different ages leaning one upon the other (Prague - Josefov).

Medieval Jewish cemeteries were founded within the walled city (e.g. Horažďovice, Cheb, Nový Jičín, Prague, Rožmberk n. V., Sušice, Tovačov), or occasionally outside it, adjacent to the city wall (e.g. Brno, Budyně n. O., Osoblaha, Uherský Brod, Znojmo). More frequently cemeteries could be founded only far away from the town or village (sometimes on the very frontier of the region), and in some cases only in unpopular places, such as next to a place of execution or a carrion-pit (e.g. Kadaň, Kožlany, Nová Včelnice, Prčice).

Contrary to Christian burial customs, where the ceremony begins in a church and cemeteries were founded next to churches, with some of the deceased even buried there, Jewish burial ceremonies are in no way related to the synagogue. In general, cemeteries are situated far from the synagogue - if a cemetery happens to be in the neighbourhood of the synagogue (e.g. Lipník n. B., Prague - the Klaus or Pinkas synagogues, Strážnice) this was either accidental or due to the limited circumstances of an overcrowded Jewish quarter.

In accordance with Judaic principles it was prohibited to leave the deceased in the house overnight. Therefore the dead body had to be taken on the day of death to a specially furnished **mortuary**, situated, in general, next to the cemetery or, occasionally (e.g. in Hroznětín) in the ghetto or village. **The Burial Society** (Hevra Kaddisha, Hebrew for "holy brotherhood") looks after the burial needs of the Jewish dead, watches over the deceased in the mortuary and provides **the ritual purification** of the body (tahara in Hebrew). In some mortuaries the stone table used for the ritual purification of the dead has been preserved (e.g. Dražkov, Jistebnice, Turnov). Because the corpse must be rinsed with warm water the mortuary has a chimney to enable heating.

Since the 19th century the mortuary often served as **a ceremonial hall** where the bereaved gathered before the burial or it was used as **a shed for the funeral coach**. In some mortuaries - ceremonial halls - we may still find the original bier of the Burial Society, a communal coffin which was sometimes used only for the transport of the deceased to the grave (e.g. in Mirotice), the entire catafalque (e.g. in Slaný, Tovačov) or the funeral coach (e.g. in Jindřichův Hradec, Městec Králové). In some towns the former mortuary has been reverently converted in **a memorial** of the vanished Jewish community (e.g. in Dobruška, Rychnov n. K.).

Monumental cemetery buildings, built in towns from the 2nd half of the

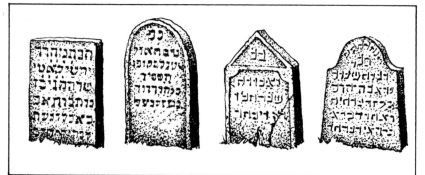

Different types of slab tombstones (stele)
from the 14th-19th cent.

19th century, were designed to suit several purposes: there used to be a ceremonial hall, a mortuary, store-rooms for the sexton and gardener; sometimes it also included the sexton's living quarters.

Sometimes, in the past centuries, an **old people's home** (e.g. in Mladá Boleslav, Osoblaha) or **a hospital** (in Prague - Žižkov) was established right next to the cemetery.

Near the entrance to the cemetery there used to be a pump or least **a lavabo** for the washing of hands after the burial ceremony. Such a lavabo has been preserved e.g. in the Prague Old Jewish Cemetery or the one in Třebíč dating from 1716-17.

In accordance with a time-honoured tradition the Kohanim (descendants of Hebrew priests) may not enter a cemetery. From the 19th century special **gates for the Kohanim** were built in the walls of some cemeteries, until then they were not even allowed to visit the graves of their relatives. These small gates were usually far away from the main entrance to the cemetery, today they are mostly walled up with the exception of e.g. the one in the cemetery in Lovosice.

Two early types of Jewish **tombstones** are to be found in the cemeteries on the territory of the Czech Republic. The most common one is the **slab tombstone** set into the ground upright (stele). The form, style of inscriptions and decorative motifs have been developing and changing in the course of time and the tombstones often reflects regional varieties (e.g. we may find slightly different types of tombstones in south-west Bohemia, in south Moravia and speak about the so-called Prague

Different types of slab tombstones
from the 17th-19th cent.

type, Osoblaha type etc.). **Wooden tombstones** used to be quite common in many regions. The life of these tombstones being limited we may today find wooden tombstones only in the collections of the State Jewish Museum.

A less common type is **a tomb** (ohel) constructed like a tent from several stone slabs and resembling an ancient sarcophagus. In some places we may find masonry tombs with a roof, resembling tiny houses (e.g. Golčův Jeníkov). These tombs appeared in our country in the Renaissance and were usually erected over the graves of significant personalities (e.g. in Brandýs nad Labem, Heřmanův Městec, Holešov, Prague - the Old Jewish Cemetery, Prague - Žižkov). There also exist remarkable Art Nouveau tombs of the above mentioned type (e.g. in Krnov).

Double tombstone from the Baroque period

Renaissance tomb

From the mid-19th century the form of Jewish tombstones began to resemble the common type or tombstones in surrounding Christian cemeteries - at present Jewish tombstones (except for a few exceptional cases) do not differ from non-Jewish tombstones typologically.

Historic Jewish tombstones are conspicuous in decoration and symbols. **The decoration** (simple plant motifs and other decorative elements) has been developing since the Middle Ages and has been influenced by the various styles in art, often reflecting different regional and local characteristics, the tradition of individual stone-cutters and is often determined by the granularity of the stone used. By tombstone **symbolics** we mean the small relief images in the upper part of the tombstone, which are mostly symbols of the descendants of specific ancient Hebrew family or tribe (blessing hands, a jug in a dish, a crown) or symbols of a trade or profession (e.g. scissors, a pincette, a book) or animals denoting family names (e.g. lions, deer, fish, birds).

The inscriptions on tombstones (epigraphs) were in Hebrew only from the Middle Ages up to the 19th century. By the mid-19th century bilingual inscriptions - Hebrew and German - began to appear in our cemeteries (or else in Yiddish, or German written in the Hebrew alphabet, such as in the cemetery in Třebíč), later Hebrew and

The most common traditional symbols: blessing hands of the Kohanim and a jug of the Levitas

Czech inscriptions followed. Some 20th century tombstones have inscriptions in Czech or German only with abbreviations of traditional Hebrew formulae. Purely Hebrew inscriptions were used on tombstones of Orthodox Jews (e.g. the tombstones of Galician refugees from the period of World War I and on some contemporary tombstones).

It usually took a long time to carve a tombstone, which would be erected a year after the burial: a short ceremony to consecrate the tombstone took place on the day of the first anniversary of the death or funeral. When speaking, for example, about "a tombstone from 1770" we mean a tombstone dated 1770 (i.e. the date of death) but completed and erected in the cemetery most probably the following year - 1771.

Some villages in Slovakia used to maintain two Jewish cemeteries: one for the Reform rite Jews (the so-called neological rite), the other for Orthodox Jews. In a number of Orthodox cemeteries the males and females are buried separately, so that even a husband and wife are not buried next to each other. This separation and special Orthodox cemeteries did not occur in the Czech lands and burials were made without regard to sex. However, even there Orthodox Jews (mainly Galician refugees from World War I) were buried in a separate place in the cemetery, at some distance of the other graves.

In some cemeteries a special part was reserved for the burials of rabbis: such group of graves is sometimes called **the rabbis' section** (e.g. Mikulov, Tachov). In some cemeteries there is a special section of children's graves, usually in rows in the edge of the cemetery. Graves of unnamed new-born babies usually bear the inscription "The child of...".

In our country it is not common to find special rows of graves of the Kohanites (their tombstones bearing the symbol of blessing hands) or of the Levites (descendants of Levi, who are required to help the members of the priestly tribe in their religious duties, whose symbol is a jug): this tradition has been maintained e.g. in the cemetery in Stráž.

In accordance with the ancient tradition Jews bring **little stones** to lay on the graves. There were even cemeteries which had a vessel full of little stones ready for the visitors (this is still the practice today e.g. in Mariánské Lázně).

A fairly large number of Jewish cemeteries with remarkable tombstones from the historical and artistic standpoint have survived on the territory of the Czech Republic. Many of the both old and new cemeteries even influenced the character of landscape. The earliest tombstones remaining in their original location (from the 15th century) may be seen in the Old Jewish Cemetery in Prague and in Kolín. Tombstones from the 16th century have survived in the cemeteries in Brandýs nad Labem, Ivančice, Libochovice, Mladá Boleslav and Stráž. Tombstones from the 17th and 18th centuries have been preserved in cemeteries in a number of towns and villages. However, the earliest and therefore the most precious tombstones, dating from the 13th and 14th centuries, originating from cemeteries which were abolished in the Middle Ages, are treasured in museums today: in Znojmo (perhaps the earliest surviving Jewish tombstone in our country, allegedly dating from 1256), in Brno and Cheb.

Jiří Fiedler

GUIDE

The aim of this guide is to show the most significant and best-preserved historical monuments which have survived the extinct or decimated Jewish religious communities on the territory of the Czech Republic. Since this territory has from early until recent times consisted of three autonomous lands (Bohemia, Moravia and Moravian Silesia) with different developments of Jewish settlement and jurisdiction, we draw attention to this historic division throughout the whole text of the guide:

Although in general the overwhelming majority of Jewish communities was in towns, a typical feature of historical **Bohemia** was a great number of rural Jewish communities, established in the 18th and 19th centuries.

In **Moravia** Jewish communities were established almost solely in towns: there existed only seven rural Jewish communities in Moravia, six of which were established in the westernmost part of the country near the Bohemian frontier.

The Jewish population in **Silesia** was expelled in the 15th - 16th centuries. Subsequently only a very small number of Jewish families was granted permission to resettle in Silesia, however, they were permitted to establish neither religious communities nor to have prayer rooms and rabbis. Prayer groups and religious congregations could be established only in the mid-19th century and originated solely in towns.

The majority of Jewish communities originated in **chartered towns** where Jews could find better opportunities of earning a living. This is why we also mention in the guide whether the town had a royal charter and we use the traditional historical denomination "town" or "small town" even in cases when a place no longer has the status of a town.

We have tried to describe at least the most significant places which are the main entries (in alphabetic order), containing a brief outline of the history of the local Jewish religious community and accompanied by brief references to the vanished Jewish religious communities and congregations in the vicinity, to concentration camps in which also Jews were interned and to the graves of the victims of the Nazis who died during the death transports in the last months of World War II. We also mention the birth-places and graves of famous Jews, and places where they lived or worked.

Since many names of towns and villages are mentioned in earlier sources by their former (historical) Czech or German language version, and also because former inmates of concentration camps knew mostly only the German names of the locations, we have also added the former Czech and German language version after the current names (italic type).

Distances are given in kilometres and measured in a direct line from the historical centre of the town. In the case of Prague the former Jewish Town represents the city centre.

Small town in Moravia, 110 km SE of Prague, 85 km W of Brno, 16 km SW of the district town Jihlava. Chartered most probably in the 13th cent.

Jews are said to have settled in B. in the 1st half of the 15th cent. and a J. community was established at that time. In the 18th and 19th cent. up to 190 J. lived in B. but their number dropped to 31 persons of the J. faith in 1930. The J. community was not revived after World War II.

The Jewish quarter, E of the main square, N of the road leading to Buková, forms a remarkable urban whole

Club. The synagogue's Classicist exterior has been preserved.

The cemetery is set on a knoll, 500 m W of the main square. The earliest preserved tombstones date from the Baroque period, from the 1st quarter of the 18th cent. Burials took place until World War II.

There are two châteaux from the 16th - 18th cent. in B. and an 18th cent. Baroque church.

The following J. communities used to be in the vicinity: **Horní Cerekev** /Ger. *Ober-Zerekwe, Lobeskirchen* (small town 5 km W, a synagogue from 1867, pulled down in 1951-52, a cemetery with tombstones from the 18th cent.).

with a small square and several narrow lanes. The J. quarter consisted of about 15 houses, most of which have been preserved.

The synagogue in the square of the former J. quarter was built on the site of an older synagogue. The building was completed in 1794, altered in 1825. Services were held until World War II. In 1958-74 it was used by the Hussite Church, in 1984-85 converted into a meeting place of the Horticultural

Town in Bohemia, 90 km S of Prague, 20 km SW of the district town Tábor. Chartered probably in 1323.

A J. community existed here as early as the 17th cent. Its population numbered about 80 persons (15 families) in the 18th and 19th cent. but by 1930 the number dropped to 32 persons of the J. faith. The J. religious congregation was not reestablished after World War II.

The Jewish street, today's street Široká, used to be along the town wall, N of the square. There was no enclosed ghetto in the town, J. lived in 6 neighbouring houses, on the N side of the street. The houses, mostly rebuilt in the 19th cent., have been preserved. A **Jewish school** was in a house left of the synagogue until the 19th cent.

The synagogue is in the street Široká, among former J. houses. Orientated towards NNE. Built after 1827 in the neo-Romanesque style. Services were held there until World War II. Since 1973 it has been used as a museum of fire protection.

The cemetery, adjacent to the outer side of the town wall, NW of the square. Remarkable tombstones from the last quarter of the 17th cent. Burials until World War II.

B. has a number of remarkable historical monuments: a Renaissance château (formerly a 13th cent. castle, rebuilt in the 16th cent.), Gothic churches and a Gothic monastery, remains of a town wall. Museum of pottery and ceramics. Peat baths with ferrous mineral springs, established in the 18th cent.

The following J. communities used to be in the vicinity: **Stádlec** /Ger. *Stachletz* (small town 9 km N, a J. street with a mid-19th cent. synagogue, an early 19th cent. cemetery); **Týn nad Vltavou** /Ger. *Moldautein* (town 9 km SSW, the J. community and cemetery ceased to exist in the 17th cent.); **Neznašov** (10 km SW, the village used to have a large J. population, former J. houses have survived, a cemetery from the 18th cent., the roof of an early 18th cent. synagogue collapsed in 1927, the walls were pulled down in 1973); **Koloděje nad Lužnicí** /Ger. *Kaladei* (6 km SW, the village was mostly J. in the past, some of the former J. houses have survived, a cemetery with tombstones from the early 18th cent., a synagogue from 1695-97 was pulled down in 1948). Koloděje n. L. is the native village of Alfred Radok (1914-1976 Vienna), producer of the National Theatre and the Prague Laterna Magika and his brother Emil Radok (1918), author of

the Laterna Magika stage. - The Czech - J. writer and publicist Bohdan Klineberger, pseud. Antonín Rataj, (1859-1928 Prague) was born in **Rataje**, a village 6 km NNW.

BĚLEČ   3

Village in Bohemia, 65 km SE of Prague, 18 km NE of the district town Tábor.

There was no J. community in B., the cemetery belonged to the Mladá Vožice J. community. (The town **Mladá Vožice** lies 2 km SW of B. A J. community was established in the town as early as the beginning of the 18th cent., ceased to exist during the Nazi occupation. Several J. houses have been preserved in the former J. street N of the square, a synagogue from about the 2nd half of the 19th cent. was pulled down after 1960.)

cent., a cemetery from the 1st half of the 19th cent.); **Bendovo Záhoří** (5 km SSW, a prayer room recorded in the 19th cent.); **Oldřichov** /Ger. Ullershof (6 km WNW, a J. community existed here in the 18th cent.); **Neustupov** (small town 12 km NW, a 17th cent. cemetery, a synagogue from the 1st half of the 19th cent. was pulled down after 1919, the birthplace of the Czech-J. poet Josef Rosenzweig-Moir [1887-1943 in a concentration camp]); **Zvěstov** (10 km NNW, a J. community existed here in the 18th cent.); **Načeradec** (small town 9 km NE, a synagogue from mid-19th cent., a 17th cent. cemetery; colonel Rudolf Bejkovský [1917-1979 Nový Knín], one of the commanders of the Czech army in the USSR during World War II, came from N.); **Pravonín** (13 km NE, a prayer room recorded in the 18th - 19th cent., a cemetery with tombstones from the 1st

The cemetery is set on the edge of a forest, 2 km NE, between the village Vilice and a seclusion called Elbančice. Founded before 1723, the oldest preserved tombstones date from the 2nd half of the 18th cent. Burials until World War II. At present, reconstruction works are being carried out in the oldest part of the cemetery.

The following J. communities and religious societies used to be in the vicinity: **Babčice** (9 km SE, a rebuilt synagogue from about the mid-19th

half of the 19th cent.); **Chmelná** (16 km NE, remains of a synagogue from about the 18th cent., the grandfather of the composer Gustav Mahler was born in Ch.); **Miřetice** (17 km NE, a prayer room is said to have existed here in the 19th cent.). - The Czech - J. writer František Kafka (1909) was born in **Louňovice pod Blaníkem** (10 km N).

*1 km **Šelmberk**, ruins of a Gothic castle with a look-out-tower; 11 km N **Blaník**, a wooded hill (639 m) with a look-out-tower, linked with the famous* *legend of the Blaník Knights. There are several noteworthy châteaux and churches in the vicinity.*

BENEŠOV 4

District town in Bohemia, 40 km SE of Prague. Chartered as early as the first half of the 14th cent.

Jewish families are mentioned in B. in the 16th cent., a J. community is recorded in the 18th cent. The J. population numbered 237 in 1930. The J. community was not revived after World War II.

(**The synagogue** was built in 1845 and demolished in 1976.)

The old cemetery - 100 m NW of the main square, in the street Československé armády, near the Hvězda department store. Founded in the 17th cent., burials until 1883. The cemetery has been recently converted into a memorial park. Several tombstones were left there, the others transferred to the new cemetery.

The new cemetery - 500 m NE of the main square, next to the municipal cemetery. Founded in 1883, funerals until World War II. Grave of 13 French prisoners from a death transport in 1945. Several tombstones of historical value were transferred here from the old cemetery after 1984.

Ruins of a Gothic cathedral, one Gothic and one Baroque church are to be found in the town.

The following J. communities and religious societies existed in the vicinity: **Bystřice** /Ger. *Bistritz* (small town 6 km S, a prayer room existed in the 19th - 20th cent.); **Zahrádka** /Ger. *Sachradka* (9 km SW, a prayer room allegedly existed here in the 17 cent.); **Maršovice** (12 km SW, a prayer room allegedly existed here after World War I); **Neveklov** (town 11 km WSW with a rebuilt synagogue from the 17th cent. and a cemetery from the 18th cent.); **Netvořice** (small town 12 km WNW, a prayer room recorded before World War II); **Týnec nad Sázavou** /Ger. *Teinitz* (town 8 km NW). - In the village of **Václavice** (5 km W) the Chief Rabbi Richard Feder (1875-1970) was born. In **Bystřice** the Nazis set up a detention camp for persons from mixed marriages (about 1000 internees). A grave of three victims from a railway transport in January 1945 is to be found at the local cemetery. A grave of 5 victims from a railway transport from Auschwitz is to be found at the cemetery in **Čerčany** (7 km NNE).

*2 km SW lies the noteworthy **Konopiště Castle** (the former castle was built in the 14th cent., rebuilt in the 19th cent.) with rich interior furnishing and collections; 8 km NW **Týnec nad Sázavou** with a Romanesque rotunda and a Romanesque keep; 6 km N **Poříčí nad Sázavou** with two Romanesque churches; 7 km SE a Baroque château **Jemniště** with collection of 17th cent. Dutch maps, plans and vedutas.*

BLEVICE 5

Village in Bohemia, 20 km NW of Prague, 12 km NE of the district town of Kladno.

The cemetery is at the S end of the village, near the road to Zákolany. Founded allegedly in the 17th cent. - the earliest preserved tombstone dates from the early 18th cent. Burials until World War II, mostly people from Velvary and Kralupy nad Vltavou. The cemetery has recently been repaired. There was no J. community in Blevice. The cemetery belonged to the J. community of **Ješín** and later to the **Velvary J.** community.

The following J. communities and religious societies used to exist in the vicinity: **Koleč** (2 km SW, a prayer room recorded in the 19th cent.); **Ješín** (7 km NW, a J. community of unknown origin existed here until the 2nd half of the 19th cent., a synagogue from about the 18th cent. was pulled down after 1970); **Velvary** (town 8 km N, a rebuilt synagogue from the 1930's, the municipal museum houses a great collection of paintings by George Kars); **Mikovice** /Ger. *Minkowitz* (4 km ENE, a prayer room existed here before 1874); **Kralupy nad Vltavou** (town 6 km NE, a synagogue from the 2nd half of the 19th cent., converted into a prayer hall of the Protestant Church, the painter George [Jiří] Kars [1880-1945 Geneva] was born in Kralupy and the Czech-J. poet Josef Rosenzweig-Moir [1887 Neustupov - 1943 in a concentration camp] lived in the town); **Kamýk** /Ger. *Kamaik*, part of the village **Velké Přílepy** (7 km SE, a rebuilt synagogue from the 1st half of the 19th cent.); **Roztoky** (town 12 km SE, a prayer room existed here in the 19th - 20th cent., Emil Utitz [1883-1959 Jena], a German-J. poet, aesthetician and philosopher, was born in Roztoky and Josef Korner-Prag [1880 in Rohatec - 1950 Prague], a German-J. historian, lived here from 1945).

*4 km S rises the hill **Budeč** with remains of a Premyslid settlement and a church from the 10th - 12th cent.; 10 km S **Okoř**, ruins of the Gothic castle.*

BOSKOVICE 6

Town in Moravia, 170 km SE of Prague, 32 km N of Brno. Chartered in the 15th cent.

Jews settled in Boskovice perhaps in the 15th cent. The Boskovice J. community represented one of the largest communities in Moravia, a famous centre of Talmudic study. Many significant rabbis were active in B. - e.g. Yehuda Oppenheim who came from Worms in the early 18th cent., Nehe-

mia Jaffe from Cracow in the 1st half of the 18th cent. and Isachar Beer Bloch from Hamburg at the end of the 18th cent. 1973 persons of the J. faith (37% of the total population) are recorded in 1848. In the mid-19th cent. the number of Jews declined as many left for Vienna and Brno. The J. population in Boskovice numbered 395 in 1930, the majority of whom perished during the Nazi occupation. The J. community was revived after 1945 but later ceased to exist owing to a decrease in members. B. is the native town of the German-J. writer and playwright Hermann Ungar (18931929 Prague) and Moritz Zobel, the editor of the Berlin *Encyclopaedia Judaica.*

The ghetto (today's Bílkova and Plačkova streets and their vicinity, S of the main square) was most probably established in the 15th cent. and is noteworthy from the town-planning point of view. It consisted of about 150 houses with up to 2,000 inhabitants and used to be the seat of the Moravian Chief Rabbi. Until 1919 it was an independent self-governing community. The J. quarter is almost intact (mostly rebuilt in the 19th cent.) and has been declared an urban conservation area. The original **gate** has been preserved in the eastern wall.

The synagogue (called S. Major) on the main street of the ghetto, was built in the late 17th cent., rebuilt in the neo-Gothic style in the 19th cent. Services until World War II. At present the building serves as a store-house, plans

1875 Szeged), the pioneer of J. emancipation and reform Judaism in Hungary.

*10 km SE, near the village Sloup, is the famous complex of stalactite caves **Moravský kras** (Moravian Karst); 10 km SW **Lysice**, a Baroque château, surrounded by a remarkable park, interior open to public.*

BRANDÝS NAD LABEM

Town 20 km NE of Prague. Chartered in the early 14th cent.

A J. community existed in B. most probably in the 16th cent. Jews settled

have been made to reconstruct the synagogue. (Until recently there existed the so-called Synagogue Minor in the ghetto and other prayer halls used to exist here earlier.)

The cemetery lies on the W outskirts, 750 m WSW of the synagogue. One of the largest J. cemeteries in Moravia. The oldest tombstones date from the late 17th cent. (The museum houses several tombstones from the abolished older cemetery.)

The small town **Černá Hora** /Ger. *Schwarzenberg* (10 km SW) is the birthplace of Rabbi Leopold Löw (1811-

originally around the synagogue (NW of the square, beyond the town proper). A small **ghetto** existed in the town in the 17th - 19th cent., on the square called Krajířské náměstí, N of the main square. The J. population of Brandýs numbered 300 in the 19th cent. but the number dropped to 60 in 1930. After World War II the J. community ceased to exist. The J. surname Brandeis was most probably derived from the town's name.

The synagogue is between the main square and the municipal cemetery, NW of the old city centre. Built in

1828-1829 on the site of an earlier synagogue. Services until World War II, at present used as a store-house.

The cemetery lies 500 m NW of the main square, in the street leading to Kostelec nad Labem. Founded in 1568, many valuable Renaissance and Baroque tombstones, one Renaissance ark-shaped tomb. Burials until World War II.

lav with three remarkable churches (Romanesque and Baroque) and a Gothic gate. St. Wenceslas (Bohemian prince) was assassinated here in 935.

The following J. communities and religious societies existed in the vicinity: **Líbeznice** /Ger. *Rotkirchen* (12 km W, a prayer room existed here in the 19th-20th cent.); **Zlonín** /Ger. *Slonin* (11 km WNW, a prayer room may have

existed here in the 19th cent.); **Kostelec nad Labem** /Ger. *Elbekosteletz* (town 7 km NW with a cemetery from the late 16th cent. and tombstones from the mid-19th cent., a synagogue from the 2nd half of the 19th cent. was pulled down about 1952); **Lysá nad Labem** /Ger. *Lissa* (town 13 km E, a prayer hall from the 2nd half of the 19th cent., converted into a dwelling house, remains of a cemetery from the 2nd half of the 19th cent.); **Jirny** (8 km SSE, a prayer room recorded in the 19th cent.). - The Czech-J. writer Vojtěch Rakous (1862-1935 Prague) was born in the village **Starý Brázdim** (5 km W).

*5 km SW **Jenštejn**, ruins of a Gothic castle with a look-out-tower; 12 km ESE **Přerov nad Labem**, a small town with an open-air museum of folk architecture and a Renaissance château; 7 km SE **Čelákovice** with a Renaissance stronghold converted into a museum.*

Brandýs has a significant Renaissance château, remains of a Renaissance bridge over the Elbe and Gothic-Renaissance churches. On the other side of the river (2 km NE) is the town Stará Boles-

BRNO 8
(Ger. *Brünn*)

District town in Moravia, 185 km SE of Prague. The town originated by uniting several Christian settlements and a Jewish settlement in the 1st half of the 13th century. From the 17th cent. until 1949 it was the capital of Moravia.

Jews had lived in Brno before the town was founded. Jews of the formerly large community were expelled in 1454, their synagogue and cemetery were destroyed. The present J. community originated in the mid-19th cent. In 1930 its population stood at 10,202 persons of the J. faith, about 8,400 persons perished during the Nazi occupation. The J. religious congregation was revived in 1945. Its present address: Hybešova ul. 14, 602 00 Brno.

Many Jews born in Brno have significantly contributed to the fields of economics, politics, science and culture. Let us mention e.g. some **writers and playwrights**: Philipp Langmann (1862-1931 Vienna), Leo Greiner (1876-1928 Berlin), Ernst Weiss (1882-1940 Paris), Oskar Jellinek (1886-1949 Los Angeles), Felix Langer (1889-1980 London), Ernst Lothar (1890-1974 Vienna), Hans Flesch-Brunningen, pen-name Vincent Brun (1895-1981 Vienna); in the field of **music** e.g. the violin virtuoso Heinrich Wilhelm Ernst (1814-1865 Nice), called "second Paganini"; composers and conductors, such as Walter Klein (1882-1961 San Anselmo, USA), Hans Gál (1890), Erich Wolfgang Korngold (1897-1957 Hollywood), Pavel Haas (1899-1944 Auschwitz) and Eitan Otto Lustig (1899-1970 Tel Aviv), the musicologist Paul Stefan (1879-1943 New York); in the field of **drama and film** e.g. Fritz Grünbaum (1880-1941 Dachau), Albrecht Viktor Blum (18881959 Mexico City), Friedrich Richter (1894), Hugo Haas (1901-1968 Vienna); in the field of **visual arts** e.g. painters Elisabeth Weingarten (1884-??) and Clara Epstein (1884-??), the painter of old Jerusalem Ludvík Blum (1891-1974 Haifa) and the artist of the ghetto in Terezín Otto Ungar (1901-1945 Blankenhain).

Arnošt Wiesner (1890 Malacky - 1971 Liverpool), a well-known architect, lived in B. in 1919-39. It is the native town of the well-known Austrian philosopher and philologist Theodor Gomperz (1832-1912 Vienna). The renowned philologist Roman Jakobson (1896 Moscow - 1982 Boston) lectured at Brno University in 1933-38.

Jakob Frank (1726-1791), leader of the anti-Talmudic Jewish Christian sect - the so-called Frankists - lived in Brno in 1773-86.

The synagogue is in the street Skořepka No. 13. It is a Functionalist style building, built in 1935-36 (architect Otto Eisler) with a traditionally designed interior (formerly an Orthodox rite synagogue).

The synagogue is still used today. (The so-called Velká synagóga [The Great Synagogue] at the corner of Spálená and Přízova streets was burnt down and demolished during the Nazi occupation. There used to be several other synagogues and prayer-rooms in Brno).

The cemetery lies 2 km E of the synagogue, the entrance is from Nezamyslova street. Founded in 1852, twice enlarged, the urn grove dates from 1936. The neo-Romanesque ceremonial hall dates from 1900, renovated in 1982. Over 11,000 graves and over 9,000 tombstones. The oldest tombstones (transferred to the cemetery from an unknown place) date from the late 17th cent. The monument in memory of 13,000 victims of the Nazis dates from 1950. Let us mention some of the significant personalities buried here: the German-J. poet and playwright Alois Jeitteles (1794 Prague - 1858), whose poems were set to music by L. van Beethoven, the German-J. writer and philosopher Hieronymus Lorm (1821 Mikulov - 1902), the founding father of the leading Czech newspaper *Lidové noviny*, journalist Adolf Stránský (1855 Habry - 1931), the actor Hugo Haas (1901-1968 Vienna), the Chief Rabbi of Bohemia and Moravia Richard Feder (1875 Václavice - 1970)

and many others. The Moravian Museum at the Brno Castle houses several 14th cent. tombstones from a former medieval cemetery.

There are many historical monuments in Brno (two castles, noble palaces, churches and the like), several museums and galleries. The historical core of the town has been declared a protected urban area.

*13 km SE, near the village **Prace**, is a monument and museum commemorating "the battle of the three emperors" (Napoleon won the battle here over the Austrian and Russian armies in 1805); 12 km S **Rajhrad**, a small town with an 11th cent. monastery, rebuilt in the 18th cent., today an art gallery.*

Jihlava. A small J. quarter with a synagogue stood there as early as in the 1st half of the 17th cent. 50 houses of Jewish ownership (420 people) are recorded in the mid-19th cent.: the northern part of the town was mostly Jewish. The J. population numbered only 33 persons of the J. faith in 1930. After World War II the J. religious congregation was not revived.

The synagogue in the former small J. quarter - a ghetto - beyond the N side of the square. Built perhaps in the 17th cent., redesigned in 1888 - the structure was extended and a women's gallery was added to the western side. The synagogue is not used today, there is a well-preserved wooden aron ha-kodesh.

BRTNICE   9
(Ger. *Pirnitz*)

Small town in Moravia, 125 km SE of Prague, 12 km SE of the district town Jihlava. Chartered in the 13th cent.

Jews settled in B. most probably in the 14th cent., a J. community was established about the 1st half of the 15th cent. after the expulsion of J. from

The old cemetery - 1 km NE of the square, near the road to Panská Lhota. Founded before 1600, the oldest legible tombstones date from the 17th cent. Several remarkable tombstones.

The new cemetery - S of the old cemetery. Founded in the late 19th cent., has been repaired recently.

B. has a large Renaissance château (formerly a castle), Gothic and Renaissance churches, a Renaissance town hall, a Baroque stone bridge with statues and other places of interest.

5 km NE Rokštejn, ruins of a Gothic castle.

BRUMOV   10

Small town in Moravia, 280 km SE of Prague, 30 km SE of the district town Zlín. Chartered in 1500. At present it forms one part of the twin-town Brumov - Bylnice.

A J. community was established here most probably in the 18th century. The J. population numbered about 60 persons of the J. faith in the 19th cent., only 21 in 1900 and 5 in 1930. The religious congregation was abolished in the early 20th cent.

The cemetery lies on a knoll 1,500 m N of the square, 300 m W of the road to Valašské Klobouky. Founded in the 18th cent., burials until World War II. Repaired in 1985. An example of a small, non-enclosed rural cemetery.

(A prayer-hall used to be in house No. 728, J. Polácha St. but was abolished in the early 20th cent.)

The following J. societies used to exist in the vicinity: **Valašské Klobouky** (town 5 km N, a prayer room existed here in the 19th - 20th cent.); **Slavičín** (town 11 km W, a prayer room existed here in the 19th - 20th cent.). - The well-known Viennese actor and librettist Julius Brammer (1877-1943 Juan-les-Pins, France) was born in the village of **Sehradice** (16 km NW).

A ruin of a Gothic castle can be found in Brumov. B. is a tourist gateway to the wooded chain of mountains the White Carpathians (the highest peak - 970 m).

Town in Bohemia, 65 km SW of Prague, 15 km S of the district town Příbram. Chartered in the first half of the 14th cent.

A J. community was established in B. most probably in the 16th cent. The J. population numbered 190 persons of the Jewish faith in the mid-19th cent., in those days Březnice was the seat of the district rabbi. In 1930 its population stood at 30 persons of the J. faith, after World War II the religious congregation ceased to exist.

Joachim von Popper (died 1795), a well-known Prague trader and financier and one of the first Jews to be raised to the nobility, was born in Březnice.

The Jewish quarter, called Lokšany, was founded by the owner of the château and town - Ferdinand of Lokšany in 1570. Enlarged to its present size most probably in the 18th cent. Situated north of the main square, it has a regular ground plan, two squares and two streets. It used to be an enclosed ghetto, connected with the town by one narrow street and a gate. It consisted of 21 - 24 houses, mostly preserved and rebuilt in the Empire style. The largest house is the so-called Popper palace with an enclosed courtyard. The enclosed character of Lokšany has been recently disturbed by the construction of a new driveway and several demolitions, however, it still represents a unique example of ghetto town-planning in Europe.

The synagogue stands in the centre of the ghetto's larger square. Built in 1725, rebuilt after 1820. At present the synagogue is used as a store-house, though the furnishing has mostly been preserved. Plans have been made to convert the synagogue into a concert and exhibition hall.

the 17th century. Burials until World War II.

The town has a noteworthy Renaissance château with collections open to the public and two 17th cent. churches.

The following J. communities and religious congregations existed in the vicinity: **Kamenná** (8 km NNE, a prayer room from 1709, rebuilt in 1822, converted into a garage; an 18th cent. cemetery); **Milín** (small town 11 km NE, a prayer room existed here in the 18th - 20th cent.); **Zalužany** (9 km ESE, an Empire style synagogue from the 1st half of the 19th cent. and a cemetery with 18th century tombstones); **Mirovice** (town 7 km SE, a 17th cent. cemetery and a rebuilt synagogue from the late 18th cent.); **Svučice** (6 km SSE, a prayer room recorded in the 18th cent.); **Drahenice** (4 km S, a prayer room recorded in the 19th cent.).

*8 km NW **Rožmitál pod Třemšínem**, a small town with a Renaissance château; 10 km NE near the village **Konětopy** is a monument commemorating the end of World War II in Europe (the last battle took place here on May 11, 1945).*

The cemetery is of great historical value, situated 1500 m N of the main square, E of the road to the village Přední Poříčí. Tombstones dating from

Town in Moravia, 240 km SE of
Prague, 55 km SE of Brno, 17 km NE
of the district town Hodonín. Chartered
most probably in the 1st half of the
14th cent.

A J. community with a synagogue is
said to have existed in B. as early as in
the 14th cent. 67 J. families are recorded in the 17th cent., in the mid-19th
cent. about 965 J. lived here in 88 houses. The Jewish population stood at 416
in 1900 and dropped to 138 in 1930.
After World War II a synagogue group
was established but soon ceased to
exist owing to decrease in members.

The Austrian composer Karl Gold-
mark (1830 Keszthely - 1915 Vienna)
spent his early childhood in B. where
his father was a cantor.

The cemetery lies 300 m E of the
square, next to the municipal cemetery.
Tombstones from the 17th cent. and
many valuable Baroque tombstones. A
monument in memory of the victims of
the Nazis was dedicated in the cemetery in 1956. A ceremonial hall was
built in the 19th cent., restored in 1985.

(The historical core of the J. quarter
was NW of the square, between the
square and the château: several houses
have survived. The last synagogue from
1863 was demolished in 1958.)

*The town has a Baroque church from
the early 19th cent. and a 19th cent.
neo-Gothic château.*

The following J. communities and
religious societies used to exist in the
vicinity: **Ostroh** /formerly *Uherský Ost-*

roh, Ger. *Ungarisch-Ostra* (town 9 km ENE, a synagogue from about the 16th cent., pulled down by the Nazis, a J. street, a 19th cent. cemetery with tombstones from the 16th cent., transferred here from an older cemetery); **Veselí nad Moravou** (town 8 km ESE, an 18th cent. cemetery, a small ghetto - a J. street, a 19th cent. synagogue); **Kyjov** /Ger. *Gaya* (town 11 km WNW, two cemeteries - from 17th and 20th cent. - destroyed by the Nazis, the ghetto and the synagogue were destroyed during the war in 1945, the native town of the painter Emil Singer [1881-1942 concentration camp Izbica] and of the Ger. - J. poet Sonka [Hugo Sonnenschein, 1890-1953 Mírov]); **Kostelec** (11 km NW, remains of an 18th cent. cemetery); **Ždánice** /Ger. *Steinitz* (town 21 km NW, a prayer room existed here in the 19th - 20th cent.); **Žeravice** (a small town 6 km NW, a J. religious society recorded in the late 19th cent.); **Kory čany** /Ger. *Koritschan* (a small town 17 km NW, a J. street with a rebuilt synagogue, a cemetery with tombstones from the 17th cent., the birthplace of Sigmund Kollisch [1816-1886 Hodonín], a Ger. - J. revolutionary journalist, poet, writer and playwright). - In **Svatobořice** (13 km W) a barrack camp for J. refugees from Galicia was set up during World War I (at least 7,000 people passed through the camp) and during the Nazi occupation family members of refugees and those of mixed marriages were deported here.

ČÁSLAV   13

Town in Bohemia, 70 km ESE of Prague, 10 km SE of the district town Kutná Hora. Founded and chartered about 1260.

Up to the mid-19th cent. only one single Jewish family was allowed to reside in Čáslav. When the Jews granted civic equality under law in the mid-19th cent. Jews from the neighbouring villages started to move to Čáslav. A J. religious congregation was founded in 1870 and it numbered about 300 per-

sons of the J. faith. The congregation numbered 119 in 1930 and ceased to exist after World War II.

The film director Miloš Forman (1932), resident in Hollywood at present, and the sculptor and graphic artist Aleš Veselý (1935) were born in Čáslav.

The synagogue stands NE of the main square in Fučíkova street. Built in 1899-1990 in the so-called Moorish style, wooden painted both the ceiling and women's gallery. Services were held here until World War II, today it serves as exhibition space - Gallery of Jindřich Prucha.

A Jewish section was established in 1884 in the municipal **cemetery** (the northern periphery of the town, in the street leading to Chotusice).

The town has a remarkable Gothic church, remains of the city fortification wall and other places of interest.

8 km **Kačina**, *a remarkable Empire château housing a museum on the history of farming; 7 km ENE* **Žehušice**, *an Empire-style château with white stags in the park; 7 km SE the* **Žleby** *château, rebuilt in the period of Romanticism, interior open to the public; 14 km SE* **Lichnice**, *ruins of an extensive Gothic castle.*

ČESKÁ LÍPA 14
(Ger. *Böhmisch-Leipa*)

District town in Bohemia, 65 km N of Prague. Chartered in the 13th cent.

A Jewish community existed in Č. L. most probably as early as in the second half of the 16th cent. The community numbered 40 J. families in the 17th cent., 600 persons of the J. faith in the late 19th cent. and only 301 persons in 1930. A synagogue group was established after World War II, its members were mostly former soldiers of the Czechoslovak foreign army from Subcarpathian Ruthenia. Subsequently, the synagogue group, considerably reduced in number, ceased to exist.

Hugo Salus (1866-1929 Prague), a German - J. poet, was born in Č. L.

Jewish houses and a synagogue were built beyond the city wall, in the **Jewish Street** along the eastern city wall. In the mid-19th cent. the ghetto consisted of about 50 houses, some of them have been preserved. The last synagogue, built on the site of an earlier synagogue in 1862-63, was burnt down and demolished by the Nazis in 1938.

The old cemetery lies 500 m NNW of the main square, near a park. Founded before 1574, tombstones from the 17th cent. Burials until 1905. The cemetery was seriously damaged by the Nazis, most of the tombstones were removed. (The new cemetery, built in 1905, with a grave of 17 J. prisoners victims of a death march, was abolished after 1980.)

The following places of interest are to be found in Č. L.: the ruins of a Renaissance château, a small Renaissance château, Gothic, Renaissance and Baroque churches.

The following J. communities and religious societies used to exist in the vicinity: **Rumburk** /Ger. *Rumburg* (town 30 km N, a prayer room existed here in the 19th - 20th cent.); **Varnsdorf** (town 25 km NNE, with a prayer room until 1983); **Jablonné v Podještědí** /Ger. *Deutsch-Gabel* (town 18 km NE, a J. community and a cemetery existed there most probably in the 16th - 17th cent.). - J. prisoners, victims of a death march from the concentration camp in Schwarzheide, are buried in the cemetery in **Horní Chřibská** (19 km N). Two small labour camps for J. women were set up 20 km north in **Jiřetín pod Jedlovou**/Ger. *Sankt Georgenthal* in 1944-45. A similar camp existed in 1943-45 in the village **Dolní Podluží** /form. *Dolní Grunt*, Ger. *Nieder- Grund* (21 km NNE).

*10 km NNW **Kamenický Šenov**, a small town with a museum of glassmaking and a protected rock formation Kamenné varhany; 8 km N **Nový Bor**, a town with a museum of glassmaking; 7 km NNE **Sloup**, a rock castle, (later a hermitage); 7 km E **Zákupy**, a small town with a château built in the style of the so-called second Rococo, open to the public; 12 km SE **Máchovo jezero**, a great lake and a popular summer resort.*

ČESKÉ BUDĚJOVICE 15
(Ger. *Budweis*)

District town in Bohemia, 125 km S of Prague. Founded and chartered in 1265.

Jews settled in Č. B. in the 14th cent. In the 15th cent. there was a large J. community with a synagogue and a cemetery in the town. In 1505 nine Jews were accused of ritual murder and burnt alive and thirteen J. were drowned. The following year 23 J. children were taken away from their parents and baptized by force, the remaining Jews were expelled from the town and the Gothic synagogue was converted into a Catholic chapel (the remains were demolished in 1908), two cemeteries were also destroyed. Jews were not permitted to reside in the town from 1506 to 1848.

A modern J. religious congregation was established in 1856, subsequently increasing in number. Its population numbered 969 persons of the J. faith in 1890 and 1,138 (3% of the total population) in 1930. After World War II there was a synagogue group in the town which ceased to exist in 1970 owing to a decline in members.

Norbert Frýd (1913-1976 Prague), a Czech-J. writer, was born in Č. B. The Czech poet, graphic artist and physician Karel Fleischmann (1897 Klatovy - 1944 Birkenau) lived in the town. 129 prisoners from Auschwitz who had died in a railway transport were cremated in the local crematorium in January 1945.

The cemetery, 1500 m E of the main square, in the street Pekárenská.

Founded in 1866, burials also after World War II. A monument in the memory of the Nazi victims (resembling an ark-shaped tomb) was dedicated in the cemetery in 1950.

(The synagogue, built in 1888 by the famous Viennese architect Max Fleischer, was blown up by the Nazis in 1942.)

There are many interesting pieces of architecture in the town: keeps, churches from the 13th up to the 19th centuries, a Baroque town-hall, arcaded houses, a museum with rich collections. The historical core of the town has been declared an urban conservation area. The town is also well-known for its brewery.

In January 1945 about 180 prisoners of a railway transport were cremated and 4 prisoners buried in the cemetery in **Poříčí** (village 6 km SSW). Many of these victims were shot by the Nazis here.

*9 km N **Hluboká,** a château, built in the Windsor style, housing a gallery with an excellent collection of fine arts; 13 km SE **Trocnov,** the native place of the Hussite leader Jan Žižka,; 13 km S **Římov,** a place of pilgrimage, which is supposed to resemble Jerusalem as far as the configuration of the grounds and architecture are concerned.*

ČESKÝ KRUMLOV   16
(Ger. *Krumau*)

District town in Bohemia, 140 km S of Prague, 25 km SW of České Budějovice. Chartered in the early 14th cent.

Several J. families lived in Č. K. in the 14th cent. The small J. community (6 families) was expelled in 1494. A maximum of 3 Jewish families were permitted to reside in the town in the course of the 17th - 19th cent. When the Jews were granted civic equality under law a modern religious society (later a religious congregation) was established in 1855. 111 persons of the J. faith are recorded in Č. K. in 1930. After World War II the religious congregation was not revived.

The synagogue, 400 m SE of the main square, in the street Švermova. It

was built in 1908-09 (arch. Kafka), services were held until 1938. The interior of the synagogue was destroyed in 1938 after the occupation of the town by the Nazis. After the liberation, in 1945, it served as an interconfessional Christian church for the soldiers of the American army, later, until 1968, as a Hussite Church. At present it is used as a store-house. Plans have been made to convert the building into a cultural centre.

The cemetery lies on a hill 900 m ENE of the main square, adjoining the municipal cemetery. Founded in 1891, burials until 1938, the last urn was brought here in 1967 from the USA.

Due to its numerous historical monuments the town has been declared an urban conservation area. The town has an extensive Renaissance château open to the public, many Gothic, Renaissance and Baroque ecclesiastic and secular buildings. Č. K. is a picturesque town situated between meanders of the Vltava river.

A religious community used to be in **Rožmberk nad Vltavou** /Ger. *Rosenberg* (small town 18 km S, a synagogue from the 17th - 19th cent. was pulled down after 1966, remains of a small J. quarter, remains of an old cemetery from about the 14th cent. with tombstones from the 18th cent., the new

cemetery from 1883). Religious societies with prayer rooms used to exist in **Velešín** (small town 11 km E, a prayer room recorded in the 19th cent.); **Kaplice** (town 15 km SE, a prayer room is said to have existed here in the 19th - 20th cent., 163 prisoners from Auschwitz who had died in a railway transport were buried here in January 1945); **Vyšší Brod** /Ger. *Hohenfurt* (small town 22 km S, a prayer room is said to have existed here in the 19th - 20th cent.); **Frymburk** /Ger. *Friedberg* (small town 20 km SE, a prayer room is said to have existed here in the 19th - 20th. cent.). - Near the village **Netřebice** (10 km ESE) there is a grave of 46 prisoners, near the village **Omlenice** (13 km SE) a grave of 63 prisoners and in the small town **Horní Dvořiště** (24 km SSE) a grave of 14 prisoners who died during a railway transport from Auschwitz.

*12 km NNW towers the **Kleť** mountain (1,083 m) with a look-out-tower and a restaurant accessible by cableway; 18 km NNE the ruins of a Gothic castle **Dívčí Kámen**; 12 km NE a Gothic monastery **Zlatá Koruna**, open to the public.*

ČESKÝ TĚŠÍN 17
(Ger. *Tschechisch-Teschen*)

Town in Silesia, on the Czech-Polish frontier, 300 km ESE of Prague, 30 km SE of Ostrava. Originally Č. T. used to be the industrial suburb of the ancient town of Těšín (Ger. *Teschen*, Pol. *Cieszyn*). In 1920 Těšín was divided by a new frontier between Czechoslovakia and Poland. The western suburb became an independent town in Czechoslovakia, named Český Těšín.

Jews settled in Těšín as early as in the Middle Ages. After the division of the town in 1920 the synagogue and cemetery remained on the Polish territory. The newly established religious congregation in Č. T. was very large (1021 persons of the J. faith are recorded in 1921) and therefore it had 3 modern synagogues built and a cemetery established. Two of the synagogues were demolished and the cemetery suffered serious damage during the Nazi occupation. The majority of Jews from Č. T. perished during the war but after the liberation in 1945 Jews from eastern Czechoslovakia and Poland settled in the town. A synagogue group was established but later ceased to exist owing to a decline in members. -

The Czech - J. writer Ludvík Aškenazy (1921-1986 Bolzano), officer in the Czechoslovak army in the USSR, was born in Český Těšín.

The synagogue is in the center of the town, in Božkova street. Built in 1928, services held until 1939, revived after World War II. The building was converted into a cultural centre for Polish citizens.

The cemetery is 1 km NW of the town centre, in Hřbitovní street, adjoining the municipal cemetery. Founded in 1924, the ceremonial hall was built in 1926. Burials until 1969. (The historically valuable cemetery with several thousands of tombstones is on the Polish side of the frontier.)

A J. community used to be in **Jablunkov** (town 22 km SE with a cemetery from the 2nd half of the 19th cent., a prayer room existed here in the 19th - 20th cent., the native town of the painter, sculptor and art historian Otto Schneid [1900 - resident in Canada], founder of an art museum in Vilnius.)

Westward are two dams and popular resorts - Těrlická přehrada (9 km) and Žermanická přehrada (10 km); there are several noteworthy wooden churches in the surrounding countryside - e. g. in the small village Nýdek (14 km SE, from the 16th cent.), in Guty (9 km S, from the 16th cent.), Albrechtice (8 km NW, from the 18th cent.). 12 km S of the town is the gateway to the popular mountain range Beskydy (the highest peak 1,324 m).

ČKYNĚ 18
(during the Nazi occupation in Ger. *Kieselhof*)

Small town in Bohemia, 120 km SSW of Prague, 16 km SSW of Strakonice. Chartered in 1537.

There exists no documentary record of the precise number of J. living in Č. in the early 17th cent. A small J. community (about 10 families) existed here in the 18th and 19th cent. By the end of the 19th cent. its population grew to about 40 families (240 persons). In the mid-19th cent. the Jews began to move to larger cities and in 1897 the seat of the J. congregation was transferred from Čkyně to Vimperk. Only 3 J. families (11 persons) lived in Č. in 1930.

Čkyně is the native town of Alois Zucker (1842-1906 Prague), a famous attorney and dean of the Prague Faculty of Law, member of the Czech Academy of Sciences and Arts, the first president of the National Union of Czech Jews (founded in 1894).

The synagogue is in the S part, between the main road and the railway station, house No. 105. Built in the Empire style in 1828, regular services held until 1895, occasional services until World War I. The synagogue was sold in 1922 and later converted into a workshop.

The cemetery is 500 m SE of the synagogue, near the road to Hradčany. The oldest preserved tombstone dates from 1688, burials until 1942. The total of about 500 burials. Remarkable Baroque tombstones. The cemetery has been repaired recently.

The following J. communities used to be in the vicinity: **Volyně** (a synagogue pulled down about 1903); **Dub** (13 km E, a rebuilt J. street - a village ghetto - with a rebuilt synagogue and

an early 18th cent. cemetery); **Vlachovo Březí** /Ger. *Wällisch-Birken* (town 9 km SE, the 18th cent. timber framed synagogue was converted into a dwelling house, it was the last wooden synagogue in Czechoslovakia; tombstones from the 1st half of the 18th cent. are to be found in the cemetery); **Vimperk** /Ger *Winterberg* (town 8 km SW, the synagogue from 1926 was destroyed by the Nazis). - In **Volary** /Ger. *Wallern* (town 23 km SSE), 95 J. girls, victims of a death march from the concentration camp Ravensbrück, were buried in the spring of 1945; the monument from 1990. Thirteen women, victims of a death march, are buried near the village **Polka** /Ger. *Elendbachel* (19 km SSW). - The German-J. poet and prose-writer Hilda Kohner-Bergmann (1878-1947 Astorp, Sweden), was born in **Prachatice** (town 16 km SE).

2 km E Lčovice, a Renaissance-Baroque château; 8 km SW Vimperk, a town with a Renaissance-Baroque château and other interesting historical monuments, a gateway for exploring the popular Šumava range of mountains.

DĚČÍN 19
(formerly *Děčín-Podmokly*, Ger. *Tetschen-Bodenbach*)

District town of Bohemia, 80 km N of Prague, on the Elbe river. Two formerly independent towns - Děčín (chartered in the 13th cent.) and Podmokly (became a town in 1901) - form the core of the present Děčín.

Jews settled in D. before 1537, later they were probably expelled and subsequently, in the mid-19th cent., granted permission to resettle in the town. A religious society was established in 1887 and changed into a religious congregation in 1895. 496 persons of the J. faith are recorded in Děčín and Podmokly in 1930. After World War II some J. from the eastern part of Czechoslovakia settled in the town. A synagogue group with a small prayer room was active here after the war but was abolished later owing to a decrease in members.

ghetto in D. but almost all the J. houses were concentrated NE of the square, by the street leading to Český Šternberk. In the early 20th cent. the J. began to move to larger towns and in 1930 only 20 persons of the J. faith are recorded. The J. religious congregation was abolished in 1930.

The synagogue was in the street Šternberská, NE of the square. Built in the mid-19th cent. Empire style elements, a semicircular apse. Services were held here until the 1930s (only during great festivals). After 1957 the building was converted into a hairdresser's.

The synagogue is in the Podmokly quarter (on the W bank of the Elbe), in Žižkova street, 400 m NW of the railway station. It was built in 1906-07 in the Art Nouveau style. Services were held here until 1938; one of the smaller rooms was converted into a prayer room in 1945. Today synagogue houses a record office.

(No traces were left of the two cemeteries in the town.)

The dominant feature of the town is a château (formerly a castle, rebuilt in the 17th - 18th cent.); there are several churches from the 17th and 18th cent. and two noteworthy bridges from the 16th and 17th cent. in the town.

12 km W the rock formation Tiské stěny (a rock labyrinth); 7 km NW the mountain Děčínský Sněžník (726 m) with a chalet and a look-out-tower; 11 km Hřensko, a starting point for exploring České Švýcarsko - a region of sandstone rocks; 8 km SE Benešov nad Ploučnicí, a town with two Renaissance châteaux from the 16th cent., open to visitors.

DIVIŠOV 20

Small town in Bohemia, 45 km SE of Prague, 13 km E of the district town Benešov. Chartered in 1545.

Jews settled in D. before 1685, a J. community was established in 1776. About 20 J. families lived here in the mid-19th cent. There was no enclosed

The cemetery lies 2 km NE of the synagogue, near the road branching off to the village Měchnov. Founded about 1776, well-preserved legible tombstones from the late 18th cent.

There is a Baroque church from the 18th cent. in Divišov.

The following J. communities and religious societies used to exist in the vicinity: **Černé Budy** /Ger. *Schwarzbuda, Klosterdorf,* a part of the small town **Sázava** (10 km N, a prayer room recorded in the 18th - 20th cent.); **Kácov** (small town 11 km E, a prayer room recorded in the 19th - 20th. cent); **Rataje nad Sázavou** /Ger. *Ratais* (small town 8 km NE, a synagogue from 1860 was pulled down in about 1922); **Trhový Štěpánov** /Ger. *Markt-Stiepanau* (small town 13 km SE, a cemetery with tombstones from the 18th cent., a synagogue of unknown origin, pulled down most probably in the 1st half of the 20th cent.); **Zruč nad Sázavou** (town 17 km SE, a prayer room from the 19th cent., converted into a flat); **Vlašim** (town 9 km S, remains of a mid-19th cent. cemetery, a synagogue from the 2nd half of the 19th cent. was pulled down after 1984, the birthplace of the Viennese painter Salomon Benesch [1867 - about 1942 in the concentration camp Malý Trostinec]).

4 km Český Šternberk, a castle, built in the 13th century and redesigned later, open to visitors.

DLOUHÁ VES   21
(also known as *Stará Dlouhá Ves*, Ger. *Altlangendorf*)

Village in Bohemia, 115 km SW of Prague, 27 km SE of the district town Klatovy, 4 km S of Sušice.

There are no records of early Jewish settlement in D. V. There was a large J. community in the 1st quarter of the 18th cent. (about 20 families, i. e. the majority of inhabitants) with a synagogue and a cemetery. 37 J. families are recorded in D. V. in the mid-19th cent. - J. houses were in the centre of the village, between the château and the church. After the mid-19th cent. J. began to migrate to towns, the religious congregation was abolished most probably at the beginning of the 20th cent. Only 13 persons of the J. faith lived in D. V. in 1921.

The cemetery is 300 m SE of the Catholic church. The oldest preserved tombstones date from the 1st half of the 18th cent. During World War II it was destroyed by the Nazis, who also took away the tombstones. After the liberation in 1945 the Nazis had to return the tombstones and reconstruct the cemetery under the supervision of Czech soldiers.

(The synagogue was built in the Empire style, burnt down in 1937 and consequently demolished.)

The following J. communities and religious societies with prayer rooms used to exist in the vicinity: **Kašperské Hory** /Ger. *Bergreichenstein* (town 7 km SSE, a prayer room existed here in the 19th - 20th cent., the native town of the painter, graphic artist and poet Josef Hahn [1917 - resident in the USA]); **Kundratice** (5 km SW, a prayer room recorded in the 18th - 19th cent., 12 Jewish women, victims of a death march, were buried in April 1945 in the 19th cent. cemetery, destroyed by the Nazis); **Hartmanice** (small town 5 km SW with a 19th cent. synagogue); **Prostřední Krušec** /Ger. *Mittel-Körnsalz* (3 km WSW, a prayer room recorded in the 19th. cent.).

In the Otava river and in the vicinity of the village gold was washed in the Middle Ages; 4 km E Albrechtice and 3 km S Mouřenec with 13th cent. churches; 5 km SE Kašperk, ruins of a Gothic castle; 4 km N Sušice, a town with many historical monuments.

DOBRUŠKA 22
(Ger. *Dobruschka*,
also *Guttenfeld*)

Small town in Bohemia, 125 km ENE of Prague, 16 km NW of the district town Rychnov nad Kněžnou. Chartered before 1320.

Jews are mentioned in D. before the mid-16th century. A small J. community used to exist here in the 17th cent., about 10 J. families are recorded in the mid-19th cent. Only 39 persons of the J. faith lived in D. in 1930. After World War II the J. congregation ceased to exist.

The synagogue is among the former (today rebuilt) J. houses in the square Šubrtovo nám., E of the main square. Built in the neo-Gothic style in the mid-19th cent. on the site of an earlier synagogue. Services were held here until the Nazi occupation. At present it is used by the Czech Brethren's Protestant Church.

The cemetery in Křovická street, N outskirts of the town. Founded in 1675, the oldest preserved tombstones date from the end of the 17th cent., several notable Baroque tombstones. A common grave of J. soldiers, who died in 1866, during the Prussian-Austrian war. In the former mortuary there is a small exhibition on the history of the Dobruška J. community and the cemetery.

The town has a Renaissance town hall, churches from the 16th - 18th cent. and other historical monuments.

4 km SW is **Opočno**, a town with a remarkable 16th cent. Renaissance château surrounded by a park, open to the public; 6 km N **Nové Město nad Metují**, an urban conservation area with Renaissance houses and fortification walls, a Renaissance château from the 16th - 17th cent. and Art Nouveau interiors, open to visitors; 6 km NNE **Slavoňov** with a 16th cent. wooden framework church; eastwards is the wooded range of mountains **Orlické hory** (the highest peak 1,115 m).

DOBŘÍŠ 23

Town in Bohemia, 40 km SW of Prague, 15 km NE of the district town Příbram. Chartered in 1569.

A J. community existed in the town as early as in the 1st half of the 17th cent. (a Burial Society, Hevra Kaddisha, is mentioned in 1645). 26 J. families are recorded in the 1st half of the 19th cent., only 88 persons of the J. faith in 1930. Only 8 persons survived the Nazi occupation and after World War II the community was not revived. There was no ghetto in D., J. houses were scattered throughout the whole town.

The synagogue is on the corner of the street Československé armády, W part of the square. Built in the neo-Romanesque style in 1904. The main wall faces the north, which is a unique exception in Czechoslovakia. Services were held here until World War II. After 1945 it was converted into a in cultural centre (it houses a concert and exhibition hall, a library etc.)

(**The old synagogue** from 1777 was used until 1904 and pulled down in 1960.)

The cemetery, of unknown origin, lies on a hill, 1500 m NE of the square. The earliest legible tombstone dates from 1650. Modern tombstones were removed from the cemetery during the Nazi occupation. The total of about 1000 burials.

There is remarkable Baroque château from the 18th cent. with a large park, open to visitors in D.

The following J. communities and religious societies used to exist in the vicinity: **Mníšek** (small town 11 km NE with a rebuilt synagogue from the 2nd half of the 19th cent.); **Nový Knín** /Ger. *Neu-Knin* (small town 9 km E, a prayer room existed here in the 19th - 20th cent.); **Čím** /Ger. *Tschim* (15 km E, a prayer room recorded in the 19th cent.); **Čelina** /Ger. *Tschelina* (11 km SE, a small village ghetto with a rebuilt synagogue from the 19th cent. and a cemetery with early 19th cent. tombstones); **Druhlice** (6 km S, a prayer room recorded in the 19th cent.); **Trhové Dušníky** /form. *Německé Dušníky*, Ger. *Deutsch-Duschnik* (13 km SW, a prayer room existed here in the 19th cent., the birthplace of the German - J. poet and prose-writer Moritz Hartmann, pseud. Maurizius Pfaffe [18211872 Oberdöbling, Austria]); **Příbram** /Ger. *Pibrans, Przibram* (town 15 km SW with a cemetery from the 2nd half of the 19th cent., the synagogue from 1873-74 was pulled down in 1969).

W and S lies the wooded mountain range **Hřebeny** *(the highest peak - 690 m); 11 km SE on the Vltava river is the* **Slapy** *dam, a popular resort (swimming, water sports); 15 km SW* **Příbram** *with a museum housing an exhibition of the history of the local mines (an open-air museum of mining), near the town is a well-known Catholic place of pilgrimage called* **Svatá Hora** *(a remarkable church and monastery from the 17th - 18th cent.).*

DOLNÍ KOUNICE   24
(Ger. *Kanitz*)

Small town in Moravia, 185 km SE of Prague, 18 km SW of Brno. Chartered most probably in the 14th cent.

Jews settled in D. K. as early as in the 2nd half of the 14th cent. A fairly large J. community must have existed there in the 1st half of the 15th century (the first cemetery was founded then). 111 J. families (over 600 people) lived in D. K. in the mid-19th cent. (almost a quarter of the total population). The J. population numbered only 53 in 1930. After World War II the religious congregation was not revived. Ancestors of the Austrian chancellor Bruno Kreisky came from Dolní Kounice.

The Jewish quarter - a ghetto - built in the 16th cent. W of the main square, near the present bus station. A part of the ghetto has been preserved, formerly it consisted of over 30 one-storey-houses.

The synagogue was built in the Renaissance style in the mid-17th cent. on the small square of the J. quarter. Services were held here until World

War II. Later it served as a store-house.

The new cemetery is set on a slope, 120 m S of the synagogue. Founded in 1680. Many remarkable tombstones dating from 1688 up to World War II. Tombstones of the Kreisky family are to be found here. (The earlier, medieval cemetery, today without tombstones, has been converted into a garden.)

D. K. has a Renaissance château (formerly a castle from the 14th - 17th cent.), the ruins of a 14th cent. Gothic monasterial church and several other churches.

4 km NW is a noteworthy iron railway viaduct built in 1868-70 over the Jihlava river; 7 km NW Ivančice, a town with a number of Gothic and Renaissance historical monuments.

DOMAŽLICE   25
(Ger. *Taus*)

District town 135 SW of Prague, 50 km SW of Plzeň. Chartered between 1262-65.

From the 14th up to the 19th cent. only a few Jews were permitted to settle in Domažlice, 3 families at the most. J. families from the surrounding villages began to migrate to the town in the mid-19th cent. and in the 1860s a religious society was established which became a religious congregation in 1873. The J. population in D. numbered 69 persons of the J. faith in 1930. The religious congregation was not revived after World War II.

The cemetery is on the N outskirts, 1 km N of the square, near the road leading to Třebnice. Founded in the 1860s, burials until 1941. A part of the cemetery has recently been taken up

owing to the construction of a new road.

(A synagogue from the 1880s was demolished in 1939-40.)

The historical centre with a great number of historical monuments has been declared an urban conservation area: e. g. the castle called Chodský hrad (from the 13th cent., rebuilt in the 18th cent., housing a museum of the Chodsko region), Gothic and Baroque churches and ancient arcaded houses. Folklore festivals of the Chodsko region are held in D. every summer.

The following J. communities and religious societies used to exist in the vicinity: **Poběžovice** /form. *Ronšperk*, Ger. *Ronsberg* (town 12 km NW with remains of a 17th cent. cemetery, destroyed by the Nazis, a synagogue from the early 19th cent., demolished by the Nazis, Rabbi Baal Shem, founder of the Hasidic movement, is said to have lived in the town in 1744); **Mutěnín** /Ger. *Muttersdorf* (small town 18 km NW, a cemetery from the 17th cent., devasted by the Nazis, a 19th cent. synagogue, demolished by the Nazis); **Meclov** /Ger. *Metzling* (8 km NNW, a synagogue from 1856); **Radonice** (6 km NE, a prayer room existed here in the 19th cent.).

Folk customs have survived to a certain extent in the region, which is also well-known for its typical folk pottery and textile manufacture. 2 km SW Veselá hora or Vavřineček with a Baroque pilgrim chapel, with wide views over the surrounding countryside; 4 km W Újezd, a village with a memorial hall of Jan Sladký - Kozina, the leader of a peasants' revolt in the 17th cent.; 9 km SW the Výhledy hill (706 m).

DOUDLEBY NAD ORLICÍ   26

Village in Bohemia, 130 km E of Prague, 6 km S of the district town Rychnov nad Kněžnou.

There are no records of early J. settlement, the earliest documentary record mentions a synagogue in 1777. In the mid-19th cent. 46 J. families (over 300 people) are recorded in the village, forming about one third of the total population. From the end the 19th cent. J. began to migrate to large towns and abroad (mainly the USA). Only 2 persons of the J. faith lived here in 1930. After 1860 J. settled in the nearby town **Kostelec nad Orlicí** /Ger. *Adlerkosteletz* (4 km NW) and thus from the end of the 19th cent. the J. community became known as "Kostelec n. O. - Doudleby". The religious congregation was not revived after World War II.

The Jewish quarter consisted of about 30 houses, its groundplan structure has survived. The village ghetto lies on the S part of D., on the left (south) bank of the Orlice river, along the street leading to Příkazy, about 250 m SW of the château.

The Baroque-Classicist **synagogue** was built in 1820-21 on the site of an earlier synagogue, in the S part of the J. quarter, in Švermova street. Services were held here until the Nazi occupation. In 1951-54 it was converted into a house of prayer of the Hussite Church.

(There was no cemetery in Doudleby nor Kostelec n. O., J. were buried in Vamberk.)

The following J. communities and religious societies with prayer rooms used to exist in the vicinity: **Choceň** (town 12 km SSW, a prayer room existed here in the 19th - 20th cent.); **Přestavlky** (5 km SW, a prayer room allegedly existed here in the 19th cent.). - **Kostelec nad Orlicí** (4 km NW) is the birthplace of Egon Ledeč (1889-1944 Auschwitz), a violin virtuoso, concert-master of the Czech Philharmonic Orchestra. - 18 prisoners who had died in a railway transport from Auschwitz were buried in January 1945 in **Brandýs nad Orlicí** (12 km SSE).

There is a Renaissance château in D. dating from the 16th - 17th cent. with rich sgraffito decoration and an exhibition of West European and Bohemian lace-making.

2 km NE Vamberk with a museum of Bohemian folk and modern lace-making; 4 km SE Potštejn, ruins of a Gothic-Renaissance castle; 6 km NW Častolovice, a small town with a Renaissance château, open to visitors.

DRAŽKOV 27

Village in Bohemia, 50 km S of Prague, 18 km E of the district town Příbram.

There exist no documentary records of early J. settlement. In the mid-18th cent. the J. population numbered 6 families, there was a prayer room and a cantor in D. About 20 J. families lived here in the mid-19th cent., the number dropped to 8 in the early 20th cent. The last two citizens of the Jewish faith died during the Nazi occupation. The religious congregation ceased to exist most probably in 1893.

The synagogue was built in 1852, in the E part of the village, house No. 33, near the road to Skrýšov. Services were held here until 1932. Later it was rebuilt and at the present time it is the

seat of the local authorities and the health centre.

The cemetery is set in a wood, about 2 km SW of the village, on a hill called Radobylka, south of the road to Kamýk nad Vltavou. There are no documentary records of its foundation, the earliest legible tombstone dates from 1681. Many Baroque tombstones. The last burial was in 1936.

The following J. communities and religious societies used to exist in the vicinity: **Kamýk nad Vltavou** /Ger. *Kamaik* (small town 2 km SW, a prayer room existed here in the 19th - 20th cent.); **Smolotely** (11 km SW, a prayer room recorded in the 19th - 20th cent.); **Bohostice** (12 km SW, a prayer room recorded in the 19th - 20th cent., a cemetery with tombstones from the 18th cent.); **Zduchovice** (6 km WSW, a prayer room recorded in the 19th cent.); **Hřiměždice** /form. *Vermeřice*, Ger. *Wermeritz* (4 km N, a prayer room recorded in the 19th cent.); **Třebnice** (5 km E, a prayer room existed here in the 19th - 20th cent.); **Petrovice** (small town 11 km SE, a synagogue from the second half of the 19th cent., converted into a seat of the standard farming cooperative); **Klučenice** (12 km SSW, a prayer room recorded in the 19th cent.); **Zahořany** (12 km SSW, a prayer room existed in **Lašovice** in the 19th cent.).

*There are many historical monuments in the vicinity - strongholds, châteaux, churches and ruins of castles; 2 km W the **Slapy** dam on the Vltava river (swimming, water sports); 5 km E **Třebnice**, a village with a château from the 18th - 19th cent., the birthplace of the Austrian marshal Josef Václav Radetzky (1766-1858); 8 km SE towers a well-preserved medieval castle **Vysoký Chlumec**.*

DRMOUL   28
(Ger. *Dürrmaul*)

Village in Bohemia, 125 km W of Prague, 4 km SW of Mariánské Lázně.

Individual J. families lived in D. as early as the late 16th. cent., 18 families are recorded in the mid-18th. cent. and 29 in the mid-19th cent. The J. population numbered only 36 persons of the J. faith in 1930. The Drmoul religious congregation existed from the 17th

cent. until the annexation of the Czechoslovak border areas by Germany in 1938.

Isaac Mayer Wise (orig. Weis, born in 1819 in Lomnička - died in 1900 in Cincinnati, USA), a prominent rabbi and founding father of American Reform Judaism, spent a part of his childhood in Drmoul. The Drmoul Jewish community is depicted in the memoirs of the Czech - J. writer Norbert Frýd (1913-1976), whose grandfather was a native of Drmoul.

Jewish houses were built towards the centre of the extensive village green with a synagogue and a J. communal house in the centre. (The synagogue from 1803 and the communal house were demolished in 1981.)

A beautiful **cemetery**, set in a wood about 1,500 m W of the village, 400 m N of the village Panský Vrch, on a hill about 600 m high. There are about 500 tombstones here, the earliest one dates from the late 17th cent. The Baroque and Empire style granite tombstones mirror local folk art.

*9 km NNW **Lázně Kynžvart**, a spa with mineral-water-springs, a Classicist château of the Austrian chancellor Metternich (remarkable collections and a fine park, open to the public), ruins of a Gothic castle; 4 km NE **Mariánské Lázně**, a famous spa with mineral-water-springs; 9 km SE **Planá**, town with many historical monuments from the 14th cent.*

DŘEVÍKOV   29

Small village in Bohemia, 105 km SE of Prague, 20 km S of the district town Chrudim.

In the mid-18th cent. so many J. families settled in Dřevíkov that Jews formed an overwhelming majority of its inhabitants. The village had a total of 30 J. families in the mid-19th cent. but towards the end of the century the community numbered only 20 persons of the J. faith and the remaining J. families migrated to towns before 1930. The religious congregation from the second half of the 18th cent. ceased to exist about 1894.

The Jewish street, dating from the mid-18th cent., leads eastwards from the village green. The houses are mostly small one-storey buildings with no outbuildings since J. did not engage in farming but mostly earned their living by trading. Moreover, J. were not free to build houses so they had to enlarge the floor space by an additional storey. The former Jewish **school** in the E part of the street has been preserved.

The **synagogue** is at the E end of the J. street, No. 43. It was built in the mid-18th cent. and rebuilt in the 19th cent. Services were held here until the late 19th cent., later it was converted into a dwelling house.

The **cemetery** is set in a wood, 500 m NW of the village green. The earliest preserved tombstones date from the mid-18th cent. The mortuary was built in the second half of the 19th cent. when the cemetery was extended. The cemetery was restored in the 1970s and fragments of damaged Baroque tombstones have been embedded in the walls of the former mortuary.

The nearest J. community was in **Hlinsko** (town 5 km E, the synagogue from 1904 was converted into a municipal museum, the cemetery dates from the late 19th cent.) - **Lipka** (8 km NW) is the birthplace of Stanislav Schulhof (1865-1919 Prague), an Esperantist poet and translator.

*Dřevíkov is a part of an extensive open-air museum of folk art, which includes several other villages in the neighbourhood with remarkable pieces of folk architecture. The following are open to the public: 2 km W **Možděnice** (a smithy and a cartwright's workshop); 1 km N **Svobodné Hamry** (a water-driven hammer-mill, a timber framed inn); 1 km E **Veselý Kopec** (a water mill and other folk architecture); 2 km SE **Králova Pila** (a water mill and a sawmill).*

9 km NE is the site of the former village **Ležáky** which was liquidated by the Nazis in 1942 (now a museum).

District town between Moravia and Silesia, 285 km ESE of Prague, 20 km S of Ostrava. It is a twin-town, formerly consisting of two separate towns: **Frýdek** (founded in the 14th cent. on the Silesian, northern bank of the Ostravice river) and **Místek** (founded before 1267 on the Moravian, southern bank).

Jews were granted permission to settle in F. - M. as late as the mid-19th cent. Each town had its own independent religious congregation but shared one house of prayer. In 1893 the two communities merged into one. The Frýdek-Místek congregation numbered 432 persons of the J. faith in 1930. After World War II the religious congregation was not revived.

The **cemetery** is in the SE part of Frýdek, in Těšínská street, leading to the village Dobrá. Founded in 1882, the entrance gate built in the Art Nouveau style. Burials also after World War II. The ceremonial hall has been converted into a prayer hall of the Seventh Day Adventists.

(A **synagogue** was built in Frýdek in 1865, and demolished by the Nazis in 1939.)

Frýdek has a Renaissance château (an exhibition on ecology and ethnography) and there are churches and other historical monuments from the Renaissance and Baroque periods in both parts of the town.

The nearest religious society was in **Frýdlant nad Ostravicí** /Ger. *Friedland* *a. O.* (10 km S, a prayer room allegedly existed in the town in the 19th - 20th cent.).

*6 km N **Řepiště**, a village with a 16th cent. wooden church; 4 km NE **Sedliště**, a village with a 17th cent. wooden church; southwards lies the attractive **Beskydy** range of mountains, popular with tourists (the highest peak - 1,324 m) and there are several dams - resorts in the neighbourhood of F. - M.: e.g. **Žermanická přehrada** (8 km NE), **Olešná** (3 km SW).*

GOLČŮV JENÍKOV 31

Small town in Bohemia, 80 km SE of Prague, 25 km NNW of the district town Havlíčkův Brod. Became a small town before 1461 and a town in 1913.

Jews settled in G. J. most probably in the Middle Ages, a J. community and a synagogue are recorded only in the mid-17th century (earlier records were destroyed during a fire). G. J. was an important J. centre in the 18th - 19th cent. (over 500 persons of the J. faith) with a tradition of Talmudic studies. Isaac Mayer Wise (orig. Weis, born in 1819 in Lomnička - died in 1900 in Cincinnati, USA), the founding father of the American Reform Judaism, began studying in 1835 in the renowned local yeshivah of Rabbi Aron Kornfeld. The English politician and philanthropist Sir Moses Montefiore (1784-1885) visited the yeshivah in 1842. Most of the J. families migrated to large towns at the turn of the 19th and 20th cent., the J. population numbered only 79 persons in 1930. The G. J. community had a rabbi until 1930. After World War II the J. religious congregation ceased to exist and was not revived.

G. J. is the birth-place of the significant Judaist Friedrich Thieberger (1888-1958 Jerusalem) and his sister Gertrude Urzidil (1898-1977 New York), a Ger. - J. poetess married to the writer Johannes Urzidil.

The Jewish quarter was fairly extensive, spreading from the S of the square to the W, most probably with a me-dieval core. It was not a compact ghetto, Christian houses were scattered among the J. houses. There were about 50 houses in J. ownership in the 19th cent. Most of the J. quarter has survived up to the present. Remains of a ritual bath are preserved in the basement of the former **school**, house No. 189; house No. 159 is the former rabbi's house. An Orthodox **prayer-room** of Galician refugees used to be in house No. 15 on the S side of the square during World War I.

The synagogue is in the centre of the J. quarter. It was built in the Moorish-Romanesque style in 1870 on the foundations of an earlier synagogue. It served as a synagogue until World War II, after the war it served as a prayer hall of the Hussite Church and the Czech Brethren's Protestant Church. Since 1977 it has served as a depository of the State Jewish Museum. The aron ha-kodesh has been preserved.

The cemetery is 750 m NW of the synagogue. It is said to have existed as early as in the early 14th cent., the oldest preserved tombstones date from the early 18th cent. Remarkable Baroque tombstones and three ark-shaped tombs are to be found here. Burials also after World War II.

The town has a 17th cent. stronghold, churches and chapels from the 17th - 19th cent. and other historical monuments.

An ancient J. community used to exist in **Habry** /Ger. *Habern* (a small town 7 km S with a cemetery with legible early 18th cent. tombstones, a synagogue built in 1825, today a cinema); a religious society used to be in the village of **Dobrovítov** (11 km SW, a 19th cent. prayer house, converted into a dwelling house).

*3 km E **Klášter**, a Baroque château and an 18th cent. church; 12 km E **Seč**, a dam and a popular resort with sporting facilities; 8 km N **Žleby**, a small town with a château from the period of Romanticism, open to the public; 10 km NE the extensive ruins of the **Lichnice** Gothic castle.*

HAVLÍČKŮV BROD · 32
(formerly *Německý Brod*, Ger. *Deutsch-Brod*)

District town in Bohemia, 95 km SE of Prague. Chartered in the 13th cent.

Jews settled in H. B. in as early as the early 14th cent. but were expelled from the town in the mid-15th cent. Jewish families were permitted to resettle there only in the mid-19th cent. The religious society changed to an autonomous J. religious congregation in 1884. 170 persons of the J. faith are recorded in 1900 and 146 in 1930. After World War II the religious congregation was not revived.

The prayer room used to be on the 1st floor of the house No.157 in the street Dolní. Services were held here until the Nazi occupation. Since 1945 it has been used by the Czech Brethren's Protestant Church.

The cemetery is about 1 km W of the square, in the street leading to Perknov. Founded in 1890, the ceremonial hall was built in 1891. Many graves of Galician refugees from World War I. The last burial was in 1939.

Typhus cemetery, a small grove amid-fields beyond the municipal cemetery, 2 km NNW of the main square, W of the road to Radostín. It was founded during World War I as a burial ground for Jewish refugees from Galicia, victims of a typhus epidemic. Dozens of simple, uniform tombstones have a survived there until today.

The town has a Renaissance town hall from the 15th cent., five churches from the 13th up to the 18 cent. and other historical monuments.

The following J. communities and religious societies used to exist in the vicinity: **Rozsochatec** (9 km NNE, a prayer room recorded in the 17th - 18th cent.); **Chotěboř** (town 14 km NNE, a prayer hall from the late 19th cent., converted into a flat, a late 19th cent. cemetery); **Libice nad Doubravou** (18 km NNE, a prayer room is said to have been in the 19th cent.); **Česká Bělá** /Ger. *Biela, Böhmisch-Bela* (small town 9 km NE, a prayer room from the 19th cent., changed to a flat). - In **Lípa** (village 6 km SSW) a J. detention work camp was set up in 1940 and closed in 1943 (the prisoners were sent to Auschwitz), a memorial tablet from 1985.

*4 km E **Pohled**, a former monastery from the 15th - 17th cent.; 10 km E near the village **Žižkovo Pole** stands a monument commemorating the place where the Hussite leader Jan Žižka died in 1424.*

A compact **ghetto** existed in today's Havlíčkova street (NE of the square) and its neighbourhood. There were about 60 houses in J. ownership here in the 19th cent., some of them have been preserved.

The synagogue is in the centre of the former ghetto, on the W side of Havlíčkova street. It was built about 1728 and entirely rebuilt in 1870 in the neo-Romanesque style. Women entered the synagogue's high gallery over a bridge through a connecting passage from the next house No. 46-47 which used to be **a school and a rabbinate**. Services were held there until World War II, today it serves as a store-house. The aron ha-kodesh has been preserved.

The cemetery is in Havlíčkova street,

HEŘMANŮV MĚSTEC 33
(Ger. *Hermannstädtel*)

Small town in Bohemia, 90 km ESE of Prague, 9 km W of the district town Chrudim. Founded and chartered in the 14th cent.

Jews lived in H. M. as early as the 15th cent., in the 17th cent. there was a fairly large community here with a prayer room. 63 J. families (277 persons) lived in the town in 1724, in the mid-19th cent. the community numbered 700 persons of the J. faith. Only 54 persons of the J. faith are recorded in 1930. Only 6 women returned from concentration camps after the war.

on the NE side of the former ghetto. It is said to have been founded in the 16th cent., several times extended. There are many remarkable Renaissance, Baroque and Empire tombstones here and several ark-shaped tombs, the oldest preserved tombstone dates from 1647.

The town has a château and a church from the 18th cent. and other historical monuments.

The following J. communities or religious societies used to exist in the vicinity: **Chrudim** (town 9 km E, a prayer room existed here in the 19th - 20th cent., with a cemetery from 1889); **Hoješín** (15 km S, a prayer room recorded in the 18th - 20th cent., remains of a cemetery with 19th cent. tombstones, liquidated in 1980); **Zdechovice** (16 km NW, a prayer room recorded in the 18th cent.); **Přelouč** (town 13 km NW with a synagogue from 1860, converted into a church of the Hussite Church, the old cemetery from 1681 was liquidated in 1874, a new cemetery from 1887).

*5 km NW **Svojšice**, ruins of a Gothic stronghold; 6 km NW **Choltice**, a village with a 17th cent. château and a wooden windmill, open to the public; 9 km **Chrudim**, a town with several churches and houses from the 14th up to the 17th cent.; 10 km ESE **Slatiňany**, a small town with a château from the 16th - 19th cent. famous for its hippological museum; 12 km S **Seč**, a dam and a popular resort (water sports); 10 km SW **Lichnice**, ruins of a Gothic castle.*

HLUBOKÁ NAD VLTAVOU   34
(formerly *Podhradí*,
Ger. also *Frauenberg*)

Small town in Bohemia, 115 km Ŝ of Prague, 9 km N of the district town České Budějovice. Chartered in the 15th cent.

The first J. families came to H. about 1645, towards the end of the century there existed a J. community with a prayer room. The community numbered about 130 persons of the J. faith in the mid-19th cent. and the number dropped to 20 in 1930. A J. religious congregation was established in the mid-18th cent., its statutes date from 1785. The religious congregation ceased to exist after World War II.

A small **Jewish quarter** used to be in today's Tyršova street, SW of the square (i.e. between the Catholic church and a pond called Židovský rybník). Some of the original houses have been preserved.

The synagogue was built in 1907 in Tyršova street No. 15. Services were held there until World War II. Since 1945 it has been used by the Hussite Church, the original furnishing has not been preserved.

The cemetery is 400 m NW of the synagogue, near a petrol station, by a pond called Munický rybník. Founded in the mid-18th cent., tombstones dating from 1750 to 1941.

Hluboká nad Vltavou is well-known for its château rebuilt in the English Windsor Gothic style in the 19th cent. (interiors open to the public, housing a gallery of Czech Gothic and modern art).

9 km S České Budějovice, a town with many historical monuments from the 13th up to the 18th cent.; 2 km SW Ohrada, a Baroque château from the 18th cent. (housing a museum of forestry, hunting and fishery); 10 km W Plástovice, Vlhlavy and other villages in the vicinity with many remarkable pieces of folk architecture from the 1st half of the 19th cent.

HODONÍN   35
(Ger. *Göding*)

District town in Moravia, 235 km SE of Prague, 55 km SE of Brno. Chartered in the 13th or 14th cent.

A J. community existed in H. in as early as the 1st half of the 17th cent. Most J. families of the fairly large community were expelled from the town in the 18th cent. Only 13 J. families were granted permission to reside in H. in 1798-1848. The J. population increased considerably in the mid-19th cent., 983 persons of the J. faith are recorded in 1910, thereafter the number of Jews declined as a result of J. migration to cities. Over 220 persons died during the Nazi occupation. The religious congregation was reestablished after the liberation and later changed to a synagogue group with a prayer room which no longer exists.

(**A ghetto** used to exist S of the main square, next to the château. It was separated from the rest of the town by the Morava river branch. It consisted of about 30 houses, though only 13 houses are recorded in the 18th cent. Demolished after World War II, today a housing estate.)

(**A synagogue** was built in the former ghetto in the 17th cent., rebuilt in the 19th cent., Moorish style elements were added. Destroyed during the Nazi occupation.)

The old cemetery used to be 700 m W of the city centre, in the street leading to Lužice. Founded most probably in 1620, burials until 1920. Most of the valuable tombstones were transferred to the new cemetery in 1974, and the cemetery was converted into a park bearing the name of the writer Gabriela Preissová; a few tombstones were left as a symbol and a new memorial with a Czech-Hebrew inscription in memory of those buried there was erected.

The new cemetery is 2 km NE of the city centre, adjoining the municipal cemetery. It was founded in 1920, tombstones from the old cemetery (18th - 20th cent.) were brought here in 1974 Hodonín district. The cemetery is still used.

Hodonín is the native town of the first Czechoslovak president T. G. Masaryk. There is an inconspicuous Baroque château in the town.

The following J. communities and religious societies used to exist in the vicinity: **Skalica** /Hung. *Szakolca* (town 7 km E with an 18th cent. synagogue, converted into a house, an old cemetery with tombstones from the 18th cent. and remains of a new cemetery from the 2nd half of the 19th cent.); **Holíč** (town 5 km SE, a synagogue from the last third of the 18th cent., pulled down after 1970, the cemetery from the early 18th cent. became extinct before 1960, a new cemetery from the 19th cent. with remains of a ceremonial hall from 1930); **Kopčany** (7 km S with a 19th-cent. cemetery, a rabbinate recorded in the 19th cent., the birthplace of the Viennese painter and graphic-artist Maria Schmalfuss-Adler [1863-1947 Hollywood]); **Moravská Nová Ves** (10 km SE, a prayer room existed here in the 19th - 20th cent.). - **Rohatec** (5 km NE) is the native village of the German - J. literary historian Josef Körner-Prag (1888-1950 Prague).

*The **Morava** river, 1 km S and SE of the town, forms a natural border between Moravia and Slovakia; 7 km E **Skalica**, a Slovak town with many historical monuments (fortification walls, a Romanesque rotunda from the 12th cent., churches from the 14th up to the 18th cent.); 5 km SE **Holíč**, a Slovak town, famous for its faience, manufactured there in 1743-1827, a château from the 16th - 18th cent. and other historical monuments; 5 km SW **Mikulčice**, extensive excavations of a settlements with unearthed remnants of ten churches from the 9th cent., a museum: Mikulčice was an important centre of the Great Moravian Empire in the 9th - 10th cent.; 11 km N **Milotice** with a Renaissance-Baroque château from the 16th - 18th cent., open to the public.*

HOLEŠOV 36
(Ger. *Holleschau*)

Town in Moravia, 240 km SE of Prague, 15 km NE of the district town Kroměříž. Chartered as early as the 15th cent.

Jews lived in H. as early as the 15th cent. The Holešov community represented one of the largest J. communities in Moravia in the 18th - 19th cent. - 265 J. families were permitted to reside in the town. 1,694 persons of

the J. faith are recorded in H. in 1848, later the number declined as many families migrated to larger towns. The J. quarter suffered serious damage during pogroms in 1774, 1899 and in December 1918 (the last pogrom in Czechoslovakia, two dead). Only 273 persons of the J. faith are recorded in 1930. About 200 J. perished during the Nazi occupation, only 14 persons returned to the town after the war. The religious congregation was re-established after 1945, subsequently changed to a synagogue group, which no longer exists.

The Czech poet Max Winder (1845 Kolín - 1920 Kolín) lived in H. in 1895-1919 and it was the childhood home of his son Ludwig Winder (1889 Šafov - 1946 Baldock, England), who wrote in German under the pseud. G. A. List.

An extensive **ghetto** (consisting of about 50 houses in 4 streets) used to exist in the NW part of the town. A greater part of the ghetto has survived: rural type one-storey houses from the 18th cent. and a two-storey school at No. 132.

A Renaissance **synagogue**, called Shakh synagogue (Šachova) used to be in the centre of the former ghetto. Built about 1560, extended in the 17th cent., the interior decorated with remarkable ornamental painting dating from 1737. The almemar is an example of excellent black-smith's work. Services of the Orthodox rite were held here from 1893 until the 1920s, later it was converted into a flat. The building was restored in 1960 - 64 and at pre-

called Shakh (Šach, most probably born in Lithuania, died in 1663), the author of *"Sifse Kohen"*, published in 1662. The Jellineks of Vizovice (producers of the famous export - also kosher - plum brandy) are buried here. A memorial tablet with the names of 250 Nazi victims from the town and vicinity. The last burial was in 1975.

The town has a significant château from the 16th - 18th cent., open to the public, and other sights.

A Jewish community with a 17th cent. synagogue is said to have been in **Dřevohostice** (a small town 11 km N); a religious society used to be in **Bystřice pod Hostýnem** (10 km NE). There is a J. section in the communal cemetery called "Lesní hřbitov" (forest cemetery) in **Zlín** (12 km SSE).

9 km NE Hostýn, a hill - 735 m, a Catholic place of pilgrimage with a Baroque church from the 18th cent.; 11 km SE Lukov, extensive ruins of a medieval castle; 12 km SSE Zlín, a town with a museum of historical and contemporary footwear; 13 km S Malenovice, a well-preserved medieval castle with a museum; 3 km NW Rymice, a village with valuable popular architecture (a windmill, dwelling houses - interiors open to visitors).

sent it house a museum with a permanent exhibition "The History of Jewry in Moravia".

(**A new synagogue** for services of the Reform rite, was built in 1891-93; burnt down and demolished by the Nazis.)

The cemetery is on the N side of the former ghetto, in Zámecká street. There are no records of its origin, the oldest legible tombstone dates from 1647. It was extended in the 18th cent. In the W part is the so-called rabbinic knoll with graves of rabbis. Visitors from all over the world visit the grave of Rabbi Shabtai ben Meir ha Kohen,

Small town in Bohemia, 80 km SE of Prague, 12 km NW of the district town Pelhřimov. Chartered as early as the mid-13th. cent.

A J. community with a synagogue and a cemetery existed here in as early as the 1st third of the 17th cent. 21 J. families are recorded in H. in 1723, 25 J. families in the mid-19th cent. and only 12 persons of the J. faith in 1930. One single man survived the Nazi occupation. Owing to the decrease in congregation members in the late 19th cent. and the early 20th cent. the religious congregation was abolished before 1920.

A compact **Jewish quarter** existed SE of the square, between the square and the bridge over Trnávka. It consisted of 20 houses built in the Baroque and Classicist styles, partly preserved today. **A school** used to be in No. 138 (the building has been modernized).

(A synagogue from 1800 was demolished in 1939.)

The cemetery is on the E bank of Trnávka, 300 m SW of the bridge. It existed as early as the 1st third of the 17th cent., the oldest preserved tombstone dates from the mid-17th cent., burials until 1940. The total of about 300 tombstones, mostly Baroque and Classicist styles. In the middle of the cemetery there is an elevation, allegedly graves in several layers.

There are a Gothic-Baroque church and a Baroque Catholic rectory in H.

The following J. communities and religious societies used to exist in the vicinity: **Pacov** (town 8 km SW, a synagogue probably from the early 19th cent. used as a storehouse today, a cemetery from 1680, with late 18th cent. tombstones); **Lukavec** (small town 10 km NW, an Empire style synagogue was pulled down in 1952, a cemetery with tombstones from the 1st half of the 18th cent.); **Čechtice** (small town 12 km NNW, the former prayer room in the château has been converted into a classroom); **Košetice** (small town 5 km N, a synagogue from around the 1st half of the 19th cent., converted into a house, a cemetery with tombstones from the late 17th cent.); **Křivsoudov** (small town 13 km N, a J. community existed here in the 18th - 20th cent.); **Studený** (10 km NNE, a cemetery from 1700 belonging to the Křivsoudov community); **Dolní Kralovice** /Ger. *UnterKralowitz* (an inundated town 17 km NNE, at the bottom of the Želivka dam: there used to be a J. street, an 18th cent. synagogue and a cemetery from about the 17th cent. in the town).

There are many châteaux and small country manors in the vicinity. 5 km E **Červená Řečice** *with a Renaissance château decorated with 17th cent. sgrafitos; 10 km NNW* **Růžkovy Lhotice,** *a Baroque château with a memorial of composers Bedřich Smetana (1824-1884), Gustav Mahler (1860-1911).*

HOŘICE 38

Town in Bohemia, 90 km NE of Prague, 20 km SE of the district town Jičín. Chartered as early as the 14th cent.

J. lived in H. as early as the beginning of the 17th cent. A J. community with a prayer room existed here most probably in the 2nd half of the 17th cent. 32 J. families are recorded in 1723, over 50 families (350 persons) in the mid-19th cent. and only 73 persons of the J. faith in 1930. The religious congregation was not revived after World War II.

Hořice is the birth-place of the Ger.-J. writer and philosopher Fritz Mauthner (1849-1923 Meersburg, Germany).

The Jewish quarter incorporated the present Karlova street (leading from the square to the N) and Tovární street, branching off Karlova street tot the W. It consisted of about 20 houses.

The synagogue is in Tovární street. Built in 1767 on the site of an earlier synagogue, extended about 1860 and rebuilt in the neo-Romanesque style.

Services were held until the Nazi occupation. Since 1956 it has been used by the Hussite Church.

The old cemetery is in Karlova street, N of the J. quarter, 500 m N of the square. Founded allegedly in the 2nd half of the 17th cent., the earliest preserved tombstones date from the late 18th cent. Valuable Baroque tombstones. Graves of J. soldiers who died during the Napoleon wars and the Prussian-Austrian war (1866). Burials until 1897.

(The new cemetery from 1897 was liquidated in 1967.)

The local school of sculpture and sto-ne-cutting where many notable sculptors studied, was founded in 1884. The school gallery has a large collection of sculpture and sculptures are also to be found in the town's parks, squares and cemeteries.

The following religious congregations used to exist on the slopes of the Krkonoše mountains: **Vrchlabí** /Ger. *Hohenelbe* (town 28 km N, a cemetery from the early 20th cent., destroyed by the Nazis, the birth-place of Paul Nettl [1889-1972 Bloomington, USA], a musicologist); **Hostinné** /Ger. *Arnau* (town 20 km NNE, remains of a cemetery from 1884).

*A battlefield of the Prussian-Austrian war (1866) with a great number of tombstones is to be found 10 - 15 km SE; a lookout-tower and museum in the village of **Chlum**; 7 km NNW Lázně Bělohrad, a small spa with mineral-watersprings; 10 km NNE Zvičina, a hill (671 m) with a chalet and a lookout-tower giving wide views over the country.*

HOŘOVICE 39

Town in Bohemia, 50 km SW of Prague, 19 km SW of the district town Beroun. Chartered in the first quarter of the 14th cent.

J. settled in H. as early as the 15th cent. but were not permitted to reside in the town during the 17th and 18th centuries. In the mid-19th cent. 6 J. families lived in H., later others came from the surrounding villages. A religious congregation was established in 1875. 50 persons of the J. faith are recorded in 1930. The religious congregation was not revived after World War II. The surnames Horvitz and Horowitz are most probably derived from the name of the town.

The synagogue is in Valdecká street, S of the square, a simple building dating from 1903. Services were held there until the Nazi occupation. Since 1947 it has been used by the Czech Brethren's Protestant Church. There is a memorial tablet from 1903 and a show case in the building displaying documents on the J. community.

(There was no cemetery in Hořovice, people were buried in the Praskolesy cemetery.)

The town has a Baroque château from the 18th century with Empire style interiors, open to the public, and a noteworthy park.

Many J. communities and religious societies used to exist in the vicinity: **Praskolesy** (4 km NE, a prayer room from 1838, converted into a flat; a cemetery from the mid-19th cent., birth-place of the Czech - J. writer Jiří Weil [1900-1959 Prague]); **Lochovice** (a small town 6 km ENE, a prayer room from the mid-19th cent., converted into a flat); **Hostomice** (a small town 10 km E, in the 19th - 20th cent. the prayer room used to be in private houses, a cemetery from the 1st half of the 19th cent.); **Běštín** /form. *Běchčín*, Ger. *Bieschtin* (9 km SE, a small synagogue rebuilt into a dwelling house); **Terešov** (16 km NW, the last synagogue, most probably from the turn of the 18th and 19th cent. was pulled down after 1960, remains of a J. street, a cemetery from the 17th or 18th cent.); **Prašný Újezd** (19 km NW, remains of a Jewish street, a synagogue unknown of origin burnt down in 1907, subsequently pulled down); **Zvíkovec** (20 km NW, a prayer room allegedly existed here in the 18th - 19th cent.); **Hřešihlavy** /or Řešohlavy, Ger. *Rescholau* (22 km NW, a J. street, a synagogue from around the 1st half of the 19th cent. was pulled down in the early 20th cent., a cemetery from the 1st half of the 19th cent.).

6 km Žebrák, ruins of a Gothic castle and Točník, a Gothic-Renaissance castle, interiors open to the public.

HRADEC KRÁLOVÉ 40
(Ger. *Königgrätz*)

District town in Bohemia, 100 km ENE of Prague. H. K. became a royal city in the 13th cent.

Several J. families settled in the town towards the end of the 14th cent. A tiny ghetto, consisting of 3 or 4 houses, used to be at Kavčí plácek near the ramparts on the NE outskirts. Jews were expelled from the town in 1542 but a rabbi and a prayer room are mentioned here again in the mid-17th cent. In 1652 J. were driven out of the town again. Only a few J. families lived in H. K. in the 18th and early 19th cent. A modern religious congregation was established in 1860. 425 persons of the J. faith lived here in 1930, only 16 persons returned to the town after World War II.

The J. religious congregation was revived in 1945 but later ceased to exist owing to a decrease in congregation members.

Jan Pita, a tailor and leader of a Christian-Jewish "Old Testament" sect, active in the vicinity of Nový Bydžov, was burnt alive here in 1748. H. K. is the birth-place of Pavel Fraenkl (1904 - 1985 Oslo), a Czech-J. literary historian, Ota Dub (1909-1987 Prague), a Czech-J. writer and Viktor Fischl, today known as Avigdor Dagan, (1912), a Czech-J. poet and prose-writer, resident in Israel since World War II, were also born in H. K.

A prayer hall used to exist in 1888 - 1905 in the courtyard of the rabbi's house in No 67, Rokytanského street on the W side of the town's historical centre.

The synagogue is near the E side of the town's historical centre, the house No. 395, on the corner of Pospíšilova

and Československé armády streets. It was built in 1904-5 by architect V. Weinzettel in the Art Nouveau style with oriental elements. Services were held there until World War II. After 1945 the synagogue was used for a short time, at present it houses the Scientific Library (interior rebuilt).

The cemetery lies in the Pouchov suburb, 2 km NE of the town's historical centre, next to the municipal and military cemeteries. Founded in 1877, extended in 1911, still used today. A modern ceremonial hall was built in 1930. A memorial in memory of the Nazi victims was dedicated in the cemetery in 1950.

The historical centre with an abundance of historical monuments has been declared an urban conservation area: churches from the Gothic up to the Baroque periods, palaces and burghers' houses. A timbered Greek-Catholic church of the eastern type has been transferred here from Slovakia. The western part of the town is an excellent example of town planning with remarkable pieces of architecture from the 1920s and 1930s.

*8-12 km NW, between the villages Horní Přím and Hořiněves, is a **battlefield** of the Prussian-Austrian war (1866) with many monuments; a lookout-tower and a museum are to be found in the village of **Chlum**.*

HRANICE   41
(Ger. *Weisskirchen* or *Mährisch-Weisskirchen*)

Town in Moravia, 245 km ESE of Prague, 23 km NE of the district town Přerov. Chartered in 1276.

The first J. families were granted permission to settle in H. at the beginning of the 17th cent., the number of J. increased after the arrival of refugees from the Ukraine in the mid-17th century. 120 J. families (about 650 persons) were permitted to reside in the town in the 1st half of the 19th cent. 800 persons of the J. faith are recorded after the mid-19th cent., thereafter the number of J. proceeded to decline.

Only 192 persons of the J. faith are recorded in 1930. Only 14 J. returned to the town after World War II. The Hranice religious congregation was revived in 1945 but later changed to a synagogue group. A prayer room used to be here until 1969, services were also attended by visitors to the spa Teplice nad Bečvou.

Hranice is the birth-place of Jakob Julius David (1859-1906 Vienna), a German-J. writer and Isidor Singer (1859-1939 New York), publisher of the twelve-volume *Jewish Encyclopaedia* and founding father of the American League for the Rights of Man.

The ghetto was founded in the 17th cent. in today's Janáčkova street, leading from the NW corner of the square to the château. It consisted of about 17 houses. No. 728 used to be the seat of the religious congregation and the rabbinate until 1936, No. 733 was the school, No. 740 the ritual bath - mikveh.

The synagogue stands between house No. 728 and the town's wall. It was built in the neo-Romanesque style in 1863 - 64 on the site of an earlier synagogue. Services were held there until the Nazi occupation. Since 1943 it has housed a municipal museum.

The cemetery is in Palackého street, NE of the synagogue and the château. Founded most probably in the mid-17th cent., the earliest legible tombstone dates from 1686. Burials until 1956. Julius Freud (died 1858), the brother of the famous psychoanalyst Sigmund Freud, is buried there.

A Renaissance château from the 16th - 17th cent., Renaissance houses and other sights are to be found in the town.

*2 km S **Teplice nad Bečvou**, a spa with mineral springs and a karst: a 244 m deep chasm (the deepest one in Czechoslovakia) and aragonite caves.*

HROUBOVICE   **42**
(formerly also *Roubovice*, Ger. *Raubowitz*)

Village in Bohemia, 115 km SSE of Prague, 16 km SE of the district town of Chrudim.

Jews settled here as early as the beginning of the 18th cent. Almost half of the population in the village was Jewish (52 families) in the mid-19th cent. Only 30 persons of the J. faith are recorded in 1930. Only 2 persons of the J. faith returned to the village after World War II. A religious congregation was established towards the end of the 18th cent. and abolished in the late 19th cent.

Jewish houses and a synagogue stood in the middle of the village, along a brook. About 30 houses were in J. ownership in the mid-19th cent. Most of them have been rebuilt and preserved.

(A Baroque synagogue and a J. school were demolished in 1979).

The cemetery is set on a slope near a wood, on the N side of the village. Noteworthy Baroque and Empire style tombstones from the mid-18th cent. Burials also after World War II.

The following J. communities existed in the vicinity: **Zájezdec** (7 km NW, an Empire style synagogue was pulled down in 1925, a cemetery with tombstones from the end of the 18th cent.,

one third of the population in the village was Jewish); **Přestavlky** (8 km NW, a synagogue from the 1st half of the 19th cent., converted into a dwelling house, a cemetery with tombstones from the 18th cent., one third of the population was Jewish, the birth-place of the Czech-J. publisher and journalist Viktor Vohryzek [1864 - 1918 Pardubice]). - Ludwig August Frankl (1810 - 1894 Vienna), an Austrian poet and literary historian and Hanuš Fantl (1917 - 1942 Mauthausen), a Czech-J. poet, were born in **Chrast** - a small town 4 km NW.

*3 km NE **Luže**, a small town with a Catholic pilgrim church from the 17th cent. and other sights; 6 km SE **Rychmburk**, a well-preserved medieval castle; 4 km NW **Chrast**, a small town with a château from the 17th - 18th cent., housing a museum.*

HUMPOLEC   **43**
(Ger. *Gumpolds*)

Town in Bohemia, 90 km SE of Prague, 15 km NE of the district town Pelhřimov. Chartered as early as the 1st quarter of the 14th cent.

Several J. families lived in H. as early as the 14th cent. but were later expelled from the town. A J. community originated in the early 18th cent. 10 J.

expelled from the town. A J. community originated in the early 18th cent. 10 J. families are recorded in H. in the early 18th cent. and over 300 persons of the J. faith in the mid-19th cent. The number of J. dropped to 89 in 1930. The community was not revived after World War II.

The notable American conductor Josef Stránský (1872-1936 New York) was born in H. Franz Kafka's grandfather Jakob Löwy came from H. as well as the painter and writer Ernst Mandler (1886-1964 France).

The ghetto, consisting of 30 houses, called the Jewish Town, was built in the S part of the town most probably in the 18th cent. Some of the houses, today rebuilt, have been preserved.

The synagogue was in the centre of the former ghetto, in the street U vinopalny. Built after the mid-18th cent., extended and rebuilt with neo-Gothic windows in the 2nd half of the 19th cent. Services were held there until the Nazi occupation. Since 1961 it has been used by the Hussite Church. The former J. school, No. 492, adjoins the synagogue.

The cemetery is 1 km NE of the synagogue, near a field path. Founded in 1719, extended in the 19th cent. About 1,000 tombstones, a great number of Baroque and Empire style tombstones. Burials until 1941.

H. has a 600 years old tradition of draper's trade and textile manufacture, it was called "the Czech Manchester". A 13th cent. Gothic church and other sights are to be found here as well as a museum of the American anthropologist Aleš Hrdlička (1869-1943 Washington), a native of Humpolec.

A religious societies used to exist in **Věž** /Ger. *Wiesch* (7 km NE, a prayer room recorded in the 19th cent.) and **Želiv** /Ger. *Seelau* (10 km SWW, a prayer room recorded in the 19th - 20th cent.). The famous composer Gustav Mahler (1860-1911 Vienna) was born in **Kaliště**, a village 7 km NW.

*8 km NNE **Lipnice nad Sázavou**, a small town with a medieval castle, open to the public; the grave and museum of the famous Czech writer Jaroslav Hašek (1883-1923, the author of "Good Soldier Schweik". 1 km E **Orlík**, ruins of a Gothic castle; 10 km SWW **Želiv**, /Ger. Seelau a remarkable monastery from the 12th - 18th cent.*

CHEB 44
(Ger. *Eger*)

District town in Bohemia, 145 km W of Prague, near the frontier with Germany. Chartered in the 1st half of the 12th cent. Cheb and its vicinity used to be a part of Germany, it was annexed by Bohemia in 1332.

The history of the Cheb J. community is very dramatic. A J. community must have existed in Ch. as early as the 2nd half of the 13th cent., because its synagogue is said to have been destroyed by fire in 1270. In the 13th - 14th cent. J. families lived in several streets around today's street called Židovská (Jewish), W of the main square. This large J. community allegedly ceased to exist in 1350, after a bloody pogrom (we are told that the name of the street Zavražděných [= massacred] refers to that time). - A second, small J. community and a new "Jewish Street" came into existence in 1352 and in 1364 King Charles IV granted the community the right to build a synagogue and to found a cemetery. However, in 1430 the Jews of Cheb were expelled from the town again, the synagogue was taken away from them and the cemetery closed. - In 1435 Jewish families resettled in the town and in 1463 King George of Poděbrady permitted the third community to build a new synagogue and a cemetery. Jews were driven out of the town again, this time in 1502.

The fourth J. community was established in Ch. at the end of the 17th cent. but left the town in the mid-18th century for unknown reasons. - It was only after the Jews were granted civic equality under law in the mid-19th cent. that J. families settled in the town again. The modern (fifth) religious congregation was established in 1862 and its population soon began to increase: 60 J. families (280 persons) are recorded in 1890, 491 persons of the J. faith in 1930. After World War II the religious congregation was re-established for a short period of time.

Cheb was a famous centre of J. learning in the Middle Ages.

The greatest scholar here was Rabbi Nathan (lived in the 2nd half of the 14th cent. and the 1st half of the 15th cent., died and buried in Jerusalem), whose Talmudic School was renowned throughout the whole of central Europe.

The German-J. poet Hugo Zuckermann (1881-1914) and Paul Löwy-Levi (1891-1970 Tel Aviv), a pioneer of puppet theatre and a stage designer, were born in Ch.

(There used to be several **synagogues** in Cheb. The most significant medieval synagogue, completed in 1375, was taken away from the community in 1430, converted into a Catholic church in 1468 and demolished in 1856. The two modern synagogues - built in 1867-69 and in 1892-93 - were demolished by the Nazis.)

(Five tombstones from the first **medieval cemetery** [the earliest from 1342] are kept in the town's museum. A memorial from 1968 commemorating the poet Hugo Zuckermann [1881-1914] is to be found on the site of the **last cemetery**, consecrated in 1872, which used to be 1,500 m S of the main square, in the street Osvobození, before it was devastated by the Nazis during World War II.)

A granite **memorial tablet** of Rabbi Meir ben Joseph from the 2nd half of the 14th cent. has been preserved and is kept at present at the castle (originally it was probably embedded in the medieval synagogue).

The city centre has been declared an urban conservation area owing to its many historical monuments: remains of a castle with buildings of the Romanesque style, remnants of ramparts, several churches from the 13th up to the 18th cent., noteworthy 14th cent. houses. There is a museum with rich collections and a gallery with a collection of Gothic sculpture in the town.

The legendary Albrecht of Wallenstein (1583-1634), imperialist generalissimo in the Thirty Years' War, was murdered in Cheb.

The following J. communities and religious societies used to exist in the vicinity: **Aš** /Ger. *Asch* (a town 20 km

NW, an Orthodox prayer hall for Galician refugees during World War I, after 1945 a religious congregation existed here for a short time whose members were former soldiers of the Czechoslovak foreign army, a transit camp for J. refugees from Poland was set up here in 1945-6); **Františkovy Lázně** /Ger. *Franzensbad* (a town 4 km NNW, a synagogue built in 1875 and demolished by the Nazis, a cemetery from 1875, destroyed by the Nazis); **Lomnička** /Ger. *Steingrub* (15 km N, a cemetery with tombstones from the 1st half of the 19th cent., seriously damaged by the Nazis, the birth-place of the great Rabbi Isaac Mayer Wise, born. Weis [1819-1900 Cincinnati, USA], founding father of American Reform Judaism); **Kynšperk nad Ohří** /Ger. *Königsberg* (a town 12 km NE, a cemetery with tombstones from the early 17th cent., seriously damaged by the Nazis, a wooden synagogue from 1803 was burnt down by the Nazis; the birthplace and grave of the painter Fritz Lederer [1878-1949] and the birth-place of the composer and pianist Erich Orlický [1911]).

*4 km SE **Jesenická přehradní nádrž**, a dam and resort with sporting facilities; 6 km SSE **Starý Hrozňatov**, a 13th cent. keep and a château from the 2nd half of the 19th cent.; 2 km W **Skalka**, a dam and resort (water sports); 3 km NW*

*Komorní hůrka, Tertiary volcano (503 m), geological reserve; 8 km NW **Ostroh** /Ger. Seeberg, a castle from the 13th - 16th cent.; 4 km NNW **Františkovy Lázně** /Ger. Franzensbad, a spa with mineral water springs, an urban conservation area; 10 km N **Skalná (Vildštejn)**, a castle from the 13th - 16th cent.*

IVANČICE 45
(Ger. *Eibenschitz* or *Eibenschütz*)

Town in Moravia, 175 km SE of Prague, 20 km SW of Brno. Chartered as early as the 13th cent.

A J. community is said to have existed in I. as early as the 13th cent., however, it is recorded only in the 15th cent. From the 18th to the mid-19th cent. 144 J. families (800 persons) were permitted to reside in the town. Only 141 persons of the J. faith are recorded in 1930. A transit camp was set up here in 1938-39 for J. refugees from the border areas annexed by Germany. The religious congregation was revived after World War II but existed only for a short time.

Ivančice is the native town of the musicologist Guido Adler (1855-1941 Vienna) and of the American composer and conductor Hugo Weisgall (1912 - resident in the USA).

The **Jewish quarter** incorporated from the 15th cent. today's Josefa Vávry street and a part of the square Komenského nám. (N of the main square). It consisted of 66 houses, most of them are rebuilt today.

The **synagogue** is in the street Josefa Vávry. Built in 1853 on the site of an earlier synagogue. One of its Thorah dated from the 16th cent. Services were held here until the Nazi occupation, today it serves as a storehouse.

The **cemetery** 300 m NW of the synagogue, in the street Mřenková. Founded about the 16th cent., extended in the 17th and 19th cent. The earliest legible tombstone is from 1552, burials also after World War II. A great number of remarkable Renaissance and Baroque tombstones.

There are a 16th cent. Renaissance château (housing a museum), an early Gothic church from the 13th cent. and burghers' houses with Renaissance portals in I.

4 km NW **Oslavany** *with a Renaissance château from the 16th cent., further NW the charming* **valley of the Oslava river** *with several ruins of medieval castles; 8 km N* **Rosice**, *a town with a 16th-cent. Renaissance château, housing a museum of bee-keeping; 3 km SE a* **railway viaduct**, *built in 1868-70 over the valley of the Jihlava river; 7 km SE* **Dolní Kounice** *with a ruin of a Gothic monastic temple and a Renaissance château; 7 km SW* **Moravský Krumlov**, *a town with a 16th-cent. Renaissance château, open to the public; 5 km WSW* **Řeznovice** *with a remarkable Romanesque church from the early 12th cent.*

JEVÍČKO   46
(Ger. *Gewitsch*)

Town in Moravia, 170 km ESE of Prague, 22 km SE of the district town Svitavy. Founded and chartered in the 13th cent.

In the 16th cent. some houses in Jevíčko were in J. ownership. A J. community is first mentioned here in 1620. 138 J. families (990 persons) were permitted to reside in J. from the 18th to the mid-19th cent. Only 86 persons of the J. faith are recorded in 1930. After World War II the religious congregation was not revived. - It is the birthplace of the J. composer Richard Fall (1882 - perhaps 1943, Auschwitz).

An urban **ghetto** originated most probably at the end of the 16th cent., consisting of about 40 houses, most of which have been preserved till the present day. The ghetto used to be N of the square, in today's Soudní street.

The **synagogue** was built in the middle of the ghetto towards the end of the 18th cent. and rebuilt in the Art Nouveau style in 1907. Services were held here until the Nazi occupation. Subsequently the interior was rebuilt and since 1953 it has been used by the Hussite Church and the Czech Brethren's Protestant Church.

A **new cemetery** was founded in 1836 in the street leading to Zadní Arnoštov, 800 m W of the synagogue. It was liquidated in the 1970s, a lapidary of preserved tombstones has been set up here. (**The old cemetery** with tombstones from the 17th cent. was liquidated in the 19th cent.)

The town has well-preserved walls, a 15th cent. watch-tower, a château from the 16th - 18th cent. and valuable churches.

The following J. communities and religious societies used to exist in the vicinity: **Svitavy** /Ger. *Zwittau* (a town 22 km NW, a synagogue from 1902 and a cemetery from 1892, both destroyed by the Nazis); **Moravská Třebová** /Ger. *Mährisch-Trübau* (a town 14 km NNW)

14 km NNW **Moravská Třebová**, *an urban conservation area with an early-17th cent. Renaissance château and a number of other sights; 8 km N* **Cimburk**, *ruins of a medieval castle; 3 km E* **Jaroměřice**, *a Renaissance château from the 16th cent. with sgraffito decoration and a Baroque pilgrim church from the 18th cent.*

District town in Bohemia, 75 km NE of Prague. Chartered about the 13th cent.

J. settled in Jičín in the 14th cent. In the 1st quarter of the 17th cent. Duke Albrecht of Wallenstein marked off a street - a ghetto - for J. to live in. 14 J. families are recorded in the town in the 18th cent., 20 J. families (67 persons of the J. faith) in the mid-19th cent., 119 persons in 1930 and about 90 in 1939. A J. community was established here about the 17th cent. After World War II the community was not revived.

The houses in Jičín were owned by Jacob Bassevi (1570 Verona - 1634 Mladá Boleslav), financier of Emperor Rudolph II, Mathias and Ferdinand II, the first Jew in Bohemia and the entire Habsburg monarchy to be raised to the nobility, a patron of the Jičín community. The Austrian writer and literary historian Karl Kraus (1874-1936 Vienna) was born in Jičín, in 1987 a memorial tablet was put up on his birthplace in Fortna street.

The Jewish street, today's Židovská street, runs parallel with the N side of the square, in the N part of the town's historical centre. The houses were mostly rebuilt in the 19th cent. The home of the Jičín community's rabbi and a school used to be in No. 100.

The synagogue is at the E end of Židovská street. There exists no documentary record of its origin, its present Classicist appearance dates from the period after the 1840 fire. Services were held here until the Nazi occupation. The municipal council bought the building in 1982 and is planning to convert it into an exhibition hall. The

Baroque aron ha-kodesh has been preserved.

The cemetery is set amid fields near a wood called Obora, 2 km NE of the square. Founded in the mid-17th cent., burials until 1949. Remarkable Baroque tombstones. A memorial tablet in memory of the Nazi victims. Ancestors of the German revolutionary Rosa Luxemburg are buried here.

Jičín has a château from the 17th - 18th cent. (housing a museum and art gallery), several churches and a gate with a tower. There is a great number of historical buildings in J., the core of the town has been declared an urban conservation area.

The following J. religious societies used to be in the vicinity: **Kopidlno** (a small town 13 km SSW, a prayer room recorded in the 19th cent.); **Libáň** (a small town 11 km SW, a small synagogue from the 2nd half of the 19th cent., today used by the Hussite Church, a J. section from 1910 in the municipal cemetery, the birth-place of the Czech-J. poet Jiří Daniel [1916-1946 Bergen-Belsen]).

Northwest of the town is a charming region with remarkable natural attractions called Český ráj (Bohemian Paradise): 5 km NW Prachovské skály, a region with sand stone rocks, called the rocktown; 2-3 km NNW military cemeteries and tombstones of soldiers fighting in the Prussian-Austrian war in 1866; 7 km N the hill Tábor (678 m) with a lookout-tower; 12 km NE Nová Paka, a town with a museum of Bohemian precious stones; 11 km SW Staré Hrady, a Renaissance château with a museum; 12 km WNW Sobotka, a town with timbered houses and a small Baroque château Humprecht, open to visitors.

JIHLAVA 48
(Ger. *Iglau*)

District town in Moravia, 110 km SE of Prague. Chartered in the mid-13th cent.

A J. community with a synagogue existed in Jihlava as early as the 14th cent. Jews were expelled from the town in 1426 and settled in the surrounding countryside, forming J. communities in Batelov, Brtnice, Police, Puklice and Třešť; the synagogue was converted into a Catholic chapel (demolished about the 16th cent.). Just a few J. families were granted permission to reside in J. until the mid-19th cent. A modern religious society was established in 1858 and changed to an autonomous religious congregation in 1876. In 1930 the J. population numbered 1,025 persons. The religious congregation was revived after the liberation in 1945, later changed to a synagogue group, which no longer exists.

German-J. writers Ernst Sommer (1888-1955 London) and Louis Fürnberg (1909-1957 Weimar) were born in Jihlava. It is also the birth-place of Julius Tandler (1869-1936 Moscow), an organizer of Austrian, Chinese and Soviet health-care and the native town of the director and actor Carl Meinhard (1875-1949 Buenos Aires). Jihlava was the childhood home of the composer Gustav Mahler (1860 Kaliště - 1911 Vienna), who lived here up to the age of 17.

(**The synagogue** from 1863 was burnt down by the Nazis in 1939 [remains demolished after the liberation].)

The cemetery is in the street U cvi čiště, 1 km W of the main square, 100 m N of the municipal cemetery. Founded in 1869 and still used today. The parents and two siblings of the composer Gustav Mahler are buried here.

The historical centre with an abundance of historical monuments has been declared an urban conservation area: several Gothic, Renaissance and Baroque churches, remains of ramparts with a watch-tower, remarkable Renaissance houses.

A J. community used to be in **Puklice** (5 km SE, several former J. houses, a synagogue, converted into a dwelling house, a cemetery with tombstones from the late 17th cent.). ·

In the village of **Střítež** /Ger. *Schrittenz* (6 km NE) is a J. cemetery with tombstones from the 1st half of the 19th cent., however, there is no documentary record of the existence of a religious congregation or society here.

JINDŘICHŮV HRADEC   49
(Ger. *Neuhaus*)

District town in Bohemia, 110 km SSE of Prague. Chartered before 1255.

Jews resided in the town towards the end of the 13th cent. and were afflicted with a pogrom in 1338. Only 2-6 J. families lived in J. H. until the 18th cent. but allegedly a small prayer room existed here in the late 16th cent. A number of J. families settled in houses along the W side of the street Kostelní in the mid-18th cent. 234 persons of the J. faith are recorded in J. H. in 1930. The J. congregation ceased to exist after World War II and was not revived.

In the 2nd half of the 19th cent. a bimonthly called *Israelitische Gemeindezeitung* was published for a short period of time in J. H.

Rabbi Michal Rachmuth, officiated as rabbi in J. H. from 1915 and wrote Czech textbooks on Jewish history and literature.

Franz Josef Beranek (1902 Břeclav - 1967 Giessen), a high school teacher in J. H., is the author of a scientific work on Yiddish dialects in Czechoslovakia (1935), the only work of its kind. J. H. is the native town of Kurt Adler (1907-1977 USA), an opera conductor, Karel Berman (1919), a well-known opera singer in the National Theatre and of the painter Robert Piesen (1921-1977 Ein Hod).

The synagogue is in Kostelní street, 150 m N of the main square. Built in the 18th cent., extended and rebuilt in the neo-Gothic style in 1867. Since 1952 it has been used by the Hussite Church (the original furnishing has not been preserved). The next building to the south was the J. school.

The cemetery is on a slope near the Nežárka river, 1 km SSW of the château, in the S outskirts. Founded allegedly in 1400, several times extended. The earliest legible tombstone dates from 1714, burials also after World

War II. The ceremonial hall was built in 1937.

J. H. has a large Gothic-Renaissance château, churches and monasteries and remarkable houses. The historical centre with a great number of historical monuments has been declared an urban conservation area.

The fóllowing J. communities used to be in the vicinity: **Nová Včelnice** /Ger. *Neu-Ötting* (a small town 12 km NNE, an early 19th cent. synagogue, converted into a dwelling house, an early 19th cent. cemetery); **Nová Bystřice** /Ger *Neu-Bistritz* (a town 15 km SE, a synagogue from 1887, converted into a youth club, remains of a cemetery from 1879, devastated by the Nazis); **Stráž nad Nežárkou** /Ger. *Platz an d. N.* (a small town 11 km SW, a synagogue from about the 1st half of the 19th cent., serving as a storehouse today, a cemetery from the 1st half of the 19th cent.); **Třeboň** /Ger. *Wittingau* (a town 23 km SW, a synagogue from the 2nd half of the 19th cent., converted into a dwelling house, a cemetery from 1900); **Kardašova Řečice** (a town 12 km NW, a synagogue from 1864-74 was pulled down in 1958-59, a small J. quarter and a 17th cent. cemetery).

KARLOVY VARY   50
(Ger. *Karlsbad,*
Engl. *Carlsbad*)

District town and a famous spa in Bohemia, 110 km WNW of Prague. Chartered by King Charles IV in 1370.

There exists no documentary record of Jews having resided in the town before the year 1499 but we know that this was the year when King Vladislav II issued an order forbidding Jews to settle in the town, which remained in effect until the mid-19th cent. (Jews trading in K. V. lived mostly in nearby Hroznětín at that time.) In 1844 or 1847 a new health centre with a prayer room was built for J. visitors to the spa. A religious society was established in 1864, which changed into a religious congregation in 1868. About 30 persons of the J. faith resided in the town in 1834, about 100 J. families in 1869 and their number gradually increased. About 2,120 persons of the J. faith (nearly 9% of the total population) are recorded in Karlovy Vary in 1930.

In 1938, when K. V. was annexed by Nazi Germany, most of the J. fled to inland Bohemia or left the country. In those days the notable Rabbi Ignaz Ziegler, who had been active in K. V. for 50 years, left the country (died in 1948 in Jerusalem).

The religious congregation was revived after 1945 (a prayer room, a mikveh and kosher restaurant were established), later changed into a synagogue group. Its present address: Československé armády 39, (3rd floor).

In 1921 the 12th and two years later the 13th Zionist Congress were held in K. V. and in 1947 the European Zionist Conference.

In the second half of the 19th cent. the Moser family established a glass-making factory in K. V., significantly contributing to the fame of Bohemian glass. K. V. is the native town of the historian and journalist Bruno Adler, publishing under the pseudonym Urban Roedl, (1889-1968 London) and of the writer and founder of the Dada movement Walter Serner (1889-1942 in a concentration camp).

The prominent ichtyologist and physician Markus Elieser Bloch (1723 Ansbach - 1799), Rabbi Mordecai ben Abraham Benet (1753 Csurgó - 1829), Professor at the Budapest rabbinic school David Kaufmann (1852 Kojetín - 1899) and the actor Max Pallenberg (1877 Vienna - 1934) came to Carlsbad for treatment and died there. The philosopher and political economist Karl Marx (1818-1883) was treated in the spa in 1874, 1875 and 1876; a Karl Marx Museum was opened here in 1960 and a monument was erected in 1988. The writer Ernst Sommer (1888 Jihlava - 1955 London) was active as a lawyer in K. V. in 1920-38, the suburb Rybáře was the childhood home of the writer Louis Fürnberg (1909 Jihlava - 1957 Weimar) and the sculptor Arnold Zadikow (1884 Kolobrzeg - about 1943

Terezín) was head of the art department in the glassworks in 1936-1938.

(The large **synagogue**, built in 1875-77 after the design of architect Adolf Wolff, was burnt down by the Nazis in 1938 and consequently demolished.)

The cemetery is 250 m NE of the main mineral water spring Vřídlo, 250 m E of the Thermal Hotel, in Krušnohorská street. Founded in 1869. Here lie visitors to the spa from various countries and also the father (died in 1916) of the Chief Rabbi of Bohemia and Moravia Richard Feder. A monument in memory of the Nazi victims and J. soldiers who had perished in World War II used to stand in 1956-83 on the site of the demolished synagogue.

There are a tower called Zámecká věž from the early 17th cent., a late Gothic and Baroque Catholic church, an Orthodox church from 1893-98 and many interesting medical buildings at the spa, and a museum of glassmaking (Moser glass) as well as an art gallery.

Many J. communities and religious societies used to exist in the vicinity: **Hroznětín** /Ger. *Lichtenstadt* (a small town 9 km N, a synagogue from about the 18th cent. was pulled down in about 1956, an extensive J. quarter, a cemetery from about the 15th cent. which suffered serious damage by the Nazis, with tombstones from the 2nd half of the 17th cent.); **Stružná** /*Kysibl*, Ger. *Giesshübel* (10 km SE, a prayer room recorded in the 19th cent.); **Bochov** /Ger. *Buchau* (a small town 14 km SE, a prayer room, converted into a flat); **Kozlov** /Ger. *Kosslau, Gosslau* (16 km SE, remains of a J. quarter, a synagogue recorded in the 18th - 19th cent.); **Údrč** /Ger. *Udritsch* (a prayer room existed here in the 19th cent.); **Útvina** /Ger. *Uitwa* (a small town 17 km SSE, remains of a cemetery from about the 1st half of the 19th cent.); **Toužim** /Ger. *Theusing* (a town 19 km SSE, a prayer room existed here in the 18th - 20th cent.); **Bečov nad Teplou** /Ger. *Petschau* (a small town 15 km SSW, remains of a ghetto and a 17th cent. synagogue, destroyed by the Nazis; the birth-place of the rocket design engineer Erwin Loewy [1897-1959 New York]); **Kamenice** /form. *Štampach*, Ger. *Steinbach* (19 km SW, a prayer room recorded in the 18th - 19th cent.); **Kostelní Bříza** /Ger. *Kirchenbirk* (21 km SW, a prayer room allegedly existed here in the 19th cent.); **Krásná Lípa** /Ger. *Schönlind* (a village inundated by the construction of the dam 21 km SW, foundations of a J. quarter and a synagogue at the bottom of the dam, a cemetery with tombstones from the 18th cent.); **Arnoltov** /Ger. *Arnetzgrün* (22 km SW, a prayer room recorded in the 19th cent., a cemetery with tombstones from the 1st half of the 19th cent.); **Loket** /Ger. *Elbogen* (a town 9 km WSW, two early-17th cent. tombstones from a demolished cemetery are to be found at the castle); **Sokolov** /*Falknov nad Ohří*, Ger. *Falkenau* (a district town 17 km WSW, a synagogue from 1897, destroyed by the Nazis; a cemetery from 1878, devastated by the Nazis; native town of the British photographer Erich Auerbach [1911-1977 London]); **Chodov** (a town 9 km WNW); **Kraslice** /Ger. *Graslitz* (a town 27 km WNW, a prayer room was established in 1913 and still existed after World War II); **Nejdek** /Ger. *Neudek* (a town 14 km NW, two prayer rooms were established in the 19th cent., later converted into flats; remains of a Jewish section from 1914 in the communal cemetery, suffered serious damage by the Nazis).

15-20 km N Krušné hory, a mountain range with numerous holiday resorts and lookout-towers (the highest peak is Klí-

*novec - 1,244 m) and **Boží Dar**, the highest situated town in Central Europe (1,028 m); 9 km NE **Ostrov**, a town with a late 17th cent. château; 6 km ESE **Andělská Hora**, ruins of a Gothic-Renaissance castle; 10 km SW **Horní Slavkov**, a town with many Renaissance buildings and a preserved medieval place of execution; 6 km WSW bizarre granite rocks **Svatošské skály**; 9 km WSW **Loket**, a charming town with an urban conservation area and a medieval castle.*

KASEJOVICE 51

Small town in Bohemia, 85 km SW of Prague, 40 km SE of the district town Plzeň. Became a small town in the 14th cent., a town in 1878.

Documentary records mention one J. family in 1570, 4 families and a prayer room in 1618. 24 J. families are recorded in the mid-18th cent., about 25 families in the mid-19th cent. and only 28 persons of the J. faith in 1930. The religious congregation merged with the Horažďovice congregation in 1921. Filip Bondy officiated as rabbi in K. in the mid-19th cent. - he was the first rabbi in Bohemia to preach in Czech.

The former **ghetto**, called Židovské Město (the Jewish Town), used to be SW of the square. Built about 1727 (before J. families used to live in their own or Christian houses scattered in the town), forming a regular urban whole, connected with the rest of the town by one narrow street. A synagogue and 4 small houses were encircled by 14 other J. houses before the mid-19th cent.

The original ground plan is mostly preserved but impaired by new streets which were built later.

Modern houses, including the building of the municipal council, were built on the site of some of the former J. houses.

The synagogue is in the centre of the J. quarter. Built in 1762 in the Rococo style, rebuilt in 1832. Services were held until the 1920s, later it housed a private Judaist and historical collection, today it serves as a small museum of

the town. The 19th-century aron hakodesh and painted ornaments in the main hall have been preserved till the present time.

The cemetery lies among fields, about 650 m N of the synagogue, 500 m NNW of the Catholic church. Founded most probably in 1704, extended in the 18th and 19th cent., repaired in the 1970s. Remarkable Baroque and Classicist tombstones from 1710.

The following J. communities and religious societies used to exist in the vicinity: **Újezdec** (8 km NE, a prayer room recorded in the 19th cent.); **Lnáře** /Ger. *Schlüsselburg* (3 km E, a prayer room allegedly existed here in the 19th cent.); **Podhůří** (5 km W, a prayer house, converted into a flat); **Nepomuk** (town 12 km W, a prayer room, converted into a flat); **Klášter** /Ger. *Kloster* (12 km WNW, a prayer room allegedly existed here in the 19th cent.); **Blovice** (town 19 km NW, a synagogue from 1904, converted into offices; a cemetery with tombstones from the late 17th cent.; the birth-place of the journalist and publicist Henri George Stephan Opper de Blowitz [1825-1903 Paris] and Adolf Kraus [1850-1928 Chicago], president of the B'nai B'rith in the USA); **Spálené Poříčí** /Ger. *Brenn-Poritschen* (a small town 19 km NW, a Rococo style synagogue from about the 18th cent. was pulled down in 1946, remains of a J. quarter, a cemetery from about the 16th cent. with tombstones from the early 19th cent.); **Těňovice** (19 km NW, a prayer room recorded in the 18th - 19th cent., a cemetery from about the 18th cent., became extinct in the 18th or 19th cent.); **Číčov** (19 km NNW, a prayer room allegedly existed here in the 19th cent.).

There is a church from the 13th - 19th cent. in K. and many historical monuments in the neighbouring villages (strongholds, châteaux, churches). 3 km E Lnáře, with a Renaissance castle and a Baroque château, 12 km W Nepomuk, a Catholic place of pilgrimage, the birthplace of St. John of Nepomuk.

KDYNĚ   52
(formerly also *Nová Kdyně*, Ger. *Neugedein*)

Town in Bohemia, 125 km SW of Prague, 10 km SE of the district town Domažlice. Chartered most probably in the 17th cent.

Two J. families are recorded in K. in 1724 and 6 families and a prayer room at the beginning of the 19th cent. Until the mid-19th cent. Jews were permitted to settle only in the small ghetto on the W side of the Americká street (remains of the ghetto were demolished in 1979). After the mid-19th cent. the number of J. increased but only 45 persons of the J. faith are recorded in 1921 and 25 in 1930. A modern religious society was established in 1840 and changed to a religious congregation in 1894. Due to a decrease in members the religious congregation merged with the Klatovy congregation in 1929.

The synagogue is in Masarykova street, W of the square. Built in 1863 in a simple style with Romanesque and Renaissance elements. When the religious congregation was abolished the synagogue was used only during festivals, the last service was held in 1936. Since 1945 it has been used by the Hussite Church. The original interior decoration and benches from the 19th cent. have been preserved. The rabbi used to live in the western part of the building which also served a school (today a rectory).

(There is no J. cemetery in K., J. from K. were buried in Loučim.)

A church from the 14th - 18th cent. is to be found in Kdyně.

The following J. communities and religious societies used to be in the vicinity: **Prapořiště** /Ger. *Braunbusch* (1 km SW, a prayer room existed here in the 19th cent.); **Všeruby** /Ger. *Neumark* (a small town 7 km SW, a synagogue from the second half of the 19th cent., demolished by the Nazis); **Loučim** (5 km ESE, a cemetery from the 1st half of the 19th cent., a prayer room existed here in the 19th cent.); **Dlažov** /Ger. *Glosau* (9 km ESE, a synagogue from 1883, converted into offices of the municipal council); **Běhařov** /or *Vihařov*, Ger. *Wihorschau* (9 km ESE, a prayer room, converted into a flat); **Janovice nad Úhlavou** (a small town 13 km ESE, a synagogue from the 1st half of the 18th cent., rebuilt into a fire engine and appliance house; a cemetery with tombstones from the early 18th cent.; the birthplace of the German-J. music critic and publicist Ernst Rychnowski [1879-1934 Prague]); **Pocinovice** /Ger. *Putzeried* (8 km SE, a prayer room, converted into a flat); **Nýrsko** /Ger. *Neuern* (a town 12 km SE, a late-18th cent. synagogue, pulled down about 1958, remains of a ghetto, a cemetery from about the 15th cent. with tombstones from the early 18th cent.; 108 women from a death transport from Auschwitz were shot near N. in the spring of 1945); **Dešenice** (15 km SE, a synagogue from the 19th cent., converted into a hairdresser's and flats).

1-3 km N ruins of Gothic castles Rýzmberk and Nový Herštejn; 4 km SSW Všerubský průsmyk near the village of Brůdek (scene of the defeat of the Bavarian army in 1040, a Baroque church from the 2nd half of the 17th cent.).

KLADNO   53

District town in Bohemia, 23 km WNW of Prague. K. became a small town in 1561, a town in 1870.

The first J. family was granted permission to settle in K. only at the beginning of the 19th cent. and only 3 J. families lived in the town in the mid-19th cent. After 1850 the number of J. inhabitants considerably increased: J. investors and businessmen played an important part in the development of mines and industrial enterprises. 430 persons of the J. faith lived in the town in 1900 (many others in nearby villages), only 210 are recorded in 1930. The first public prayer room was opened in 1864. The Jewish religious society received official recognition in 1884 and was converted into a religious congregation about 1893.

The religious congregation was reestablished for a short period of time after World War II.

The synagogue in Plk. Stříbrného street, 50 m S of nám. Revoluce square. Built in 1884 in an eclectic style with dominant neo-Renaissance elements. Services were held there until 1939 when the religious congregation brought the synagogue into service of the Hussite Church so as to save it from being destroyed by the Nazis.

Since 1939 it has been used by the Hussite Church. The original wooden gallery, stone stairs to the apse (where an aron ha-kodesh used to be) and the Ten Commandments in the W gable of the building have survived.

The cemetery is 900 m NNE of the synagogue, in Slánská street (leading to the Švermov neighbourhood), next to the municipal cemetery. Founded in 1889, it is still used today. A modern ceremonial hall was built in 1938, serving as a prayer room from 1939.

Kladno has an 18th-cent. Baroque château with a museum, a Baroque chapel, an art gallery and is noted for its coal mines and metallurgical industry.

The following J. communities used to be in the vicinity: **Hostouň** (7 km SE, a synagogue from the 1st half of the 19th cent., pulled down after 1950, an old cemetery with tombstones from the 18th cent., a new cemetery from 1856); **Unhošť** (town 7 km SSE, an early 20th cent. prayer room in a private house, today used as a storeroom); **Velká Dobrá** /Ger. *Gross-Do-bray* (4 km SW, a synagogue from 1805, pulled down before the mid-20th cent.); **Slaný** /Ger. *Schlan* (town 9 km N, a synagogue and a J. school from 1865, today housing archives, a cemetery from 1881 with a ceremonial hall from 1931); **Zlonice** (a small town 15 km N, a prayer room recorded in the 18th - 19th cent., a cemetery from about the 17th cent. with tombstones from the 2nd half of the 18th cent.).

*6 km **Lidice** (memorial of a village massacred by the Nazis in 1942, a museum and a garden of roses from all over the world); 10 km WSW **Lány** (the grave of the first Czechoslovak president T. G. Masaryk (1850-1937) and his family); 5 km WNW **Libušín** - a Slavonic settlement from the 9th - 10th cent. with a Gothic-Baroque church and a wooden belfry (part of the original fortifications reconstructed); 15 km NW **Třebíz**, an open air museum of folk architecture, exhibition of folk sacral art.*

KOJETÍN 54

Town in Moravia, 225 km ESE of Prague, 16 km SW of the district town Přerov. Chartered at the end of the 13th cent.

The first J. families are said to have settled in K. as early as the 12th cent. A J. community was established most probably in the 15th cent. after the expulsion of J. from several Moravian royal cities. The community numbered already 52 J. families in 1566 who had settled in a separate street. In the 17th cent. the community's population increased after the arrival of refugees from the Ukraine and Vienna. From the late 18th cent. up to the 19th cent. only 76 J. families were granted permission to reside in K. 506 persons of the J. faith are recorded in 1857, 198 in 1900 and only 72 in 1930, 83 persons were deported to Terezín. The religious congregation was not revived after World War II.

Rabbis of Kojetín included, e.g. Eleazar Fleckeles (1754 Prague - 1826 Prague) and Jakob Brüll (1812 Rousí-nov - 1889 Kojetín). Richard Feder (1875 Václavice - 1970 Brno), Chief Rabbi of Bohemia and Moravia, was rabbi of Kojetín in 1903-06. Kojetín is the native town of David Kaufmann (1882-1899 Karlovy Vary), Professor at the Budapest rabbi school and author of many Judaist works.

The ghetto used to exist as early as the mid-16th cent. in a curved street between the square and the western walls (today's Husova street), consisting of about 50 houses.

Most of the houses have been rebuilt. A school, a meeting hall and a ritual bath used to be in the communal house No. 796, built in 1867 (today's rectory of the Hussite Church).

The synagogue is in the N part of Husova street, along the former walls. It must have existed in the 16th cent. as it was renewed in 1614. It was destroyed by fire in the mid-17th cent., and acquired its present appearance in the first half of the 18th cent. Services were held here until the Nazi occupation. Since 1953 it has been used by the Hussite Church (today its orientation turned 180°). The building has Renaissance type vaulting and stucco decoration of later date. A ceramic ritual lavabo - kijor - has been walled over in the vaulted anteroom (today used as a columbarium).

The cemetery 700 m NNW of the synagogue, in Olomoucká street, leading to the village Uhřičice. The origin of the cemetery in unknown, it was extended in 1574 and several times later on. The earliest legible tombstone dates from 1795, burials until 1942.

There is Baroque church from the late 17th cent. in K. and other historical monuments.

*5 km **Chropyně**, a town with a Renaissance-Baroque château, today housing a museum and an exhibition of the works of the Czech Cubist painter Emil Filla (1882-1953).*

KOLÍN 55

A district town in Bohemia, 55 km E of Prague. Chartered in the second half of the 13th cent.

Jews resided in K. as early as the 14th cent. Later on they were expelled and not permitted to resettle in the town from 1541 to 1564. 33 J. families are recorded in K. in 1574, 138 (in 38 houses) in 1718, 313 (in 52 houses) in the first half of the 19th cent. and 1,700 persons of the J. faith in 1854. The number of J. dropped in the following years, only 430 persons are recorded in 1930. 2,202 persons were deported to Terezín from Kolín and its vicinity in 1942 and only about 105 persons survived the Nazi occupation. The religious congregation was revived after World War II but later ceased to exist.

Many famous rabbis and authors of Judaist works were active in Kolín. Let us mention, e.g. in 1782-1802 Eleazar Kalir (about 1739 Eisenstadt - 1802 Kolín) or in 1802-10 Benjamin Volf ha-Levi Boskovic (about 1740 Boskovice - 1818 Bonyhád). In 1917-42 and 1945-54 Richard Feder (1875 Václavice - 1970 Brno), later Chief Rabbi of Bohemia and Moravia, was active in Kolín.

The Kolín J. community gave birth to many significant personalities in the field of culture, politics and economics. Let us mention, e.g. Bernard Illowy (1812-1871 Cincinnati), a prominent Orthodox Rabbi in the USA, Max Winder (1845-1920 Kolín), a Czech-Jewish poet, Otokar Fischer (1883-1938 Prague), a Czech-Jewish poet and literary historian, Camill Hoffmann (1879-1944 Auschwitz), a German-Jewish poet, Joseph Popper-Lynkeus (1838-1921 Vienna), a writer, philosopher and technician, and members of the Petschek family, well-known bankers (Julius 1856-1932 and Ignaz 1857-1934).

The ghetto existed most probably from the 14th cent. in Židovská street (today's Na hradbách and K. Světlé streets) and in Zlatá ulička, between the square and the W walls. Before the mid-19th cent. it consisted of approximately 52 houses, some Baroque and Classicist houses have been preserved. **The school**, built in the Classicist style, used to be in the street Na hradbách No. 157/12 (the synagogue is accessible through the school). Above the entrance of the house No. 152/7 in the street Na hradbách there is a Hebrew date 1732-33; in K. Světlé No. 46 there is a room in the loft with a movable ceiling, used during the sukkot festival.

The synagogue in the street Na hradbách, between house No. 157/12 and the former city walls. The building began in 1642 on the site of an older synagogue (which stood there before 1587) and was completed only in 1696. In the early 18th cent. the structure was elongated towards the west, and later a northern aisle was added. The synagogue has a Baroque E gable, a Baroque aron ha-kodesh most probably from 1696 and stucco decorated vaulting. Services were held here until the Nazi occupation, and again from 1945 until

about 1955. The chandelier and a part of the furnishing have survived and are kept today in Temple Emmanuel in Denver, USA. Plans have been made to convert the building into a concert hall.

The old cemetery is WNW of the square. The main entrance is in Kmochova street, the present entrance in Sluneční street (entrance open on request by the Regional museum). The earliest preserved tombstones date from the 1st half of the 15th cent., burials until 1887. The cemetery was extended several times in the 17th, 18th and 19th cent. Prominent rabbis and scholars are buried here: e.g. Bezalel ben Jehuda Liva-Löw (1599), son of the Prague Rabbi Jehuda ben Becalel Liva-Löw. Remarkable Renaissance and Baroque tombstones. Over 2,600 tombstones illustrate developments from the 15th to the 19th cent.

The new cemetery is in the neighbourhood Zálabí, in Veltrubská street, leading to the village Veltruby, 1 km N of the bridge over the Elbe river. Founded in 1887, it is still used today. During World War II it suffered serious damage. A monument in memory of six victims of a death transport in 1945. A monument in memory of the 480 Nazi victims from the Kolín district was dedicated in the cemetery in 1950. The ceremonial hall also served as a prayer hall (the aron ha-kodesh was transferred from here to the Northswood synagogue near London in 1982). The ceremonial hall was pulled down in 1989.

A Gothic church from the 13th - 14th cent., other churches, remains of a Renaissance castle and noteworthy Baroque houses are to be found in K. The historical centre with its medieval ground plan and an abundance of historical monuments has been declared an urban conservation area.

The following J. communities and religious societies used to exist in the

vicinity: **Zásmuky** (a small town 14 km SW, a synagogue from the 2nd half of the 19th cent., today used by the Czech Brethren's Protestant Church, the birthplace of Rudolf Illový [1881-1943 Terezín], a Czech-J. poet); **Bohouňovice II** (19 km SW, a prayer room recorded in the 19th cent.); **Libodřice** (8 km WSW, a prayer room existed here in the 19th cent.); **Kouřim** /Ger. *Gurim* (town 15 km WSW, a J. section from the late 19th cent. at the municipal cemetery); **Plaňany** (small town 13 km WNW, a synagogue from about 1864, today serving as a Hussite Church). In the village **Velim** (8 km NW) there is a grave of 3 prisoners who died during a railway transport from a concentration camp in January 1945.

Several rural strongholds and manors have been preserved in the Kolín region. 15 km WSW Kouřim, a town with many historical monuments and an open air museum of folk farm buildings, open to the public.

KOLINEC 56

Small town in Bohemia, 110 km SW of Prague, 15 km SE of the district town of Klatovy. Chartered in the 13th cent.

Jews are first mentioned in K. in 1654, 4 J. families are recorded in 1724, 16 J. families in 8 houses in the 1st half of the 19th cent. (J. houses and a synagogue stood W of the château, between the street leading to the village Ujčín and the one leading to Hrádek.)

The number of J. declined after the mid-19th cent., the religious congregation ceased to exist towards the end of the century and the congregants joined the Klatovy J. religious congregation. 20 persons of the J. faith are recorded in K. in 1921, only 4 in 1930.

The cemetery lies 200 m SE of the J. quarter and the château, on a steep slope by the road to Hrádek. Founded allegedly in the 14th cent., the oldest legible tombstone dates from the 1st half of the 18th cent. It was extended twice in the 19th cent. Burials until 1939. It belongs among the most beautifully situated J. cemeteries in Bohemia.

(The Classicist **synagogue** from the late 18th or early 19th cent. was destroyed by fire in 1931 and consequently pulled down.)

There are a church from the 13th cent. and a château from the 16th - 19th cent., rebuilt and converted into a modern school, in K.

The following J. communities and religious societies used to exist in the vicinity: **Nalžovské Hory** /form. *Stříbrné Hory*, Ger. *Silberberg* (a small town 8 km NE, a prayer room allegedly existed here in the 19th - 20th cent.); **Velhartice** (a small town 5 km SW, a synagogue from the 1st half of the 19th cent., converted into a fire station; a cemetery from 1858 with a monument in memory of the Nazi victims); **Běšiny** (9 km W, a prayer room recorded in the 19th cent.); **Strážov** /Ger. *Drosau* (a small town 14 km W, the last synagogue was built in 1808 and pulled down in 1954, a Jewish street, a cemetery with tombstones from the mid-18th cent.); **Chlístov** /Ger. *Klistau* (6 km WNW, a synagogue of unknown origin was pulled down in 1965-66, a cemetery from the 2nd half of the 19th cent.).

There is a great number of historical monuments in the vicinity of K. (rural strongholds, châteaux and churches); 5 km SW Velhartice, ruins of a Gothic castle.

KOSOVA HORA 57
(Ger. *Amschelberg*)

Small town in Bohemia, 50 km S of Prague, 35 km E of the district town Příbram. Chartered most probably in the 14th cent., another charter granted in 1744.

Jews are first mentioned here in 1570 (2 men or 2 families). A list from 1674 of family members of 18 J. families (54 persons) has been preserved. The J. population numbered 16 J. families in 1724, 37 families living in 23 houses in the 1st half of the 19th cent. 400 persons of the J. faith are recorded in 1870 (about 35% of the total population). Later the number of J. declined; 47 persons in 1921 and 32 in 1930. The religious congregation was abolished about 1893 and the congregants joined the nearby Sedlčany religious congregation. (A ritual bathhouse, a burial society and a cantor remained active in K. H.). Friedrich Adler (1857-1938 Prague), a German-J. poet, playwright and translator, is a native of K. H.

The Jewish quarter used to be in the NW part of the town, by the road leading to the village Červený Hrádek. It consisted of 25-30 houses, a very small square and a synagogue in the centre. It represents a noteworthy urban whole, most of the houses, today rebuilt, have been preserved.

The synagogue stands on the small square of the former J. quarter. Built after 1740 on the site of a former synagogue destroyed by fire. Services were held there until World War I. Its furnishing has not survived. The rabbi's house adjoins the synagogue on the western side. At present the whole building is in private ownership and is going to be restored.

The cemetery lies 450 m SSE of the synagogue, 300 m SSW of the château. Founded allegedly in 1580, the oldest legible tombstones to be found there today date from the second half of the 18th cent. Extended in 1907 for the last time, burials until World War II.

There are a Renaissance château and a church from the 13th - 18th cent. in K. H.

The following J. communities used to exist in the vicinity: **Sedlčany** (town 3 km W, a synagogue converted into a workshop); **Vrchotovy Janovice** /Ger. *Janowitz-Markt* (7 km ENE, a J. community and a prayer room existed there in the 18th cent.); **Votice** (town 11 km ESE, a synagogue was built in 1724 and pulled down in 1949-50, remains of a ghetto, a cemetery from the 16th cent. with tombstones from the early 18th cent.); **Prčice** (small town 9 km SE, a part of a small twin town **Sedlec-Prčice**, a synagogue from the 2nd half of the 19th cent., converted into a workshop, a precious cemetery with tombstones from the 2nd half of the 18th cent.).

A small detention camp was set up near **Živohošť** (11 km NNW) towards the end of World War II. In the cemetery in **Olbramovice** (12 km ENE) there is a mass grave of 82 prisoners from a railway transport from a concentration camp who were shot here in May 1945. One woman was buried in the cemetery in **Votice** and one man in **Červený Újezd** (14 km SE) - victims of a transport in January 1945. A memorial tablet commemorating 27 prisoners from a death transport shot in 1945 is to be found in the village **Křešice** (10 km E).

1,5 km W Červený Hrádek, a château, rebuilt in the Romantic style housing a regional museum; 7 km ENE Vrchotovy Janovice, a château, rebuilt in the Romantic style, surrounded by a remarkable park, an exhibition commemorating the poets Karl Kraus (1874-1936) and Rainer M. Rilke (1875-1926). There are strongholds, notable churches, châteaux and manors in the nearby villages.

KOSTELEC U KŘÍŽKŮ 58
(Ger. *Kreuz-Kosteletz*)

Village 22 km SSE of Prague.

There exist no records of early J. settlement. The first prayer room was established in 1714. Four J. families (18 persons) are recorded in 1724, 5 J. families in the mid-18th cent. and 7 in the mid-19th cent. (30 J. families are recorded in the vicinity in the mid-19th cent.) A rabbi lived in K. in the mid-19th cent., a religious society and a cantor are recorded in 1872. The religious society ceased to exist in the early 20th cent. Only 3 persons of the J. faith are recorded in 1921.

The cemetery of unknown origin is 750 m WSW of the Catholic church, near the road to Jílové. The earliest legible tombstone dates from 1724. Many Baroque and Classicist tombstones. The cemetery was extended in the 1880's.

Burials until World War II (from the region between the southern suburb of Prague and the Sázava river).

(The last **prayer room**, built in 1846, was demolished in the 1st half of the 20th cent.)

There is a Romanesque rotunda from the 12th cent. with a 19th cent. nave in the village.

The following J. communities and religious societies used to be in the vicinity: **Strančice** (8 km NE, a synagogue from 1849, today used as a storehouse, remains of a 19th cent. cemetery; the birth place of the electrical engineer Emil Kolben [1862-1943 Terezín], one of the founders of the Prague machine works ČKD [formerly Czech-Moravian-Kolben-Daněk]); **Říčany** (town 10 km NE, a prayer house from the 1880's, converted into a fire station); **Pyšely** (small town 8 km ESE, a synagogue from the 2nd half of the 19th cent., converted into a workshop). - Three prisoners were buried in **Říčany** and two prisoners in the village **Mirošovice** (11 km E) - victims of a railway transport from Auschwitz in January 1945.

5 km WSW Jílové u Prahy, a town with a small museum of gold mining and historical monuments from the mid-14th cent.

KRNOV 59
(Ger. *Jägerndorf*)

Town in Silesia, near the Polish frontier, 230 km E of Prague, 50 km NW of Ostrava. Chartered as early as the 1st half of the 13th cent.

The earliest documentary record of J. settlement dates from the 2nd half of the 14th cent. J. were expelled from the Krnov principality in 1535 and left K. by the end of the century. The modern history of J. settlement begins in the mid-19th cent. - 5 J. families lived in the town in 1848, a religious society was established in 1853. The J. population numbered 17 families in 1860 and in 1877 the religious society became an autonomous religious congregation. 534 persons of the J. faith are recorded in 1900, only 378 in 1921 and 318 in 1930. After the annexation of K. by Germany in 1938 most of the J. were driven out of the town. After World War II the religious congregation (with a small prayer room) was revived, later changed to a synagogue group (active until 1958).

above the aron ha-kodesh. Services were held there until 1938, the furnishing was destroyed by the Nazis, during the Nazi occupation it served as a market. One of the few synagogues on the territory annexed by Germany which was not demolished in 1938. Since 1960 it has been used for storing records.

The cemetery lies 1,500 m SE of the synagogue, in Opavská street, entrance from the street V osadě. Founded in 1873, burials until 1968. Noteworthy tombstones, an Art-Nouveau ark-shaped tomb from 1910.

There are churches from the 14th - 18th cent. in K., Renaissance and Baroque houses and a part of Renaissance remodelled town walls.

There used to be a religious society in the district town of **Bruntál** /Ger.

The synagogue is in the E part of the town's centre, at the corner of Gottwaldova and Barvířská streets. Built on the site of the town walls in 1871. It is a neo-Romanesque building with two towers, a choir used to be

Freudenthal (20 km SW, a prayer room, converted into a flat; remains of a late 19th cent. cemetery, demolished by the Nazis). - The small town **Město Albrechtice** /Ger. *Olbersdorf Stadt* (12 km NW) is the birthplace of František Gel

(1901-1972), a Czech-J. writer and journalist.

2 km SE Cvilín, a hill with a lookout-tower, ruins of a castle and pilgrim church; westward the wooded mountain range Hrubý Jeseník (the highest peak is 1,492 m).

KROMĚŘÍŽ   60
(Ger. *Kremsier*)

District town in Moravia, 230 km SE of Prague, 60 km ENE of Brno. Chartered in the 2nd half of the 13th cent.

Most probably there was only one J. family in the town in the 1st half of the 14th cent. A J. community with a synagogue existed in K. in the early 15th cent. During the Swedish invasion in 1643 the vast majority of J. of the K. community was massacred, the synagogue and most of the houses were pillaged: over 70 Jews perished, including Rabbi Mordecai ben Moshe. In the 18th and the half of the 19th cent. 100-106 J. families (542 persons in 1830) were granted permission to reside in K. 783 persons of the J. faith are recorded in 1880, 611 in 1900 and only 383 in 1930. The religious congregation was revived after World War II (no longer exists).

Names of almost forty rabbis active in K. are recorded from the early 15th cent. Many came from abroad: Germany, Austria, Poland and Hungary. The most prominent modern rabbi in K. was Adolf Frankl-Grün (1847 Uherský Brod - 1916 Kroměříž), author of many historical and theological works. The German-J. writer and historian of J. communities in Moravia Max Grünfeld (1856-1933 Brno) and the German-J. poet and art historian Adolf Donath (1876-1937 Prague) were born in K.

The Jewish quarter used to be SE of the town centre, in today's Moravcova and Tylova streets. J. families resided here most probably in the 15th cent. Towards the end of the 17th cent. an order was issued to build a separation wall with 3 small gates to form an enclosed ghetto. (Remnants of this wall, today registered as a historical monument, are to be found between Moravcova street and the church Nanebevzetí P. Marie.) The ghetto consisted of 34 houses, a synagogue and a town hall.

(A medieval **synagogue** used to stand until the 17th cent. in Vodní street. The second synagogue, dating from the 2nd half of the 17th cent., in Moravcova street, was demolished in 1908. The third synagogue, built in 1908-10 on Komenského square, was demolished by the Nazis in 1942.)

The J. town hall is in Moravcova street No. 259. Built in the early Baroque style in 1867-88, most probably after the model of the Italian architect G. P. Tencalla. From the 18th cent. till 1880 it used to house a J. school. It was restored in 1974-80 and another storey was added, today the building houses the district cultural centre.

The cemetery lies 1,500 m SSW of the J. town hall, in the street Osvoboditelů, leading to Vážany suburb. Opened in 1928, devastated by the Nazis, still used today. A monument in memory of the 300 Nazi victims of the Kroměříž region. The ceremonial hall from 1928 (with columns imitating an ancient temple) is used by the municipal cemetery today. (The first cemetery of unknown origin, with tombstones from 1535 up to 1849 became extinct in 1882. The second, founded most probably in the 18th cent., was used until 1927; devastated by the Nazis during World War II and consequently ceased to exist.)

The historical centre of K. with a great number of historical monuments has been declared an urban conservation area: a remarkable Baroque château from the turn of the 17th and 18th cent. (housing a famous art gallery), two remarkable 17th cent. parks, several churches from the 13th up to the 18th cent., Renaissance and Baroque houses.

LIBEREC 61
(Ger. *Reichenberg*)

District town in Bohemia, 90 km NNE of Prague. Became a small town in 1454, a town in 1784.

J. lived in L. most probably as early as the 14th and 15th cent. 60 J. families fled from Prague to Liberec in 1582 to escape plague. L. was a centre of the draper's trade and a numerous group of J. dealers formed in the town but as they had not been granted the right of permanent residence they could not establish a J. community. Jews were expelled from L. and the entire estate in 1799 (only 14 men were permitted to stay). 6 J. families are recorded in the town again in 1823. After the mid-19th cent. the J. population gradually increased: 30 J. families in 1861, 314 persons of the J. faith in 1869. The J. population numbered 1,392 in 1930.

A religious society was established in 1863 (in 1861 a room was rented and converted into a prayer room), an autonomous religious congregation was re-established after World War II: 1,211 persons of the J. faith resided in L. in 1946 (37 citizens, survivors of concentration camps, 1,174 post-war settlers among which were 182 members of the Czechoslovak army-in-exile). The newly established religious congregation, considerably reduced in numbers, consequently changed into a synagogue group.

The address of the present prayer room: Matoušova 453/12 (corner of Vaňurova street). The prayer room was restored in 1987, a memorial tablet in memory of the victims of the Nazis.

L. is the birth-place of Richard Breitenfeld (1869-1942 Terezín), an opera singer, active in Germany.

The cemetery is 900 m N of centre (the town hall) in Ruprechtická street (corner of Květnové revoluce street). Opened in 1865, a new part in 1896. The cemetery is still used today. The ceremonial hall dates from 1900 (today a storehouse). Many graves of Galician refugees from World War I. A grave of 11 women prisoners from the labour camp in Bílý Kostel n. Nisou.

(The neo-Renaissance synagogue from 1889 was burnt down and demolished by the Nazis in 1938.)

Liberec has a Renaissance-Baroque château (an art gallery in the park), several churches from the 16th up to the 20th cent., three timber-framed houses from the mid-17th cent., a town hall, built in 1888-93, resembling the town hall in Vienna.

The following J. communities used to exist in the vicinity: **Jablonec nad Nisou** /Ger. *Gablonz* (a town 10 km SE, the synagogue, built by architect W. Stiassny in 1892, was demolished by the Nazis; the cemetery from 1882 was destroyed by the Nazis and closed in 1968 - the urns were transferred to the Liberec cemetery; Jablonec n.N. is the birth-place of the conductor Hermann Adler [1899 - resident in the USA since

1939]); **Český Dub** /Ger. *Böhmisch-Aicha* (a town 13 km SSW, a prayer room existed most probably in the 19th cent., a cemetery from about the 18th cent. was liquidated by the Nazis). - A Nazi labour camp was set up in the village **Bílý Kostel nad Nisou** /Ger. *Weisskirchen* (11 km NW), 11 women prisoners buried in the L. cemetery. **Višňová** (22 km N) is the native village of the Terezín ghetto painter Fritta (Friedrich Taussig, 1906-1944 Auschwitz). Max Brod's mother was born in **Smržovka** (small town 14 km ESE).

*NE is the wooded range of mountains **Jizerské hory** (the highest peak 1,124 m); 10 km SE **Jablonec nad Nisou** with a museum of glass and costume jewellery; 6 km SW the **Ještěd** mountain (1,012 m, hotel).*

LIBOCHOVICE 62

Town in Bohemia, 45 km NW of Prague, 13 km SW of Terezín. Became a small town in the 1st half of the 14th cent., a town in 1560.

J. families are recorded in L. in as early as the 2nd half of the 15th cent., a J. community originated most pro-

bably in the 2nd half of the 16th cent. after arrival of many J. families (allegedly from the near-by Radovesice). 11 J. families are recorded in L. in 1570, 31 in the mid-18th cent., and only 48 persons of the J. faith in 1930. The religious congregation was not revived after World War II.

The Jewish quarter used to exist from the 15th or 16th cent. in the W part of the town, SW of the square. It consisted of 27 houses in several neighbouring narrow streets (Koželužská, Nerudova and their vicinity). Some of the houses, today mostly rebuilt, have been preserved.

The cemetery is 800 m WNW of the square, W of the communal cemetery. Founded in 1583, extended in 1846. The oldest preserved tombstone dates from 1588, burials until World War II. It represents a valuable cemetery with a number of Renaissance and Baroque tombstones.

(The synagogue from the 2nd half of the 18th cent. was rebuilt in 1835 and demolished in 1985.)

L. has a Renaissance château, rebuilt in the early Baroque style in 1683-90 (with remarkable collections and a memorial of the natural scientist Jan E.

Purkyně [1787-1869]) and two Baroque churches.

A J. community used to exist in **Budyně nad Ohří** (a small town 6 km E, remains of a ghetto, a synagogue from the 1st half of the 18th cent., rebuilt in the 1st half of the 19th cent., today used as a store-house, a cemetery from 1787). A J. community is said to have been in the village of **Radovesice** (2 km ENE) whose members moved to Libochovice in the 2nd half of the 16th cent.

*3 km NNW **Hazmburk**, ruins of a Gothic castle; 6 km E **Budyně nad Ohří**, a small town with a Gothic-Renaissance château (housing a municipal museum) and other historical monuments.*

LIPNÍK NAD BEČVOU   63
(Ger. *Leipnik*)

Town in Moravia, 235 km ESE of Prague, 12 km NE of the district town Přerov. Chartered most probably about 1620.

Jews are first mentioned here in 1454. At that time some J. families that had been expelled from Znojmo settled in the town. A J. community and a synagogue must have existed in L. in the 1st half of the 16th cent. The community suffered extreme hardship during the Thirty Years' War. 34 J. houses are recorded in L. in 1667 and 48 in 1700. The community numbered 975 persons (28% of total population) in 1794. 255 J. families were granted permission to reside in the town in the 1st half of the 19th cent. 1,664 persons of the J. faith (31% of the total population) resided in L. in 1848, 1,687 in 1857 but later their number dropped: 534 persons in 1900, 154 in 1930. The religious congregation was revived only for a short time after 1945.

Since the Middle Ages J. houses were concentrated in the street running along the W walls (today's Pernštýnská street) and at the NE edge of the walled city. In the late 16th cent. J. also owned houses in other streets. There was no enclosed ghetto in the town.

Moses Löb Bloch (1815 Poběžovice - 1909 Budapest) officiated as rabbi in L. from 1856 to 1877, in 1877 he became the head-master of the Budapest rabbinical school.

The synagogue is in Pernštýnská

street, on the SW edge of the city centre. It stood there already in 1540, was extended in 1607-8 and in the 1870s. Services were held until the Nazi occupation. Since 1949 it has been in use by the Hussite Church (orientation turned 90°). Its 19th cent. exterior appearance was simplified after World War II. Late Gothic vaulting with brick ribs in the interior. It represents one of the most valuable synagogues in Central Europe.

The village **Horecko** was founded in 1813 as a Jewish colony to relieve the overpopulated J. community in the town. It lies 1 km WNW of the synagogue, near the road leading to Trnávka. Originally, it consisted of 28 uniform one-storeyed houses with a school and an alms-house. In 1839 a railway was built, dividing the village into two parts (three middle houses were pulled down). Several houses, today rebuilt, have been preserved.

The cemetery is 300 m SE of the synagogue in Zahradní street. Founded in 1883, burials also after World War II. Tombstones from the neighbouring **older cemetery**, founded in 1567 were transferred here. (There are no traces of the two other older cemeteries.)

The town has a Gothic-Renaissance church, Renaissance arcaded houses and remains of the city wall. The historical centre with a great number of historical monuments has been declared an urban conservation area.

*3 km **Helfštýn**, extensive ruins of a Gothic-Renaissance castle; 4 km S **Kladníky**, a village with an operating wooden wind-mill from the 17th cent.*

LITEŇ   64

Small town in Bohemia, 27 km SW of Prague, 8 km SE of the district town Beroun.

We have no documentary record of early J. settlement but it is said that J. settled in L. as early as the Middle Ages. Documentary records date from the 2nd half of the 17th cent. Four J. families (22 persons) are recorded in 1715, 23 families (102 persons) in 1793. A synagogue and a rabbi are recorded in 1793. J. houses were not concentrated in one particular place, there was no ghetto in L. 190 persons of the J. faith (12% of the total population) lived in L. and its vicinity in 1849, 52 in L. in 1890 and only 13 persons in 1930.

The J. religious congregation was not revived after World War II.

The cemetery is 1 km SSW of the château. Founded in 1680 as a burial ground for the whole neighbourhood, later extended. The oldest preserved tombstones date from the late 17th cent., burials until the Nazi occupation. It represents a well-preserved country cemetery. A wooden tombstone from 1843 was transferred from this cemetery to the State Jewish Museum in Prague.

The synagogue was in the S part of the square, SW of the château. Built in the 19th cent. (particulars are not known), services were held there until the 1930s. It was converted into a fire station after World War II and completely rebuilt in 1956.

L. has a Baroque château (housing a museum) and a Gothic-Baroque church.

The following J. communities used to exist in the vicinity: **Všeradice** (4 km SW, remains of a J. quarter with a synagogue from the 1st half of the 19th cent.); **Suchomasty** (6 km WSW, a prayer room and a cemetery are said to have existed here in the 19th cent.); **Tetín** (5 km WNW, a synagogue of unknown origin was pulled down in 1974, a cemetery of unknown origin,

became extinct in the 20th cent.); **Beroun** (a town 8 km NW, the former prayer hall with J. school are used today as an art and music school; a cemetery from the 2nd half of the 19th cent.).

E and S spread the wooded hills Hřebeny (the highest peak 603 m); W and N Český kras a protected region with karst formation and localities of fossils; 5 km WNW Koněpruské jeskyně, caves open to the public with remarkable stalactites and a medieval underground workshop of counterfeiters; 5 km NW Tetín, a village with 3 churches from the Romanesque up to the Baroque periods, the seat of Princess Ludmila in the 10th cent.; 8 km NW Beroun, remains of the city walls with two gates, churches from the Gothic up to the Baroque periods and other historical monuments.

LOMNICE   65

Small town in Moravia, 160 km SE of Prague, 17 km WNW of the district town Blansko, 27 km NW of Brno. L. became a small town in the early 16th cent.

J. settled in L. before 1656. A J. religious congregation was established most probably in the 1st quarter of the 18th cent. after the arrival of J. families from nearby Lysice. From the late 18th cent. to the mid-19th cent. 56 J. families were granted permission to reside in L. The J. population numbered 606 persons (over one third of the total population) in 1830 and only 306 (20% of the total population) in 1848. Many J. moved to Vienna and Brno and thereafter the number of J. proceeded to decline: 203 persons in 1880, 88 in 1900 and 30 in 1930. The J. religious congregation had a rabbi until 1919. There was a minimal number of congregants in L. in the 1930s.

The Jewish quarter was NW of the main square. It originated most probably in the 18th cent. and represents an important urban whole. It consisted of a square-shaped plaza and one street (today's nám. Josefa Uhra and ul. Josefa Uhra) with about 30 houses. On the E side of the square (opposite the synagogue) there was a rabbi's house and a Talmud Torah school. Most of the houses have been preserved (some of them rebuilt).

The synagogue is on the square nám. Josefa Uhra. The Baroque synagogue was built in 1780-85. Services were held here until the 1930s. At present it is used as a store-house.

The cemetery is set on a slope 200 m N of the synagogue. The oldest tombstone dates from 1686, burials until World War II. Many remarkable Baroque tombstones.

L. has a Renaissance-Baroque château, a significant Baroque church, a
Baroque town-hall with a tower and other Baroque historical monuments.

A religious society was in **Tišnov** /Ger. *Tischnowitz* (6 km S, a prayer room allegedly existed here in the 19th cent.).

*6 km S **Předklášteří** (suburb of Tišnov) with a former monastery from the 13th cent. (a remarkable Romanesque-Gothic portal); westwards the romantic valley of the **Svratka** river; 9 km NW **Pernštejn**, a well-preserved Gothic-Renaissance castle, open to the public.*

LOŠTICE 66
(Ger. *Loschiz*)

Town in Moravia, 185 km ESE of Prague, 25 km SSW of the district town Šumperk. L. became a small town in the mid-14th cent. and a town in the 17th or 18th cent.

J. settlement is first mentioned in L. in 1544. 7 J. families are recorded in L. in the mid-16th cent. and a J. community in 1581. 21 houses in J. ownership are recorded in 1630, only ten were inhabited after the Thirty Years' War (1656). The community increased after mid-17th cent. when J. expelled from the Ukraine and Lower Austria settled in L. 80 J. families (328 persons) in 17 houses are recorded in 1727. Until those days J. houses had stood very close to the Catholic church but in 1727 Jews were forced to move to another place and form a ghetto. 71 J. families were granted permission to reside in L. from the late 18th cent. to the mid-19th cent. (438 persons, i.e. 17% of total population, in 1848). Later the number declined: 280 persons of the J. faith are recorded in 1880, 115 in 1900, 55 in 1930. Only 11 survivors returned from the Nazi concentration camps. The religious congregation was not revived after World War II.

The ghetto used to be in the street Novosady (Ztracená street) and in one part of the two neighbouring streets, W of the square. In 1727 the emperor ordered an exchange of J. and Christian houses and a transfer of the synagogue. (The former J. quarter was by the Catholic church, NE of the square.) In the beginning the ghetto consisted of 17, later of about 25 houses. Most of the original houses were destroyed by fire in 1928. The J. town-hall was in No. 317 (the corner of Ztracená and Žádlovická streets), the school in No. 324.

The synagogue is at the S end of Ztracená street. It was built most probably in 1805 on the site of the former wooden synagogue from 1651, which had been transferred there in 1727 from the former J. quarter. A simple structure with Classicist style elements. Services were held there until the Nazi occupation, subsequently the synagogue was used as a store-house, the original furnishing has not been preserved. In 1966 - 80 it housed a municipal museum with an exhibition on the history of the J. community, today it serves as an art and music school.

The cemetery is 1,100 m SE of the synagogue, 200 m S of the road leading to Palonín. Founded in 1554, tombstones from the 17th cent. Burials also after World War II. Remarkable Baroque tombstones, an ark-shaped tomb from 1736. (In 1743 the lordship ordered thr founding of a new cemetery N of the synagogue but there is no evidence of burials there, at present it serves as an orchard.)

There are a 16th cent. Renaissance town hall and an 18th cent. Baroque church in L.

The following J. communities and religious societies used to exist in the vicinity: **Mohelnice** /Ger. *Müglitz* (a

town 3 km NNW, a prayer room existed here in the 19th - 20th cent., a J. section in the municipal cemetery, established in 1905; a grave of the victims of a death transport from the Auschwitz concentration camp, memorial tablet of the Wolf brothers, natives of L.: Kurt [killed in 1943 near Sokolovo] and Otto [tortured to death as a partisan in 1945 near Zákřov]); **Litovel** /Ger. *Littau* (a town 11 km SE, a prayer room existed here in the late 19th cent., the birthplace of the famous architect Heinrich Kulka [1900-1971 Auckland, New Zealand]).

1 km W Žádlovice, a Baroque château from the 18th cent.; 3 km NNW Mohelnice, a 13th cent. Gothic church and a 72 m high Gothic tower; 7 km SE Mladečské jeskyně, stalactite caves with preserved fireplaces from the Diluvial Period open to the public; 8 km S Javoříčko, a monument in memory of the village massacred and burnt down by the Nazis in 1945, stalactite caves open to the public; 5 km SSW Bouzov, a small town with a Gothic castle rebuilt in the neo-Gothic style, interiors open to the public.

LOUNY 67
(Ger. *Laun*)

District town in Bohemia, 55 km NW of Prague. Chartered most probably in 1253.

J. settled in L as early as the 1st half of the 14th cent. A J. community with a prayer room existed most probably in the early 15th cent. J. were expelled from the town in 1542. Only one or two J. families resided in L. from the 17th to the mid-19th cent. but the prayer room and the cemetery (from 1680) was used by J. from the vicinity. A modern Jewish religious congregation was established in 1860, receiving official recognition in 1874. 51 J. families are recorded in L. in 1880, 567 persons of the J. faith in 1890, only 205 in 1930. The J. religious congregation was reestablished for a short time after World War II.

The synagogue is in Thälmannova

street, in the NE part of the city centre. Built after the design of architect Staněk in 1871 in the Moorish style with Romanesque elements. Services were held here until the Nazi occupation. It served as a museum in 1946-54, since 1967 as archives depository. The interior furnishing has not been preserved.

The cemetery is 1 km SE of the synagogue, next to the communal cemetery. Founded in 1874-75, burials also after World War II. The ceremonial hall has Moorish style elements.

(The earliest cemetery was founded in 1680 but not the slightest trace of it is left behind. The other cemetery, used from the 1st half of the 19th cent. till 1858, became extinct about 1930.)

There is an abundance of historical monuments in L.: a remarkable late Gothic cathedral from the 16th cent., a Romanesque-Gothic church, remains of the city walls with a gate, a museum housed in a Gothic building, Renaissance houses and many other places of interest.

The following J. communities and religious societies used to exist in the vicinity: **Třebívlice** /Ger. *Triblitz* (13 km NE, a synagogue from 1860 used by the Hussite church, a cemetery from the 2nd half of the 19th cent., devastated by the Nazis); **Pátek** (10 km ENE, a prayer room existed here in the 18th cent.); **Hříškov** /Ger. *Rischkau* (8 km SE, a synagogue was built in the 18th cent., rebuilt in the 19th cent. and demolished after 1950); **Panenský Týnec** /Ger. *Jungfernteinitz* (a small town 10 km SE, a prayer room recorded in the 18th cent.); **Ročov** (a small town 11 km SSW, a synagogue was built in 1869, demolished in 1957); **Domoušice** (14 km SSW, a religious society recorded in the 19th cent.); **Postoloprty** /Ger. *Postelberg* (town 7 km W, a synagogue from the 1st half of the 18th cent., demolished after 1980, remains of a J. street from the early 18th cent., graves of the Red Army soldiers from 1945 in the new cemetery, ancestors of Karl Marx buried in the old 18th-cent. cemetery [liquidated after 1970]). Tombstones from the mid-18th cent. are to be found near the

village **Vrbno nad Lesy** (8 km SE). The cemetery belonged to the Hříškov J. community.

*North of the town unfolds **České středohoří** with many eruptive hills, offering a view of the surrounding countryside; 3 km N Červený vrch (also called Stříbrník, 272 m) with a tourist chalet; 11 km ESE Peruc (a small town with a Rococo château, housing a gallery of the Czech Cubist painter Emil Filla [1882 - 1953]); 10 km SE Panenský Týnec (a small town with remains of an uncompleted monasterial church from the 14th cent.).*

LUŽE   68

Small town in Bohemia, 115 km ESE of Prague, 18 km ESE of the district town Chrudim. Chartered most probably in the 14th cent.

Jews lived in L. most probably as early as the 2nd half of the 16th cent. 11 J. families are recorded in 1620, 17 families in the mid-18th cent. and about 55 families (300 persons) in 25 houses in the mid-19th cent. A J. community was established most probably in the 17th cent. and had a rabbi towards the end of the century. Only 32 persons of the J. faith resided in L. in 1930. Only 6 survivors returned to L. from concentration camps after the war. The religious congregation was not revived after World War II. Jiří Alter (1891-1972 Beith Yitzhak, Israel), an astronomer, was born in Luže.

The ghetto consisted of 24 one storey houses in Jeronýmova street, SW of the square. The exact time of its origin is not known. A school used to be in No. 182. Most of the houses, today rebuilt, have been preserved.

The synagogue is in the N part of Jeronýmova street, 100 m SW of the square. Built or rebuilt in the Baroque style about 1780. Services were held there until the Nazi occupation. Today it is used as a drying-house for leather. A Classicist aron ha-kodesh, an almemor with a grillwork, a chandelier and other valuable furnishings have been preserved.

19th - 20th cent., a cemetery from 1881, the Polička J. community is commemorated in the municipal museum). - A grave of four prisoners who died in a death transport in 1945 is to be found at the cemetery in the village **Zámrsk** (13 km NE).

*1 km SSE **Košumberk**, ruins of a Gothic-Renaissance castle (a small museum); 6 km SSE **Rychmburk**, a well-preserved Gothic-Renaissance castle (courtyard open to the public).*

The cemetery is set in the edge of a wood, 1,300 m ENE of the square, near farm out-buildings. Tombstones from the 17th cent., burials until World War II. The cemetery suffered serious damage by the Nazis. Remarkable Baroque and Classicist tombstones.

L. has a Gothic-Baroque church and a pilgrimage church from the 17th cent.

The following J. communities and religious societies used to exist in the vicinity: **Vysoké Mýto** /Ger. *Hohenmauth* (town 11 km NE, a prayer room existed here in the 19th - 20th cent.); **Litomyšl** (a town 20 km ESE, a cemetery from 1876); **Polička** (a town 26 km SE, a prayer room existed here in the

Small town in Bohemia, 60 km ESE of Prague, 5 km SW of the district town Kutná Hora.

J. settlement is first mentioned in 1719: 15 J. families lived in M. in those days and the community had a rabbi. 20 J. families (140 persons) are said to have lived in M. before the mid-19th cent. After 1848 J. families left to settle in the neighbouring Kutná Hora and other larger towns. Only 8 persons of the J. faith are recorded in M. in 1930. The religious congregation ceased to exist in M. towards the end of the 19th cent. and the congregants joined the Kutná Hora religious congregation.

The cemetery is 400 m SW of the square, near the road to Roztěž. Founded most probably in the 18th cent., extended in the 2nd half of the 19th cent. The oldest legible tombstone dates from the mid-18th cent., burials also after World War II. The cemetery was also used as a burial ground by the Kutná Hora community. Remarkable Baroque and Classicist tombstones.

Most of the J. houses and the synagogue were in the so-called **Jewish street** (200 m E of the square, between the street leading to the village Bykáň and the street to the railway station). Two houses have survived: a school used to be in No. 27 and during World War I there was an Orthodox prayer room for Galician refugees there. (The synagogue from about the mid-19th cent. was used until the 20th cent., demolished in 1987.)

A 15th cent. tower stronghold and a Baroque church are to be found in M.

The following J. communities used to exist in the vicinity: **Kutná Hora** /Ger. *Kuttenberg* (a town 5 km NE, remains of a synagogue from 1881, the synagogue from 1902 is used by the Hussite Church; the native town of the stage-designer František Zelenka [1904-1944 during a death march from Auschwitz] and of the Czech-J. poet Jiří Orten [1919-1941 Prague] and his brothers, theatrical artists Ota Ornest [1913] and Zdeněk Ornest [1929-1990 Prague]); **Malín** (7 km NE, a synagogue from 1859-63, pulled down after 1960); **Zbraslavice** (a small town 11 km SSW, a synagogue from 1832, converted into a garage, a cemetery from the late 18th cent. with tombstones from the early 19th cent.); **Uhlířské Janovice** /Ger. *Kohl-Janowitz* (a small town 11 km SW, a synagogue from the late 18th cent., rebuilt in 1914, used by the Hussite Church, remains of a cemetery from 1834).

2 km SSW Sion, ruins of a Gothic castle; 2 km WSW Roztěž, a château, rebuilt in the Art Nouveau style at the beginning of the 20th cent.; 4 km NW

Vysoká, a hill with ruins of an early Baroque monasterial chapel from the end of the 17th cent.; 5 km Kutná Hora, (in the Middle Ages the second most important town in Bohemia, an abundance of historical monuments from the 14th cent., several museums, a silver mine open to the public, an urban conservation area).

MARIÁNSKÉ LÁZNĚ 70
(Ger. *Marienbad*)

Town in Bohemia, 125 km W of Prague, 25 km SE of the district town Cheb. The first health resort building was built in the mid-18th cent. Chartered in 1865.

Jews were most probably not permitted to settle in M. L. until the 1820s. J. lived in the surrounding villages and did their business in the town. (Physicians Leo Isak Weis and Yesayas Weis, the great-grandfather and grandfather of the well-known American Rabbi Isaac Mayer Wise, lived in nearby Drmoul and worked in M. L.).

A small J. community is recorded in 1824, the first public prayer room was established in 1861, the community's statutes were officially recognized in 1875. In 1872 the religious congregation had 26 taxpayers, a shohet, a school with a teacher and a spa building. 405 persons of the J. faith are recorded in M. L. in 1930. After World War II the religious congregation was revived and later changed into a synagogue group. Most of the post-war congregants lived in the local J. old people's home (abolished as well as the prayer room in 1972).

In 1933 the German philosopher and publicist Theodor Lessing (born in 1872, Anderten) was killed by the Nazis in M. L.: there is a memorial tablet in Třebízského street, No. 213. The last World Conference of Agudath Israel to be held before the outbreak of World War II was also held in M. L. in 1937. In 1947 the World Conference of Agudath Israel (115 delegates from

28 countries) was held in M. L. and a yeshivah was founded but abolished soon after.

The cemetery, 2 km SW of the city centre, in Chebská street (leading to the suburb Velká Hleďsebe), near the railway. Founded most probably in 1875, extended before 1930. The cemetery is still used today. The earliest tombstones were destroyed by the Nazis. Salomon Kalischer (1843-1925), President of the Union of German Jewish Communities, and Theodor Lessing (1872-1933), a German philosopher and anti-fascist are buried there. Two historically valuable tombstones have been transferred there from the Lázně Kynžvart spa cemetery which had been liquidated by the Nazis (one dates from 1714).

The former **J. hospital** (spa building) and the first public prayer room used to be in the house Sion, Lesní street, No. 102/6. Built in 1861, the prayer room was abolished in 1930. The building was converted into flats.

(The great synagogue from 1884 was burnt down and demolished by the Nazis in 1938.)

M. L. ranks among the most famous European spas. About 40 curative and thermal springs. Spa buildings from the 2nd half of the 19th cent., an Orthodox church from 1900-01 with a porcelain iconostas, an Anglican church from 1878-79 with a memorial tablet commemorating King Edward VII, a museum with exhibitions on J. W. Goethe, F. Chopin and M. Gorki.

The following J. communities and religious societies used to exist in the vicinity: **Lázně Kynžvart** /Ger. *Königswart* (a town 6 km NW, remains of a ghetto, perhaps of medieval origin, the 18th cent. synagogue and the early 15th cent. cemetery were destroyed by the Nazis); **Úbočí** /Ger. *Amonsgrün* (11 km NW, a synagogue of unknown origin, pulled down after 1960, remains of a rural ghetto, a cemetery with tombstones from the 1st half of the 19th cent.); **Milíkov** /Ger. *Miltigau* (14 km NW, a prayer room recorded in the 18th - 19th cent.); **Malá Šitboř** /Ger. *Klein-Schüttüber* (14 km NW, a synagogue from 1808, burnt down in 1914 and consequently pulled down, remains of a cemetery with tombstones from the 1st half of the 19th cent.); **Poutnov** /Ger. *Pauten* (10 km NE, foundations of a

17th cent. synagogue, demolished in 1915, a cemetery with tombstones from the 18th cent.); **Bezdružice** /Ger. *Weseritz* (a small town 20 km ESE, remains of a J. quarter with a synagogue from the 1st half of the 19th cent., a cemetery with tombstones from the 1st half of the 19th cent.); **Lestkov** /Ger. *Leskau* (a small town 15 km SE, remains of a J. quarter); **Kořen** /Ger. *Kurschin* (16 km SE, a synagogue most probably from the 1st half of the 19th cent., converted into a dwelling house, a cemetery with tombstones from the 1st half of the 19th cent.); **Chodová Planá** /Ger. *Kuttenplan* (a small town 8 km SSE, a synagogue from the mid-18th cent., pulled down after 1970, a J. street, remains of an old J. cemetery with tombstones from the 17th cent., a new cemetery from 1890, devastated by the Nazis); **Planá** /Ger. *Plan* (a town 11 km SSE, a prayer room existed here in the 17th and in the 19th - 20th cent., no traces are left of the cemetery which is recorded in the 17th - 19th cent.). - In the village **Pístov** (6 km SE) 58 prisoners from a death march, victims of an air raid, were buried in April 1945.

*6 km NW **Lázně Kynžvart**, a spa with mineral water springs, a Classicist château with collections open to the public, ruins of a Gothic castle; 11 km E **Teplá**, a town with a remarkable monastery from the 12th - 18th cent. (interior open to the public); 11 km SSE **Planá**, a town with many historical monuments.*

MĚLNÍK   71

District town in Bohemia, 28 km N of Prague. Chartered most probably in 1274.

The earliest documentary mention of J. settlement dates from 1402. J. were not granted permission to reside in the town and its vicinity and only a few J. families (three at the most) lived there until the mid-19th cent. After 1848 J. families began to settle mainly in the northern suburbs: Podolí, Záduší, Okrouhlík and Pšovka. A prayer room was established in **Záduší** in 1850, a religious congregation in 1864 (its statutes were officially recognized only in 1878) and a synagogue and a cemetery were founded in this suburb. The religious congregation consisted of 194 taxpayers in 1872. 84 persons of the J. faith were recorded in M. in 1930. The religious congregation was not reestablished after World War II.

The cemetery lies 1 km NE of the square, in Dobrovského street, behind house No. 1743/30. Founded in 1878, burials until the Nazi occupation.

(The synagogue from 1861 - 62 was used until the Nazi occupation, demolished in the late 1960s.)

M. has a Renaissance-Baroque château (housing a gallery and a museum), a late Gothic gate, a late Gothic church with an underground ossuary, open to the public, and other churches from the 13th to the 18th cent., arcaded houses etc.

The following J. communities and religious societies used to exist in the vicinity: **Liběchov** (a small town 6 km NNW, a prayer room recorded in the 19th - 20th cent.); **Radouň** (15 km NNW, a synagogue from the 19th cent., allegedly demolished in 1980, a cemetery from 1789); **Liblice** (8 km SE, a prayer room recorded in the 19th cent., the birthplace of Emil Pollert [1877-1935 Prague], opera singer of the National Theatre); **Byšice** (a small town 10 km SE, a prayer room recorded in the 19th cent., a cemetery from 1609 with tombstones from the 1st half of the 18th cent.); **Všetaty** (a small town 11 km SE, a prayer room existed here in the 20th cent.). A cemetery with tombstones from the 18th cent. is to be found near the village **Bosyně** (8 km NE), however, there is no documentary record of the existence of a J. community here.

*6 km NNW **Liběchov**, a small town with a château from the 16th - 18th cent., housing a museum of Asian art; 7-9 km N near the village **Želízy** the sculptor V. Levý hewed great sculptures from sandstone rocks in about 1845.*

MIKULOV   72
(Ger. *Nikolsburg*)

Town in Moravia, near the Austrian frontier, 210 km SE of Prague, 43 km S of Brno. It developed into a small town in the 13th cent. and became a town most probably in the early 15th cent.

J. lived in M. as early as the 2nd half of the 14th cent., a J. community originated most probably in the 15th cent. The first precise records date from 1560: in those days 32 houses in M. were in J. ownership. A hundred years later (in 1657) 146 J. families are recorded in 98 houses. 80 J. families that had been expelled from Vienna settled in the town in 1670. 620 J. families were granted permission to reside in M. from the end of the 18th cent. to the mid-19th cent. (3,238 persons in 1804; 3,670 persons in 1848). Thereafter the number of J. population dropped as a result of J. migration to Vienna: 1,500 persons in 1869, 900 in 1900 and 437 in 1930. The religious congregation was revived for a short period after World War II. - In 1948 members of the Czechoslovak voluntary brigade were concentrated in M.

before leaving for Israel (1,280 soldiers and about 700 family members).

Until the mid-19th cent. the Mikulov community represented the second largest J. community in the Czech lands (after Prague). M. was the seat of the Chief Rabbi of Moravia from the 16th cent. till 1851 and many famous rabbis and Talmudic scholars resided here. Among the famous Chief Rabbis let us mention e.g. Yehuda ben Bezalel Liva-Löw (about 1511-1609 Prague) active in M. in 1553-73 and in 1847-51 it was Samson Raphael Hirsch (1808 Hamburg - 1888 Frankfurt am M.). M was a centre of J. education with a yeshivah

famous throughout the whole of Europe. The community had 3 synagogues and about 10 prayer rooms in the mid-19th cent. During World War I several thousand Galician refugees settled **Na Mušlově** /Ger. *Muschelberg*, 4 km ESE, where they established their own school and a prayer room. A Moravian Jewish Museum existed in M. in 1935-38. The J. surname Nasch/Nash has been derived from the J. abbreviation of the town's name (N-sh).

Mikulov is the native town of the well-known Austrian lawyer and writer Joseph von Sonnenfels (1733-1817 Vienna), the German-J. poet and prose writer Hieronymus Lorm (1821-1902 Brno), the German-J. writer and playwright Eduard Kulke (1831-1897 Vienna) and of the Berlin actor Max Pohl (1855-1935 Berlin).

An extensive **ghetto** used to exist in the western part of the town, beyond the city walls (in the streets: Husova, Zámecká, Alfonse Muchy, U staré brány and their neighbourhood). It originated most probably in the 1st half of the 15th cent. and consisted of up to 168 houses. Some of the houses have been preserved.

The Old Synagogue (or The Altschul, Upper Synagogue) is in the northern part of Husova street. Built in 1550 (according to an inscription), extended in the S part in 1689 (formerly a women's gallery), destroyed by fire in 1719. Its present appearance dates from the reconstruction after the fire (opened in 1723), restored in 1977-88. The synagogue represents the only preserved example of a synagogue of the so-called Polish (Lvov) type on the Czech territory: four columns in the centre supporting the ceiling and surrounding the bimah. Today there are plans to convert the synagogue into a concert hall with a museum on the history of the Jewish Community.

(The so-called New Synagogue, Winter Synagogue, the rabbi's house and other houses were mostly pulled down in the years of 1950-75.)

An extensive **cemetery** is sited 250 m N of the synagogue, entrance from Hřbitovní náměstí. The date of its foundation is not known, the oldest legible tombstones date from 1605 and 1618, burials also after World War II. Several times extended, in the southern old part of the cemetery there are several layers of graves. In the southern part there are two separate sections where children and rabbis used to be buried. Graves of the following rabbis

are to be found there: Petahia ben Josef (died 1637), Menachem Mendel ben Abraham Krochmal (about 1600 Cracow - 1661), Samuel Shmelke ben Hirsh ha-Levi Horowitz (1726 Czortków - 1778), Mordecai ben Abraham Benet, called Markus Benedikt (1753 Csurgó - 1829 Carlsbad, reburied in Mikulov in 1830). A grave of 21 prisoners of the local labour camp killed by the Nazis in April 1945. There is a total of about 2,500 tombstones and their style, form and decorative motifs became a source of inspiration for other south Moravian cemeteries. The ceremonial hall was built in 1895, restored in 1984.

M. has a great Baroque château (formerly a Gothic castle), churches and chapels from the 15th up to the 18th cent., Renaissance and Baroque houses. Due to the abundance of historical monuments the historical centre of the town has been declared an urban conservation area.

*1 km N **Turold**, a hill with a small stalactite and stalagmite cave; further north **Pavlovské vrchy**, a nature reserve (the highest point - 550 m), a limestone area with steppe flora and fauna and two castle ruins.*

MILEVSKO 73
(Ger. *Mühlhausen*)

Town in Bohemia, 70 km S of Prague, 22 km NE of the district town Písek. M. developed into a small town as early as the 1st half of the 14th cent., became a town most probably in the 1st half of the 15th cent.

The first J. family was granted permission to settle in M. after 1640. 8 J. families (over 50 persons) are recorded in the town in 1694, most probably they had a prayer room at that time. In 1724 the governorship issued an order that the J. population be reduced from 66 to 57 and this number was not to be exceeded. In the 1st half of the 19th cent. 13 J. families lived in 10 houses concentrated mainly on the S side of the so-called Malé náměstí (150 m NE of the main square). After the mid-19th

cent. the number of J. increased. A modern religious congregation was established in 1881. 103 persons of the J. faith are recorded in 1921, only 81 persons in 1930. The religious congregation was not revived after World War II.

The old synagogue is to be found in the basement of the house No. 387 on Malé náměstí. Built allegedly in the 18th cent., rebuilt in 1812, closed in 1919. A small stone portal has been preserved in the carriage-way of the house.

The new synagogue is in Sokolovská No. 209, 100 m NE of the old synagogue. Built in 1914-19 after the design of architect Střílek. The structure represents a unique combination of Classicist and Cubist style elements: a Pseudo-Empire front with columns and a two-wing staircase to the women's gallery, a Cubist style tympanum. Services were held here until the Nazi occupation, since 1950 the synagogue has been used by the Hussite church. The stone aron ha-kodesh has been preserved.

The cemetery is set at the edge of a wood near a seclusion called Židovna, 1,800 m ENE of the synagogue. Consecrated in 1714 (the oldest tombstone dates from that year), extended in the mid-19th cent., burials until 1942. An

Art-Nouveau ceremonial hall. Remarkable Baroque and Classicist tombstones.

M. has a former Gothic-Baroque monastery (today housing a museum) with a Romanesque basilica from the 12th cent. (remodelled in the 13th, 17th and 19th cent.), a Gothic church with a Romanesque tower from the 12th cent. at the cemetery and other historical monuments.

The following J. communities and religious societies with prayer rooms used to exist in the vicinity: **Chyšky** /form. *Malá Chyška*, Ger. *Klein Chischka* (9 km NE, a prayer room recorded in the 19th cent.); **Květuš** (9 km NE, minor remnants of a synagogue of unknown origin, pulled down after 1972; remains of a cemetery, allegedly from the 1st half of the 18th cent.); **Nadějkov** (a small town 10 km NE, a prayer room allegedly existed here in the 19th cent.); **Zběšičky** (8 km SE, a wooden house of prayer, burnt down in 1866; remains of a J. quarter, cemetery from 1750); **Veselíčko** (7 km S, a synagogue from the 1st half of the 19th cent., demolished in 1986, a J. street); **Kučeř** (8 km WSW, a prayer room existed there allegedly in the 19th cent.); **Kotýřina** (9 km NW, a prayer room recorded in the 19th cent. in the settlement **Kroupov**); **Kovářov** (9 km NW, a prayer room converted into a flat, a cemetery from the 2nd half of the 19th cent.).

MIROTICE 74

Small town in Bohemia, 80 km SSW of Prague, 15 km NNW of the district town Písek. Chartered as early as the beginning of the 14th cent.

J. settlement is first mentioned in 1547. The 1654 census mentions 4 J. men in M. (women and children were not included). 10 J. families (62 persons) are recorded in M. in 1724, 13 J. families in 11 houses in the 1st half of the 19th cent. The number of J. population began to decline in the mid-19th cent. and about 1900 the community merged with the Mirovice religious congregation and thereafter both came under the Březnice religious congregation. The J. population numbered 14 persons of the J. faith in 1930, only 4 persons survived the Nazi concentration camps.

There was no ghetto in M., J. houses formed several clusters: around the synagogue and the school and by the cemetery, where a hospital used to be, on the N side of the square.

(**The synagogue** was built in the 18th cent., seriously damaged during an air-raid in 1945 and consequently pulled down.)

The cemetery is set on a knoll 300 m N of the square, entrance from Neradovská street. Consecrated in 1681 (but the oldest tombstone allegedly dates from 1647), extended in 1740 and 1805, the last burial was in 1946. Remarkable Renaissance and Baroque tombstones.

M. has a church from the 12th cent., rebuilt in the 19th cent. and a Baroque belfry, a small museum commemorating the Czech painter Mikoláš Aleš (1852-1913) and the marionettist Matěj Kopecký (1775-1847).

The following J. communities and religious societies used to exist in the vicinity: **Rakovice** (4 km NNE, a prayer room recorded in the 19th cent.); **Orlík nad Vltavou** /Ger. *Worlik* (12 km NE, a prayer room recorded in the 19th cent.); **Varvažov** (6 km ENE, a wooden prayer house from about the 19th cent., today used as a workshop); **Písek** (dist-

rict town 15 km SE, a cemetery from 1879, devastated in 1969-70, later closed down; a synagogue from 1872, serves as a store-house today, the Czech-J. poet and prose writer Richard Weiner [1884-1937] was born and buried in Písek [after the exhumation at the J. cemetery in 1987 he was buried again in the municipal cemetery]); **Blatná** (town 11 km W, a prayer hall from the 2nd half of the 19th cent., today used as a police station). - The famous Austrian embryologist Alfred Fischel (1866-1938 Vienna) was born in **Čimelice** (4 km NE).

The Mirotice vicinity is densely a-forested, the countryside is rich in lakes and noteworthy country mansions. 10 km E Orlická přehrada, a dam on the Vltava river, a popular summer resort; 10 km E Zvíkov, an early Gothic castle from the 13th cent., today housing a museum; 12 km NE Orlík, a château from the 13th - 19th cent. with remarkable collections open to the public.

MLADÁ BOLESLAV 75
(Ger. *Jung-Bunzlau, Jungbunzlau*)

Town in Bohemia, 50 km NE of Prague. Founded and chartered in 1334.

J. settlement is first mentioned in 1471. 17 J. families are recorded in 1570, 27 families (126 persons) in 1620, 775 persons (about 50% of the total population) in 1687 and about 900 persons (18% of the total population) in the mid-19th cent. and 264 in 1930. From the beginning of the 20th cent. until the Nazi occupation the local J. religious congregation maintained remarkable Judaic collections. A synagogue group was active in M. B. for several years after the liberation.

M. B. used to be a centre of J. learning and Talmudic study, it was referred to as "Jerusalem upon the Jizera river". Names of 18 rabbis are recorded (from the 17th cent.), among them authors of significant works on religion and history.

Jakob Bassevi (Baševi) von Treuenberg, financier of the emperors Rudolph II, Matthias and Ferdinand II and the first Jew in the Austrian Empire to be ennobled, found shelter from arrest in the ghetto in 1633, a year before he died. - M. B. is the native town of the Ger.-J. prose-writer and poet Isidor Heller (1816-1879 Arco, Italy), one of the leaders of the Czech Social Democratic Party and minister of justice Alfred Meissner (1871-1952 Prague), of the Czech-J. poet and cartoonist František Gellner (1881-1914 at the Galician front) and of the painter Max Horb (1882-1907 Prague). Siegfried Kapper (1821 Prague - 1879 Pisa), a physician, poet, publicist and one of the leaders of the Czech Jewish movement, worked as a physician in M. B. in the 1860s.

Remnants of a **ghetto** in the N part of the town's historical centre (the streets: Synagogní, Starofarní, Bělská, Vodkova). 12 houses of J. ownership are recorded in 1599, 32 in the 1st half of the 19th cent. The ghetto was damaged by fire in 1761 and 1859.

(**The synagogue**, built on the site of an earlier synagogue in 1785, was pulled down in 1958.)

The cemetery is in a the S part of the of the town, in Dimitrovova street No. 165/21, 200 m SE of the castle. It existed as early as 1584, extended after 1715. The oldest legible tombstone dates from 1604, burials also after World War II. A Renaissance tombstone of Jakob Bassevi von Treuenberg (1570 Verona - 1634 Mladá Boleslav).

Many remarkable Renaissance, Baroque and Classicist tombstones. An octagonal ceremonial hall.

M. B. has a Renaissance-Baroque château (formerly a Gothic castle), housing a museum, a Renaissance town hall, several Gothic, Renaissance and Baroque churches, old arcaded houses and other historical monuments.

The following J. communities and religious societies used to exist in the vicinity: **Mnichovo Hradiště** /Ger. *Münchengrätz* (town 12 km NNE, remains of a J. street; a synagogue, built most probably in the early 19th cent., demolished during World War II, a cemetery from the 18th cent. was liquidated after 1983, the native town of the German-J. writer Leopold Kompert [1822-1886 Vienna]); **Dolní Bousov** /Ger. *Unter-Bautzen, Nieder-Bausow* (a small town 15 km ENE, a prayer room recorded in the 19th cent.); **Domousnice** (13 km E, a prayer room recorded in the 19th cent.); **Luštěnice** (9 km SSE, a prayer room recorded in the 19th cent.); **Zámostí** /Ger. *Samost,* part of the village **Písková Lhota** (4 km SSW, a synagogue from the 19th cent., converted into a dwelling house, a cemetery with tombstones from the 1st half of the 18th cent.); **Benátky nad Jizerou** /form. *Nové Benátky,* Ger. *Neu-Benatek* (town 14 km SSW, a house of prayer from 1884, converted into a dwelling house); **Dolní Cetno** /Ger. *Unter-Zetno* (6 km W, a synagogue built in 1892-73, converted into a house, a cemetery from about 1869). A cemetery, with tombstones from the 1st half of the 19th cent., which used to belong to the Domousnice religious congregation, is to be found near the village **Veselice** (14 km E).

*3 km NNW **Michalovice**, a ruin of an early Gothic castle from the 13th cent. with a lookout-tower; 3 km NNE **Kosmonosy**, suburb with a Catholic pilgrimage complex - Loretto - from the early 18th cent., a Baroque château and other places of interest; 5 km SE **Sýčina**, near by a Renaissance church from the 16th cent. with three towers; 5 km SW **Vinec**, a village with a remarkable small Romanesque church from the 1st half of the*

13th cent. There are many other interesting historical monuments in the vicinity of Mladá Boleslav.

MORAVSKÝ KRUMLOV 76
(Ger. *Kromau, Mährisch-Kromau)*

Town in Moravia, 175 km SE of Prague, 28 km NE of the district town Znojmo. Chartered in the early 14th cent.

Jews lived in M. K. as early as the 1st half of the 15th cent. (the earliest preserved documentary record dates from 1437). A J. community was established not later than the 1st half of the 16th cent. 49 J. families were granted permission to reside in the town from the 18th to the mid-19th cent., later the number of J. declined: 356 persons of the J. faith are recorded in 1830, 276 in 1856, 116 in 1900 and 34 in 1930. The religious congregation was not revived after World War II.

The names of 30 rabbis active in M. K. are recorded (from the 16th cent.). Rabbi Samuel Baeck (1834 - 1912 Leszno, Poland), a historian and publicist, father of the famous Berlin Rabbi Leo Baeck (1873 - 1956), was born in M. K.

Remains of a **ghetto** in the N part of the walled town, by the street connecting the château with the Catholic parish church. It consisted of 43-48 houses in the 1st half of the 19th cent. Most of the ghetto was demolished during an air-raid in May 1945.

(**A synagogue** was built in 1547, rebuilt in 1900 for the last time, suffered damage by an air-raid and was thereafter pulled down.)

The cemetery is 500 m SSW of the château, near a crossroad. The earliest legible tombstone dates from 1653, burials until World War II. Noteworthy Renaissance and Baroque tombstones. The ceremonial hall was converted into a dwelling house.

There is a remarkable Renaissance château from the 14th to the 16th cent. in M. K. (housing an art gallery and an exhibition of the Swiss physician and chemist Paracelsus) and three churches from the 13th to the 18th cent. This ancient town suffered severe damage during an air-raid in 1945.

MOŘINA 77
(formerly *Velká Mořina*,
Ger. *Gross-Morschin*,
Gross-Morzin)

Village in Bohemia, 20 km SW of Prague, 10 km E of the district town Beroun.

Only two J. families are recorded in 1724 (the earliest documentary record of J. settlement) and only two J. families are also mentioned in the census from the mid-18th cent. Other families settled in M. most probably in the 2nd half of the century and a J. community was established although a cemetery had been consecrated earlier. 16 J. families are recorded in the 1st half of the 19th cent., after 1848 the number of J. declined. Only 4 persons of the J. faith are recorded in 1930. After 1908 the Mořina religious congregation merged with the Beroun J. religious congregation.

M. is the native town of Jakob Eduard Pollak (1818 - 1891 Vienna), private physician of the Iranian shah, organizer of health service in Teheran and sponsor of expeditions.

A small **Jewish quarter** with a synagogue in the W part of the village, on the N side of the main road. It consisted of 8 houses, today rebuilt.

The synagogue used to be in No. 59. The synagogue existed in the mid-19th cent., abolished probably after 1907, thereafter converted into a gymnasium, rebuilt in 1928.

The cemetery lies 500 m NW of the synagogue. Established in 1735-36, tombstones from 1741, burials until the 1st third of the 20th cent. About 150 Baroque and Classicist tombstones. A tablet from the time of the cemetery's foundation with a Latin-Hebrew inscription has been embedded in the mortuary.

A Baroque church and a Baroque cemetery gate from the 18th cent. are to be found in M.

The following J. communities and religious societies used to exist in the vicinity: **Vysoký Újezd** /Ger. *Hoch-Aujest* (4 km N, a synagogue from 1877, rebuilt and converted into a dwelling house); **Hořelice** (9 km N, a synagogue was built in 1842, demolished after 1950); **Vonoklasy** (4 km E, a prayer room recorded in the 18th - 19th cent.); **Všenory** (6 km SE, a prayer room is said to have existed here in the 19th cent.); **Davle** (small town 14 km SE, a synagogue was built in 1877, demolished in 1960). A cemetery from the 2nd half of the 18th cent., which used to be administered by the Zbraslav J. community, is to be found near the village **Třebotov** (6 km NE).

3 km Karlík with a Pseudo-Romanesque church and a 12th-cent. Romanesque presbytery-rotunda; 2 km SW Karlštejn, an imposing 14th-cent. royal castle - one of the most significant castles in Bohemia (open to the public); 5 km WNW Svatý Jan pod Skalou, a former monastery with a Baroque church, two chapels, two small sanctuaries in caves; the area is a nature reserve with karst features.

MYSLKOVICE   78
(formerly *Miskovice*,
Ger. *Miskowitz*)

Village in Bohemia, 90 km ESE of Prague, 14 km SE of the district town Tábor.

The first J. family settled in M. before 1650. 3 J. families are recorded in 1706, 7 families in 1723. A J. community was established in the 2nd half of the 18th cent., the J. population increa-

sed at the turn of the 18th and 19th cent. after the arrival of J. families from Galicia. The community numbered 65 J. families (474 persons, 55% of the total population) in 1850, only 71 persons of the J. faith in 1890 and 9 persons subject to racial laws in 1939. One single man survived the Nazi occupation. After 1921 the religious congregation merged with the J. religious congregation in Soběslav.

The father of Victor Adler (1852-1918), an Austrian social democratic politician, was born in M.

The Jewish quarter, in the W part of the village, consisted of two parts separated by a pond. Most of the original 40 houses have been preserved. A **school**, with preserved original window grillwork, used to be in No. 90.

(**The synagogue** from 1770 with an adjoining rabbi's house was devastated after 1930 and pulled down in 1965.)

The cemetery is set 750 m NNE of the château on the edge of a wood. Consecrated in 1770, the oldest preserved tombstones date from that time, burials until the Nazi occupation. The cemetery has been restored recently.

There is a 17th cent. château, partly modernized, in M.

The following J. communities used to be in the vicinity: **Přehořov** (6 km SSE, a synagogue of unknown origin, pulled down in 1960, remains of a J. quarter, a mid-19th cent. cemetery); **Soběslav** (town 5 km SSW, a synagogue from the 2nd half of the 19th cent., converted into a workshop and flats).

5 km SSW Soběslav, a town with a Gothic keep, three churches from the 13th up to the 17th cent. and Renaissance houses.

NOVÁ CEREKEV   79
(Ger. *Neu-Zerekwe*)

Small town in Bohemia, 90 km SE of Prague, 8 km W of the district town Pelhřimov. N. C. developed into a small town most probably in the 1st half of the 14th cent.

Jews are said to have settled in N. C. before 1570. According to other sources J. famillies settled there only about the year 1680, a J. community and a prayer room were established about 1690. The community numbered 6 J. families in about 5 houses in 1723, 21 J. families in 14 houses in the 1st half of the 19th cent. and about 30 families (160 persons) in 1850. In the late 19th cent. the N. C. religious congregation was administered by the Pelhřimov religious congregation. By 1930 the number of J. in N. C. dropped to 20 persons. Nobody returned after the liberation.

There was no enclosed ghetto in N. C. Most of J. houses were surrounding the synagogue, some houses in J. ownership were also on the main square.

N. C. is the birth-place of Alfred Justitz (1879-1934 Bratislava, buried in the N. C.), a renowned modern painter. The Grandmother of the composer Gustav Mahler was born in N. C.

The synagogue is 120 m NNE of the square. It was built in 1855 on the site of an earlier synagogue. Built in the Moorish style, a pentagonal apse. Services were held here until the 1930s, today it is used as a store-house.

The cemetery is 100 m NE of the synagogue. Established about 1690, the oldest preserved tombstone dates from 1692. Many Baroque tombstones. A new section was founded in 1866, burials until World War II. There are more than 400 tombstones in the cemetery, including the grave of the painter Alfred Justitz (1879 - 1934). Mainly J. from Pelhřimov were buried there.

There is a Baroque church from the mid-18th cent. with a Gothic tower in N. C.

The following J. communities used to be in the vicinity - **Pelhřimov** /Ger. *Pilgrams* (district town 7 km ENE, a cemetery of unknown origin, became extinct in the 18th cent., a synagogue built around 1890, pulled down in 1966-67); **Pavlov** (8 km ESE, a building with a prayer room from the 19th cent., converted into a dwelling house, a cemetery with legible tombstones from 1804); **Kamenice nad Lipou** (town 12 km SSW, the old synagogue from 1815 was pulled down in 1938, a new synagogue was built in 1938 - the last synagogue built before the Nazi occupation - today used by the Czech Brethren's Protestant Church; a cemetery with tombstones from 1807).

7 km ENE Pelhřimov, town with many remarkable 14th cent. buildings,

an urban conservation area; 1 km SE
***Proseč-Obořiště**, a Baroque château with
a chapel open to the public; 6 km W
Kámen, a castle built in the 14th - 19th
cent.*

NOVÝ BYDŽOV   80
(Ger. *Neu-Bidschow*)

Town in Bohemia, 75 km NEE of
Prague, 24 km W of the district town
Hradec Králové. N. B. was founded
and chartered most probably in the late
13th cent.

J. settlement in N. B. is mentioned
in 1432. A J. community was established probably about 1520, several J.
families were expelled from the town in
1536. The community numbered 9 J.
families in 1570 and still in 1620. After
the Swedish invasion during the Thirty
Years' War the J. population was reduced to less than a half. 18 J. families
(73 persons) are recorded in 1650, 89
families (384 persons) in 1723, 85 families (about 10% of the total population) in the mid-19th cent., 1,024 persons (17% of the total population) in
1868 and only 84 persons of the J. faith

in 1930. The J. religious congregation
was not revived after World War II.

In the 1740s the destitute country-
men in the region of N. B. founded a
sect called the Israelites whose dog-
matics were close to Jewish religion.
Three members of this sect were executed in 1748 and many others imprisoned. Rabbi Mendl of the N. B. community was accused of being the "moral
father" of the movement and was burnt
at the stake in 1750. In the late 18th
cent. (after Emperor Joseph II issued
the Edict of Toleration) the movement
of the Israelites began to spread again
in Bohemia.

(**A Jewish quarter** - ghetto - existed
in the town most probably in the 16th
cent., E of the square. In 1638 it consisted of 11 houses, in the 1st half of
the 19th cent.   41 houses. In 1901 it
was completely destroyed by fire and
thereafter demolished with the exception of the synagogue. The site has
been converted into a park.)

The synagogue is in the middle of
the park (originally the ghetto's centre),
100 m E of the square. Built after 1568
(probably on the site of an earlier
synagogue), remodelled in 1660, 1838

and in 1902. Services were held here until World War II. In 1947 - 48 it was redesigned to be used by the Czech Brethren's Protestant Church (the main hall was divided into two storeys), restored in 1985.

The old cemetery 400 m SSW of the square, entrance from Revoluční street. Consecrated in 1520, enlarged in 1735, burials until 1885. The oldest preserved tombstone dates from 1645. Remarkable Renaissance and Baroque tombstones.

The new cemetery is 1 km WSW of the square, near the road to Skochovice, next to the municipal cemetery. Consecrated in 1885, burials until World War II.

The town has three churches (from the 14th, 18th and 19th cent.), a neo-Gothic town-hall and other historical monuments. The town's regular ground plan represents a significant example of medieval town planning.

The following J. communities used to be in the vicinity: **Barchůvek** /Ger. *Klein-Barchow, Klein-Barchau* (4 km SE, a timber framed synagogue from about the 18th cent. burnt down after 1877); **Chlumec nad Cidlinou** (town 9 km SSW, a synagogue from 1879, converted into a fire station, a J. section from the early 20th cent. in the muni-

cipal cemetery, the J. ceremonial hall used today for all funeral services).

6 km Loučná Hora, a village with an 18th cent. timber-framed church; Vysočany (3 km S) and Měník, (3 km SE) - villages with timber-framed, plastered churches from the 17th cent.; 9 km SSW Chlumec nad Cidlinou, a town with a notable Baroque château from the 18th cent., housing a museum of Czech Baroque art.

OLOMOUC 81
(Ger. *Olmütz*)

District town in Moravia, 210 km SE of Prague, 65 km NE of Brno. Olomouc was founded on the site of several early settlements and chartered in the 1st half of the 13th cent.

Jews lived on the territory of O. most probably as early as the 11th cent. An order is said to have been issued in 1060, according to which J. houses had to be concentrated in one settlement. After the foundation of the town J. lived in a separate street (today's Univerzitní street). In 1454 J. were expelled from the town and the synagogue together with the cemetery ceased to exist. In the early 19th cent. several J. tradesmen were permitted to do business in the town and stay there from Monday to Friday. J. began to resettle in Olomouc after 1848. 72 persons of the J. faith are recorded in 1857, 747 in 1869, 1,676 in 1900, 1,451 (6% of the total population) in 1930. 1,088 persons perished during the Nazi occupation.

The first modern prayer room was established in 1859. A religious society was established in 1865 and changed into a J. religious congregation in 1892. The religious congregation was reestablished after World War II and changed into a synagogue group in 1961.

Olomouc is the native town of the composer Leo Fall (1873-1925 Vienna), the architect and writer Paul Engelmann (1891-1965 Tel Aviv); the architect and painter Jaques Groag (1892-1961 Vienna), the conductor Fritz Zweig (1893-1984 Los Angeles). Andreas Ludwig Jeitteles, pseud. Justus Frey (1799 Prague - 1878 Graz), a noted journalist, poet and chancellor of the Olomouc University, worked as a physician in O. in 1837-69. Gustav Mahler (1860 Kaliště - 1911 Vienna) was a conductor of the Olomouc Theatre Orchestra in 1882-83.

The former **prayer room** used to be on the 1st floor of the J. communal house in Sokolská street No. 586/7. Services were held there from 1863 to 1897. Today it serves as a conference hall of the Association of Physical Training.

(**The synagogue**, built in 1896-97 after the design of architect J. Gartner, was burnt down by the Nazis in 1939 and subsequently pulled down.)

The present **prayer room** was established after 1955. Address: ul. Komenského č. 7.

The cemetery is 2 km WNW of the square Horní nám., forms the E part of the municipal cemetery. Entrance from třída Míru. The cemetery was consecrated in 1901 and is still used today. Tombstones from the 2nd half of the 19th cent. have been transferred here from the older cemetery. Graves of 21 prisoners - victims of a transport from Auschwitz in January 1945. A monument in memory of the victims of the Nazis from Olomouc and its vicinity was dedicated in the cemetery in 1949. Tablets with the names of all the victims are in the ceremonial hall.

(**The older cemetery** from 1867, was closed down about 1900 and converted into a park in 1920. Some of the tombstones were transferred to the new cemetery, the remaining ones were removed during the Nazi occupation.)

A religious society with a prayer room used to exist in the suburb **Pavlovičky** /Ger. *Paulowitz* (2,5 km NE of the square Horní nám.).

A private Orthodox prayer room used to exist in the suburb **Bělidla** /Ger. *Bleich* (2,5 km ENE) from the early 19th cent. until World War II.

The ancient centre with a great number of historical monuments has been declared an urban conservation area: remains of a Romanesque castle, many remarkable churches and monastic buildings, palaces and burghers' houses, a GothicRenaissance town-hall and others. Worthy of attention are also the many historical monuments in the suburbs.

A religious society used to be in **Šternberk** /Ger. *Sternberg*, a town 15 km N.

OPAVA 82
(Ger. *Troppau*)

District town in Silesia, near the Polish frontier, 245 km E of Prague, 30 km NW of Ostrava. Chartered in 1224. The seat of the Opava principality since the 15th cent., in 1742-1928 the capital of Austrian (later Czechoslovak) Silesia.

The earliest documentary mention of J. settlement dates from 1281. A J. community was established in the Middle Ages, houses in J. ownership used to be in the street Na valech. J. were expelled from all of Silesia in the course of the 16th cent. They had to leave O. in 1501, finally in 1523. No traces of the medieval synagogue are left. - J. began to resettle in O. before the mid-19th cent., the first prayer room was established in 1850. J. population began to increase, 971 persons of the J. faith are recorded in O. in 1930. The J. religious congregation was revived after World War II and was later changed into a synagogue group (active until about 1968).

O. is the native town of the artist Leo (Lev) Haas (1901-1893 Berlin) and of the film director Kurt Goldberger (1919 - resident in Munich).

(The house in which the first **prayer room** had been established in 1850 was destroyed during the war, in 1945. The **first synagogue** was built in 1855, converted into a gymnasium in 1896 and demolished by an air-raid in 1945. **The second synagogue** was built in 1896 after the design of architect J. Gartner, burnt down by the Nazis in 1938 and consequently pulled down.)

A post-war **prayer room** was established about 1945 on the ground floor of the house No. 688/7 in Čapkova street. The synagogue group did not survive and the prayer room has been used by a the Plymouth Brethern's Church since 1970.

(**The first** modern **cemetery** was founded in 1850 and closed down in 1854: those buried there were exhumed and re-interred in the second cemetery. **The second cemetery** was founded in 1854 in Veleslavínova street, burials until 1892, devastated by the Nazis: only a part of the wall has survived.)

The third cemetery, 1,700 m SW of the city centre (the theatre), forms a part of the municipal cemetery. Entrance from Otická street. Founded in 1892, still used today. The cemetery was devastated by the Nazis, restored in 1948. A grave of 25 prisoners - victims of a death march from Auschwitz. The ceremonial hall is used today for all funeral services.

Although the town suffered extreme hardship towards the end of World War II (800 houses demolished, 3,400 damaged) many historical monuments have survived and have been restored: churches from the 13th up to the 18th cent., Renaissance houses, Baroque palaces and a museum with rich collections.

A religious society used to be in **Budišov nad Budišovkou** /Ger. *Bautsch*, a town 25 km SW.

7 km E Kravaře, a Baroque Château, housing a museum with a documentary exhibition of the Ostrava Operation - one of the most important battles in 1945; 8 km ESE Štítina, an open air museum of military equipment from World War II; 12 km SE Hrabyně, memorial to the Ostrava Operation with a symbolic cemetery (stone tablets with the names of 10,000 soldiers and civilian victims of racial persecution in the Opava and Ostrava districts); 8 km SSW Hradec, formerly a castle, rebuilt into a Classicist-Romanticist Château with rich collections relating to L. v. Beethoven, F. Liszt and N. Paganini; 9 km W Nový Dvůr, an arboretum with about 1,000 trees and shrubs from all over the world.

OSOBLAHA 83
(Ger. *Hotzenplotz*)

Village in Silesia, by the Polish frontier, 230 km E of Prague, 65 km NW of Ostrava. O. used to be a town from the 13th cent. to 1945.

The earliest documentary mention of J. settlement dates from 1334 and notes several J. families who had found refuge in the suburb of O. In 1420 J. were granted permission to reside in the town. The J. community increased in the 15th and 16th cent. with the arrival of J. who had been expelled from Glubczyce (Ger. *Leobschütz*), Prudnik (Ger. *Neustadt*) and other Silesian towns. The community numbered 132 J. families in 1570, 135 J. families in 1616, 153 families (845 persons, the maximum) in 1802 and 671 persons (18% of the total population) in 1842. The number began to decline in the 2nd half of the 19th cent. About the early 20th cent. the J. religious congregation merged with the Krnov congregation. Only 13 persons of the J. faith are recorded in O. in 1930.

Osoblaha was a Moravian enclave situated in Silesia and under Moravian jurisdiction. For this reason from the 16th to the 19th cent., when J. were not permitted to reside in the surrounding Silesia, many J. found refuge in O., giving rise to a large J. community.

The Jewish quarter was established about 1420 in the N part of the town. It consisted of about 20 houses in 1570, 39 in 1800 and about 50 in 1836. The J. quarter together with the entire town was destroyed by the 1802 fire. The entire town was destroyed again towards the end of World War II. Only 3 houses have survived in the former J. quarter, at present surrounded by gardens and lawns.

(The first **synagogue** was built after 1569, burnt down before 1626. On its site a second synagogue was built in 1625, which burnt down together with 32 Torah scrolls in 1802. The third synagogue, built in 1807-8, burnt down in 1833, rebuilt later, pulled down in 1933.)

The cemetery is 150 m NNE of the square, beyond the city walls. The cemetery is said to have existed in the 12th cent. but it was most probably founded only in the 1st half of the 15th cent. It was enlarged several times, burials until the Nazi occupation. Many wooden tombstones were destroyed by the 1802 fire and the cemetery was

badly damaged in 1945. Unique tombstones of the so-called Polish type from the 2nd half of the 17th cent. have been preserved there.

The ancient town was entirely destroyed towards the very end of World War II, in 1945. Not many houses were built again after the war among the remnants of the town's walls on the medieval network of streets.

A religious society used to be in **Jeseník** /*Frývaldov*, Ger. *Freiwaldau* (35 km WSW, a prayer room existed here in the 19th - 20th cent., a cemetery from about the end of the 19th cent., destroyed by the Nazis) and a seasonal prayer room in the nearby spa **Lázně Jeseník** /Ger. *Gräfenberg*. Josef Reinhold (1855 Stryj - 1948 Jeseník), a noted balneologist, was active there. A J. community used to be in **Vidnava** /Ger. *Weidenau* (a small town 37 km WNW, a prayer room existed here in the 18th - 19th cent; a cemetery from 1854, destroyed by the Nazis). - There is a small J. section from the late 19th cent. in the municipal cemetery in **Zlaté Hory** /form. *Cukmantl*, Ger. *Zuckmantel*, a town 21 km W, the native town of the sculptress, graphic artist and goldsmith Elisabeth Turolt (1902 - 1966 Vienna). Franz Kafka was treated in a sanatorium here in 1905 and 1906. A mass grave of the victims of a death march from Auschwitz is to be found in the communal cemetery in **Bílá Voda** /Ger. *Weisswasser* (58 km WNW).

5 km N on the Polish frontier is the so-called Švédský sloup - a monument commemorating the end of the Thirty Years' War (1618-48); 4 km S Fulštejn, ruins of a Gothic-Renaissance castle; 8 km SSW Slezské Rudoltice, a Baroque château, noted for its collections on high life in the 18th cent., known then as the "Silesian Versailles"; 6 km SW Dívčí Hrad, a Renaissance château.

OSTRAVA   **84**
(formerly *Moravská Ostrava*,
Ger. *Mährisch-Ostrau*)

Town in Moravia and Silesia, 275 km E of Prague. O. consists of several formerly independent towns and small towns. The oldest one - Moravská Ostrava - was founded and chartered before 1267.

The first family settled in O. in 1508, however J. were expelled from the town in 1531. Until 1792 J. were not permitted to stay overnight in O., 4 J. families are recorded in 1800. A small prayer room was established in 1832. J. families were streaming into the town from 1848. The J. population numbered 1,077 persons of the J. faith in 1880, about 5,000 in 1900, 7,189 in 1930 and about 10,000 in 1937. Many J. left the country before the outbreak of World War II. About 4,860 persons were deported to the Nazi death camps, about 250 persons returned to O. after the liberation.

A religious society was established in 1860, and changed into a J. religious congregation in 1875. The congregation had a rabbi from 1890. The J. religious congregation was re-established in 1945. The Ostrava Jewish Religious Congregation administers congregations of the former North Moravian region. Present address: ŽNO, Revoluční třída 17, 702 00 Ostrava.

In 1899 the first J. sports club on the territory of later Czechoslovakia was founded in O. The Second Czechoslovak Maccabia (a gymnastic show), attended by 2,000 J. sportsmen, was held in O. in 1929.

O. is the native town of Joel Müller (1827-1895 Berlin), a noted Berlin rabbi and historian; Ilse Weber (1903-1944 Birkenau), a Ger.-J. poetess; Shlomo Rozen (1905), Israeli politician and minister; Josef Bor (1906-1979 Prague), a Czech-J. writer; Joseph Wechsberg (1907, resides in the USA), a journalist and publicist; Meir Marcel Färber, pseud. Meir Reubeni (1908 - resides in Tel Aviv), a playwright and poet who writes in Hebrew and German and of Pavel Blumenfeld (1914-1982 Cologne), a film director.

The present **prayer room** was established in 1978 in Revoluční tř. 17, in the central neighbourhood Moravská Ostrava.

The cemetery is in the neighbourhood Slezská Ostrava, 1500 m E of the centre of Moravská Ostrava, entrance from Na Najmanské street, a section of the new municipal cemetery. Opened in 1965, a ceremonial hall built in 1988. Many tombstones from the older cemetery were transferred there.

J. religious societies used to be in the following neighbourhoods: **Hrušov** - a small town N of the centre.(**A prayer house** was built after 1912, burnt down by the Nazis in 1939 and consequently pulled down.)

Michálkovice - a small town E of the centre. Small **cemetery** founded in 1901, burials until World War II.

Moravská Ostrava /Ger. *Mährisch-Ostrau* - town in the centre of Ostrava. (**The main synagogue** [built in 1879] and the **Orthodox synagogue** [built in 1926] were burnt down by the Nazis in 1939 and pulled down. The house with an Orthodox "Hassidic" **prayer room** was demolished by an air-raid during World War II. The post-war **prayer room** was located successively in 5 different houses.)

(**The cemetery** was established in 1872, burials until 1965. Converted into a park in 1988, some tombstones transferred to the new cemetery in Slezská Ostrava.)

Přívoz /Ger. *Oderfurt* - town NW of the centre. (**The synagogue** built about 1904, was burnt down by the Nazis and demolished.)

Slezská Ostrava /form. *Polská Ostrava*, Ger. *Polnisch-Ostrau, Schlesisch-Ostrau* - town NE of the centre. (The first three prayer rooms in Ostrava were in rented rooms: from 1832, 1857 and 1860.) - A new cemetery was founded in 1965.

Vítkovice - town SSW of the centre. (**The synagogue**, built in 1911, was burnt down by the Nazis in 1939 and demolished.)

Zábřeh nad Odrou /Ger. *Teufelsdorf* - SW of the centre. (**A prayer house** existed there in 1893, destroyed by the Nazis in 1939.)

Ostrava is Czechoslovakia's most important industrial centre (metallurgy, mechanical engineering, coal mines).

The town has few historical monuments: e.g. a Gothic church and a Baroque town-hall in the neighbourhood Mor. Ostrava, ruins of a medieval castle in Slezská Ostrava (1 km SE of the centre), a wooden church from the 16th cent. in the suburb Hrabová (7 km S).

The following J. communities and religious societies used to be in the vicinity: **Bohumín** /form. *Nový Bohumín*, Ger. *Oderberg, Neu-Oderberg* (town 9 km NE, a synagogue from 1900, demolished by the Nazis, the post-war prayer room has been converted into a music and art school; remains of a J. section from 1898 in the municipal cemetery, the ceremonial hall in the cemetery is used today as a prayer hall of the Seventh Day Adventists; the native town of the poet Arthur Zanker [1890 - 1957 Croydon, England]); **Orlová** /Ger. *Orlau* (town 10 km ENE, a Reform rite synagogue from 1900 and an Orthodox synagogue - both demolished by the Nazis, the post-war prayer room has been converted into a flat; a J. section was established in 1900 in the municipal cemetery, tombstones transferred there from the cemetery in Karviná); **Karviná-Město** /*Fryštát*, Ger. *Freistadt* (district town 18 km ENE, a synagogue from the 2nd half of the 19th cent., demolished by the Nazis; a late 19th cent. cemetery, devastated by the Nazis and converted into a park after the war); **Karviná-Doly** /form. *Karviná*, Ger. *Karwin* (a part of the town **Karviná**, 14 km E, a synagogue from the 1930s, demolished by the Nazis); **Klimkovice** /Ger. *Königsberg* (town 13 km SW, a prayer room, converted into a flat; remnants of a cemetery from the 2nd half of the 19th cent., devastated by the Nazis); **Hlučín** /Ger. *Hultschin* (town 10 km NW, a synagogue built in 1843 and demolished in 1931; a cemetery from 1814, destroyed by the Nazis, after the liberation a burial ground of the Red Army soldiers). After World War I a private prayer room was established in **Petřvald** /Ger. *Peterswald* (7 km E). - A J. labour camp (victims buried there) was set up in 1942 in the village **Pudlov** (6 km NNE).

District town in Bohemia, 95 km E of Prague. Founded and chartered before 1340.

The earliest record of J. settlement in P. dates from 1492. Until the end of the 16th cent. only a few J. families were permitted to reside in the town. The number of J. increased (about 7 families in 1645) in the early 17th cent., when a J. community and a prayer room were established. J. were expelled from the town in 1662. One J. family was granted permission to resettle in P. in 1747 (as tenants). Two J. families are recorded in 1801, 5 families in 1851, 378 persons of the J. faith in 1880, 518 persons in 1930. 28 persons survived the Nazi concentration camps and returned to the town. The J. religious congregation was re-established in 1945 and was later changed into a synagogue group (no longer exists).

Pardubice is the native town of the opera singer and producer of the National Theatre Hanuš Thein (1904-1974 Prague).

(The seat of the J. religious congregation with the first **prayer room** from 1867 was pulled down in 1958-59. **The synagogue** was built in 1879-80, extended in 1904, converted into an art centre in 1945 and pulled down in 1958-59.)

(**The old cemetery** was consecrated in 1624, enlarged in 1762, 1806 and 1837, burials until 1882. In 1939 it was closed down, the remaining tombstones were transferred to the new cemetery.)

The new cemetery is 2 km SSE of the château, in the N part of the municipal cemetery. Entrance from S. K. Neumanna street. Consecrated in 1883, still used today. Tombstones from the old cemetery (the earliest tombstone dates from 1739). A grave of 7 prisoners who died in a railway transport from Auschwitz in January 1945. A monument in memory of the Nazi victims was dedicated in the cemetery in 1948. A tablet on the wall of the ceremonial hall in memory of the Nazi victims from the neighbouring J. religious congregations. Viktor Vohryzek

(1864 Přestavlky - 1918 Pardubice), an organizer of the Czech-Jewish movement and a journalist, Stanislav Schulhof (1864 Lipka - 1919 Prague), an Esperanto poet and translator, and Hanuš Thein (1904 Pardubice - 1974 Prague), a singer and director of the National Theatre are buried here.

P. has a remarkable Renaissance château (housing a museum), two Renaissance city gates, three churches from the 16th cent., Renaissance and Classicist houses and other places of interest. The historical centre with its great number of sights has been declared an urban conservation area.

The following J. communities and religious societies used to exist in the vicinity: **Brozany** (3 km NNE, a synagogue recorded in the 18th - 19th cent.); **Býšť** (14 km NE, a prayer room recorded in the 19th - 20th cent.); **Chvojenec** (14 km NE, a prayer room is said to have existed there in the mid-19th cent.); **Holice** (town 15 km ENE, prayer rooms, converted into flats, a cemetery from 1913, the native town of the director and actor Jan Kačer [born 1936]); **Dašice** (small town 10 km E, a synagogue from about 1822, pulled down about 1958); **Bohdaneč** (town 8 km NW, a prayer room is said to have existed there in the mid-19th cent.). - Twelve prisoners - victims of a railway transport from Auschwitz - were buried in January 1945 in **Lány na Důlku** (a village 7 km W).

5 km NNE Kunětická Hora, a castle from the 15th - 16th cent. offering wide views of the surrounding landscape.

District town in Bohemia, 80 km SW of Prague. Founded and chartered about 1295.

The earliest documentary record of J. settlements dates from 1338. A ghetto, consisting of 10 houses, used to be in the NW part of the historical centre in the 15th cent. In 1504 J. were expelled from P. and forbidden to stay overnight in the town which remained valid for almost three centuries. It was only in 1790 that one J. family was granted permission to buy a house in the town. In 1821, 32 Jews were found to have been living without permission in Pilsen. Only 3 J. families are recorded in P. in 1837, 10 families in 1850 (P. was the seat of the district rabbi, a prayer room existed at that time), 41 families (259 persons) in 1854. A J. religious congregation was established in 1859. In 1870 the J. community numbered 1,207 persons, 3,094 in 1921, 2,738 in 1930. The J. religious congregation was re-established after World War II. Present address: ŽNO, Smetanovy sady 80/5, 301 37 Plzeň.

P. is the native town of Emil Lederer (1882-1939 New York), Professor of Economics; of Oskar Baum (1883-1941 Prague), the German-J. blind poet and musician, and of the harpsichordist Zuzana Růžičková (born 1928).

(No traces are left neither of **the first synagogue**, mentioned in 1409 nor of **the second synagogue**, built in 1436.)

The third synagogue is on the S edge of the historical centre, in the yard of the house where the present J. religious congregation has its seat. Built in 1857-59 after the design of architect M. Stelzer. Services were held there most probably until 1892, not used today.

The fourth synagogue stands right next to the third one. Built in 1875 (architect J. Melzer) in the neo-Romanesque style. Services were held there most probably until 1892, later used as a store-house, not used today.

The Great (fifth) Synagogue on the

W edge of the historical centre, in Nejedlého sady. Built in 1890-92 (architects M. Fleischer and E. Klotz) in the neo-Romanesque style with two towers. Services were held here until World War II. After the liberation only the smaller prayer hall was used, services until 1988. Plans have been made to convert the synagogue into a municipal concert hall and an exhibition hall showing the history of J. religious congregations in Western Bohemia.

The present **prayer room** was established in 1988. Address: Smetanovy sady street 80/5.

(**The first cemetery**, founded in 1432, ceased to exist in 1504. **The second cemetery** was consecrated in 1856, burials until the early 20th cent., tombstones removed in 1985, converted into a park.)

The third cemetery is 4 km E of the main square, in Rokycanská street, leading to the village Ejpovice, opposite the central municipal cemetery. Opened in 1898, still used today. 18 urns of prisoners - victims of a transport - were buried in the cemetery in 1945 (tombstone from 1973). A monument in memory of the Nazi victims was dedicated in the cemetery in 1951.

The historical centre with an abundance of historical monuments has been declared an urban conservation area: several churches from the 14th up to the 18th cent., a Renaissance town hall, remarkable Gothic, Renaissance and Baroque houses. Noteworthy are also the sights in the suburbs. A museum with rich collections and a gallery of children's art from all over the world. Famous for its brewery (export beer Prazdroj-Urquell) and the brewery museum.

The following J. communities and religious societies with a prayer room used to exist in the vicinity: **Liblín** (21 km NNE, a prayer room recorded in the 19th cent.); **Radnice** (town 19 km NE, a small J. quarter with a synagogue from about the late 18th cent., converted into a workshop, a cemetery allegedly from the 16th cent. with tombstones from the 2nd half of the 18th cent.; in 1843-46 Rabbi Isaac Mayer Weis-Wise [1818 Lomnička - 1900 Cincinnati], founding father of American Reform Judaism, officiated as rabbi in R.); **Osek** /Ger. *Wossek* (15 km ENE, a J. street with a prayer hall converted into a flat, a cemetery from about 18th cent. with tombstones from the early 19th cent.); **Rokycany** (district town 15 km E, the house in which a prayer room was established in 1871 was pulled down after 1981, a cemetery from the end of the 19th cent.); **Mirošov** (20 km ESE, a prayer room recorded in the 19th cent.); **Štěnovice** /Ger. *Stienowitz* (8 km SSE, a synagogue of unknown origin, pulled down after World War II, a J. quarter, a cemetery with tombstones from the 1st half of the 19th cent., birth-place of Louis E. Levy [1846-1919 Philadelphia], author of the patented "Levotype" [photochemical reproduction of engravings]); **Nýřany** /Ger. *Nürschan* (town 12 km WSW, a late 19th cent. synagogue, demolished by the Nazis); **Vlkýš** /Ger. *Wilkischen* (20 km WSW, a prayer room existed here in the 19th - 20th cent.); **Úlice** (16 km W, a prayer room

existed there in the 19th - 20th. cent.); **Kozolupy** (9 km WNW, a synagogue from about 1780 collapsed in 1927, the last remains of a cemetery from the 16th cent. were liquidated after 1980); **Bdeněves** /form. *Venousy*, Ger. *Wenussen* (10 km WNW, a prayer room allegedly existed there in the 19th cent.); **Město Touškov** /Ger. *Tuschkau Stadt* (town 10 km WNW, a synagogue from 1926, today used as a store-house, remains of a 16th cent. cemetery, destroyed by the Nazis); **Pňovany** /Ger. *Piwana* (small town 18 km WNW, a small J. quarter, a synagogue of unknown origin, converted into a house and today used as a store-house, remains of a 16th cent. cemetery, devastated by the Nazis); **Malesice** (6 km NW, a J. street with a 19th cent. synagogue, converted into a flat); **Všeruby** /Ger. *Wscherau* (small town 14 km NW, a J. quarter, a cemetery of unknown origin with tombstones from the mid-18th cent. and a grave of a woman - victim of a death march from 1945, a synagogue from the 2nd half of the 19th cent., pulled down in 1989); **Chrančovice** (18 km NW, a synagogue from about the 1st half of the 19th cent., pulled down in 1958, a J. street); **Skupeč** /Ger. *Skupsch* (23 km NW, a J. street with a synagogue from the 19th cent., rebuilt into a house); **Krašovice** (14 km NNW, a wooden prayer room of unknown origin, pulled down after World War I); **Dolní Bělá** /Ger. *Unter--Biela, Böhmisch - Neustadt* (11 km NNW, a J. quarter with a synagogue from the 2nd half of the 19th cent., rebuilt into a house). **Nezvěstice** (15 km SE) is the birth-place of the former General Secretary of the Communist Party of Czechoslovakia Rudolf Slánský (1901 - executed in 1952 Prague).

*8 km SE **Starý Plzenec**, a town with two formerly Gothic churches, site of a settlement with a late 10th cent. Romanesque rotunda; 9 km SE **Radyně**, ruins of a Gothic castle - the keep gives immensely wide views of the surrounding countryside.*

PODBŘEZÍ 87

Village in Bohemia, 125 km ENE of Prague, 12 km NW of the district town Rychnov nad Kněžnou.

J. are said to have begun settling here in 1696. A J. community is recorded in P. in 1723 (10 families, 32 persons). The J. population numbered allegedly 150 persons in 1844 (the maximum). In 1893 the J. religious congregation merged with the Dobruška religious congregation (only three J. families lived in the village), the last J. family left the village in 1924.

A small **synagogue**, between the main road and the château, 250 m S of the château. Built about the 1st half of the 19th cent. on the site of an earlier wooden synagogue. Services were held here until 1888, converted into an almshouse in 1908, inhabited until 1982, today out of use.

The cemetery is set on the edge of a wood near a brook, 450 m E of the château. Founded most probably in the late 17th cent., the oldest preserved tombstone dates from 1725, the last burial in 1924. The total of 262 tombstones of the Baroque and Classicist types. The mortuary was pulled down in 1911.

There is a Baroque château Skalka in P., rebuilt in the 18th cent., formerly a Renaissance stronghold (interior open to the public, a small exhibition on the history of the local J. community).

Orlické hory, a wooded mountain range with popular holiday resorts (the highest peak - 1,115 m).

PODĚBRADY 88
(Ger. *Podiebrad*)

Town in Bohemia, 50 km E of Prague, 8 km SE of the district town Nymburk. Chartered as early as the 2nd half of the 15th cent.

The first J. family settled in P. in the 1st half of the 17th cent. (From the 17th cent. to the lst half of the 19th cent. the whole estate was administered by the suburban community **Malé Zboží** which had a prayer room, 2 km NNW of the château.) The J. population numbered 8 families (36 persons) in 1826. A J. religious congregation and a small prayer room were established in P. before the mid-19th cent. 49 persons of the J. faith are recorded in P. in 1930. The J. religious congregation was re-established after World War II and later became a synagogue group (171 persons of the J. faith lived in the town in 1946).

A J. old people's home for 65 persons was set up in 1946 in the Luxor boarding-house (today's Purkyně Health Centre in Pavlovova street).

P. is the native town of Rudolf Fuchs (1890-1942 London), a Ger.-J. poet and writer, and of the Ger.-J. poet Franz Janowitz (1892-1917 Italian front). Franz Kafka's mother was born in P.

vices were held there until 1948. Thereafter the building was used as a museum depository and pulled down in 1958.)

(**A prayer room** was set up in 1948 in the Luxor old people's home, services were held there until 1965.)

The cemetery lies 1,500 m SW of the château, in the Kluk suburb, near the road to Písková Lhota. It forms the W part of the municipal cemetery. Founded in 1898 (until then burials in Kovanice), still used today. The older tombstones were removed during the Nazi occupation.

P. has a 13th cent. castle, rebuilt in the 16th and 18th cent., housing a memorial to King George of Poděbrady, churches from the 14th and 16th cent. P. is a well-known spa with springs of mineral water.

The following J. communities used to be in the vicinity: **Sadská** (a small town 9 km W, a prayer room existed there in the 18th - 20th cent.); the suburb of P. called **Malé Zboží** (2 km NNW); **Kovanice** (4 km NW, the old synagogue from 1786 was converted into a workshop in the 19th cent.; a new synagogue was built around 1861 and pulled down around 1900, a cemetery from 1830, Franz Kafka's grandmother is buried there); **Nymburk** /Ger. *Neuenburg* (district town 7 km NW, a synagogue built in 1891 - 92, rebuilt and converted into a municipal museum, the museum houses memorial tablets from the Křinec synagogue); **Křinec** (a small town 13 km N, a synagogue built in 1868 - 70, converted into a dwelling house, a cemetery from 1884); **Bošín** (14 km N, a prayer room allegedly existed there in the 19th cent.); **Rožďalovice** (a small town 17 km NNE, remains of a synagogue from 1815, today a small garden); **Činěves** (11 km NE, a synagogue from 1857, converted into a dwelling house); **Městec Králové** /Ger. *Königstädtel* (town 13 km NE, a synagogue from 1894, used by the Hussite Church today, a late 19th cent. cemetery).

*4 km SE **Libice nad Cidlinou**, a princely settlement of the Slavník family from the 10th - 12th cent., a model of the groundplan and a small museum.*

PODIVÍN 89
(Ger. *Kostel*)

Town in Moravia, 220 km SE of Prague, 45 km SSE of Brno, 8 km NNW of the district town Břeclav.Chartered as early as the 1st half of the 13th cent.

A J. community is said to have existed in P. as early as the beginning of the 17th cent. Only 4 J. families are recorded in P. in 1647 (after the Thirty Years' War). Polish J. families found refuge in the town at the end of the 17th cent. 42 J. families lived in the town in 1768, 81 families (412 persons) in 1787 (this number was not to be surpassed until the mid-19th cent.), 684 persons of the J. faith (the maximum) are recorded in 1857, 435 in 1900, 196

(almost 8% of the total population) in 1930 and only 143 in 1938. Only 6 survivors returned to the town after World War II, the J. religious congregation was not re-established.

Its rabbis included authors of significant theological and philosophical works, e.g. Simon Mandl (officiated as rabbi in P. in 1894-99) and Koppel Duschinsky (officiated as rabbi in P. in 1904-1907), later resident in London.

There were two **J. quarters** - ghettos - in P.: one SW of the square (over 20 houses) and the other N of the square (about 40 houses). Most of the houses have been preserved.

(**The synagogue** used to be in the southern ghetto. Built presumedly in the 17th cent., redesigned in the 1st half of the 19th cent. It suffered serious damage in 1945 and was pulled down later on.)

The cemetery on the N edge of the town, 550 m NN of the square. Consecrated about the 2nd half of the 17th cent., enlarged for the last time in 1872, damaged by the Nazis, burials also after World War II. The oldest preserved tombstone dates from 1694. Remarkable Baroque and Classicist tombstones.

(There are no traces left of **the older cemetery**, of unknown origin, closed down about the 17th cent.)

P. has a formerly Romanesque church, rebuilt in the Baroque style, and other sights.

The following J. communities and religious societies used to exist in the vicinity: **Klobouky** (town 18 km N, an Art-Nouveau synagogue from 1912, converted into a dwelling house); **Dambořice** (a small town 23 km NNE, a synagogue of unknown origin was pulled down after 1948, an extensive J. quarter, a cemetery founded presumedly in the 17th cent., tombstones from 1700); **Břeclav** /Ger. *Lundenburg* (district town 7 km SSE, remains of a ghetto with a synagogue from 1868, not used today, remains of a cemetery from about the 17th cent. with tombstones from the early 18th cent., the cemetery has been converted into a park, an interesting ceremonial hall from 1892

[architect F. Neumann]; in 1572 Yehuda ben Bezalel Löw-Liva was chairman of the synod of Moravian rabbis here; B. is the native town of Julius Lieban [1857-1940 Berlin], an opera singer and of Franz Josef Beranek [1902-1967 Giessen, Germany], author of the only scientific work on Yiddish dialects in Czechoslovakia); **Lanžhot** /Ger. *Landshut* (a small town 14 km SE, a prayer room existed there in the 19th - 20th cent.); **Lednice** /Ger. *Eisgrub* (a small town 5 km SW, a synagogue of unknown origin was pulled down after 1960, a cemetery of unknown origin was liquidated in 1980-81, several tombstones have been preserved, remains of a J. quarter); **Valtice** /Ger. *Feldsberg* (town 11 km SW, a J. community existed here in the 14th - 15th cent., re-established in the 17th cent.). - In 1942-45 a labour camp for J. prisoners from Hungary existed in the village **Poštorná** /Ger. *Unter-Themenau*, 8 km S.

2-8 km SW a remarkable complex of structures built in the Classicist and Romantic styles: in **Lednice** *- a neo-Gothic, Tudor style château (with rich collections and a museum of a gardening, viniculture and hunting), three small châteaux in the vicinity, a minaret and antiquity-like temples.*

POHOŘELICE   **90**
(Ger. *Pohrlitz*)

Town in Moravia, 190 km SE of Prague, 25 km SSW of Brno. Chartered most probably in the 13th cent.

Jews are first mentioned in P. in 1490. 50% of the 43 houses in J. ownership were deserted in the mid-17th cent. after the Thirty Years' War. The J. population numbered 453 (34% of the total population) persons of the J. faith in 1790, 769 (the maximum) in 1857, only 498 in 1900 and the number dropped to 234 (5% of the total population) in 1930. The J. religious congregation was not re-established after World War II.

A transit camp for J. prisoners from Hungary existed in the town in 1944-45 from where they were sent to Terezín and Bergen-Belsen.

The names of twelve rabbis are recorded from the 17th cent. Rabbi Moses Friediger officiated in P. in 1912-13, from 1920 Chief Rabbi in Copenhagen.

P. is the native town of Berthold Feiwel (1875-1937 Jerusalem), a German-J. journalist, translator and publicist and of Philipp Brunner (1837-1904 Vienna), an author of books for children and father of the Viennese writer Armin Brunner.

Remains of a **ghetto** in the town's centre, S of the Catholic church. The ghetto existed in the early 17th cent. and consisted of about 40 houses.

(**The old synagogue** of unknown origin was pulled down in 1853. It is said to have been the oldest synagogue in Moravia.

The new synagogue, built in 1854-55, was demolished by the Nazis.)

The cemetery is 400 m NW of the square, in Tyršova street, leading to Cvrčovice. There is no record of its foundation, the oldest preserved tombstone dates from 1676, burials until World War II. Devastated by the Nazis, restored after the war. Remarkable Baroque and Classicist tombstones.

(No traces have been left of **the older cemetery** of unknown origin.)

There is a Gothic church from the 13th - 14th cent. in P.

The following J. communities and religious societies used to exist in the vicinity: **Židlochovice** /Ger. *Seelowitz, Gross-Seelowitz* (town 9 km NE, a society recorded in the 19th - 20th cent., the birth-place of the piano virtuoso Moritz Strakosch [1825-1887 Paris]); **Hustopeče** /Ger. *Auspitz* (town 15 km ESE, a small synagogue from 1880, today used as a work-shop, a cemetery from 1886, converted into a park with some tombstones left; the native town of the architect Rudolf Hönigsfeld [1902-1977 Vienna]); **Jiřice u Miroslavi** /Ger. *Irritz* (a small town 11 km SW, seriously damaged by the Nazis, a synagogue from 1837 was demolished in 1951-52; remains of a J. street, a cemetery with tombstones from the late 17th cent.); **Miroslav** /Ger. *Misslitz* (town 15 km WSW, remains of a J. quarter, seriously damaged during an air-raid in 1945, a synagogue from 1845, converted into a cultural house, a remarkable cemetery with 17th cent. tombstones, the birth-place of the Ger.-J. playwright Jakob Herzog [1842-1915 Vienna], the writer Armin Brunner [1864-1929 Vienna] and of Ernst Müller [1880-1954 London], a poet and author of works on J. mysticism and the cabbala).

POLICE   91
(Ger. *Pullitz*)

Village in Moravia, 150 km SE of Prague, 31 km SW of the district town Třebíč.

J. families are said to have settled in P. in the 15th cent., according to other sources a J. community existed here in 1523. The earliest documentary record mentioning J. population in P. dates from 1671. About 40-50 J. families lived here in 1727 in 22 houses mostly surrounding the village green. After 1727 Jews were forced to move into a newly built ghetto. In 1769 (after a great fire in the ghetto) only 17 J. families lived in P., only 22 J. families (up to 160 persons) were permitted to reside in P. from 1787 to 1848. 43 persons of the J. faith are recorded in 1869, only 12 in 1900 and the last Jew left the village in 1913. The J. religious congregation merged with the Jemnice congregation in 1891.

The J. surname Pullitzer has been derived from the German name of the village.

A Jewish street - ghetto - leads from the centre of the village to the south, to the J. cemetery. Founded in 1728. About 25 houses on both sides of the street. The whole ghetto was demolished by fire in 1758 and subsequently rebuilt. A noteworthy urban whole, most of the houses have been preserved.

The synagogue is at the S end of the J. street. Built in 1759 in the Baroque

quarter with a J. town-hall and a school, converted into a cultural centre; a synagogue was built in 1821-22, demolished by the Nazis; a 17th cent. cemetery with tombstones from the 1st half of the 18th cent.; the Czech-J. poet Max Winder [1845 Kolín - 1920 Kolín] lived in Š. and his son, writer Ludwig Winder [1889-1946 Baldock, England], who wrote in German, was born here); **Písečné** /Ger. *Piesling* (11 km W, a synagogue from about the 18th cent., pulled down in 1948, a J. quarter, a

style on the site of an earlier wooden synagogue, which had burnt down. Services were held here until about the late-19th cent. After 1917 it was converted into a gymnasium, still used as a gymnasium today.

The cemetery is 120 m SSE of the synagogue. It is said to have existed as early as 1523. The oldest legible tombstone dates from 1681. Baroque and Classicist tombstones.

There is a Renaissance-Baroque château from the 16th - 17th cent. in P.

The following J. communities used to exist in the vicinity: **Šafov** /Ger. *Schaffa* (a small town 12 km SE, a J.

cemetery with tombstones from the 1st half of the 18th cent.); **Staré Hobzí** /Ger. *Althart* (a small town 13 km WNW, a synagogue from 1739, rebuilt into a private house in 1903 and pulled down about 1978; a cemetery of unknown origin, liquidated before 1939, remains of a J. street); **Jemnice** /Ger. *Jamnitz* (town 7 km NW, a synagogue from 1649, rebuilt in the 18th cent., demolished by the Nazis, a J. quarter, a cemetery allegedly from the 14th cent., tombstones from the 17th cent., suffered serious damage by the Nazis).

6 km Vranovská přehradní nádrž, a dam on the Dyje river with sports facili-

*ties; on the river bank - **Bítov**, a well-preserved castle from the 13th - 19th cent. (interior open to the public) and ruins of Gothic castles - **Cornštejn** and **Frejštejn**.*

the SE suburb. The J. population numbered 52 families (305 persons) in 1724, 87 in 1811, 128 families (770 persons) in 1830, the number dropped to 238 persons in 1890, the last rabbi left the town in 1920, only 51 persons

POLNÁ 92

Town in Bohemia, 110 km SE of Prague, 14 km NE of the district town Jihlava. Founded and chartered in the 1st half of the 13th cent.

Jews are first mentioned here in 1532, a numerous J. community existed in P. in the late 16th cent. The owner of the estate ordered to set up a ghetto after 1675. - J. houses with a prayer room were concentrated in the NW suburb (towards the J. cemetery). A new ghetto was established in 1681 in

of the J. faith lived in P. in 1930. The J. religious congregation was not revived after World War II.

P. is the native town of Josef Seegen (1822-1904 Vienna), a well-known balneologist who has contributed to the research of the curative effects of mineral water springs in Carlsbad and its vicinity.

The death of a Christian girl who had been murdered near P. in 1899 resulted in a wave of anti-Jewish sentiment and the infamous trial against Leopold Hilsner (1869-1928), an innocent J. citizen who was accused of ritual murder and sentenced.

The Jewish quarter - a ghetto - on the SE edge of the historical centre, 70 m SE of the main square. Built after 1680, burnt down several times in the 18th and 19th cent. It represents an interesting urban whole, consisting of 32 one-storey houses, with two squares, originally accessible by two gates. Plans have been made to restore one of the gates.

The synagogue is in the centre of the ghetto, between the two squares. It was built after 1683, several times destroyed by fire. The last alterations date from 1861 and 1863 (after a fire). Services were held here until World War II. After 1951 it was used as a store--house, in 1969 the roof and ceilings collapsed. Plans have been made to convert the synagogue into a concert and exhibition hall.

The cemetery lies 650 m NW of the main square, near a brook. It existed as early as 1597 and has been enlarged several times. The earliest legible tombstone dates from 1683, burials until World War II. Noteworthy Baroque and Classicist tombstones.

Remains of a Renaissance château (housing a museum). Three churches from the 14th up to 18th cent. and other sights are to be found in P.

Capital of Czechoslovakia. Prague Castle was founded in the 2nd half of the 9th cent. and settlements originated on both banks of the Vltava river. The first settlement with a market was on the W bank below the castle (today's Malá Strana, The Little Quarter). The settlements on the E bank were enclosed by a fortification wall in the 13th cent., resulting in an urban formation (today's Staré Město, The Old Town).

The earliest mention of a Jewish settlement dates from the early 10th cent. At least two independent J. settlements existed here in the 11th cent.: one on the W bank, most probably surrounding the square Maltézské náměstí (the settlement and its synagogue were burnt down in 1142) and the other one on the E bank, most probably around today's Charvátova street (12 houses recorded in 1067, the settlement ceased to exist about the 14th cent.). The third J. settlement originated not later than the 12th cent. in the place which later became Židovské Město (The Jewish Town). The fourth settlement (a ghetto) was established about 1348 with the foundation of Nové Město (The New Town) - at least 12 houses around today's Školská street, the settlement ceased to exist towards the end of the 15th cent. The fifth ghetto used to be in the village Libeň (4 km ENE) during the 16th or 17th cent. and became a part of Prague in 1901.

Since the Middle Ages Jews were concentrated in the densely populated ghetto (see Jewish Town), its population was 12,000 in the 18th cent. From the beginning of the 19th cent. J. businessmen (manufacturers and financiers) were also permitted to settle beyond the ghetto's borders and in 1848 the legal validity of the ghetto was abolished and Jews were free to move and reside elsewhere. The number of Jewish families in Prague increased: about 10,000 persons of the J. faith in 1848, about 27,000 in 1890, 31,751 are recorded in 1921, 35,463 in 1930, about 54,500 persons subject to racial laws in 1940. 36,500 persons, i.e. 67% of Prague's Jewish population, perished during the Nazi occupation. - Only about 300 persons from mixed marriages and people working for the Jewish Religious Congregation lived in Prague towards the end of the Nazi occupation. 7,614 persons of the J. faith are recorded in Prague again in 1947.

Ever since the Middle Ages Prague has been an important centre of J. learning: philosophy, theology, history, education and art. The Hebrew press in Prague established a reputation for excellence (the earliest print dates from 1512). Since the 18th cent. Prague was also the centre of J. enlightenment and emancipation. From the 2nd half of the 19th cent. many significant works of art, mainly literary, originated in Prague, a meeting place of Czech, German and Jewish culture. A Jewish Museum was founded in 1906, administered by the J. Religious Congregation. After 1932 many J. refugees from Germany and in 1938 from Austria streamed into Prague, seeking refuge. The Eighteenth Zionist Congress was held in Prague in 1933 organizing aid for J. refugees from Germany. In 1941 the Nazi conference on "the final solution of the Jewish problem" was held in Prague (attended by R. Heydrich, A. Eichmann, K. H. Frank and others) and thereafter the first transports of Jews from the Nazi-occupied European countries left for ghettos and extermination camps.

After the liberation in 1945 the decimated Jewish Religious Congregation resumed its activity. Prague is the seat of the Jewish Religious Congregation which also administers the Central, South and East Bohemian regions, and the seat of the Federation of Jewish Congregations in Bohemia and Moravia. Services are held regularly in the earliest preserved synagogue, the Altneuschul (observing traditional rites) and in the Jubilee Synagogue (observing the Reform rite). The Jewish Town Hall (Maislova street No. 18) is the seat of the Federation of the Jewish Congregations and the Prague Jewish Religious Congregation, it houses a kosher restaurant and the editorial office of the monthly *Roš chodeš* and other publications.

The State Jewish Museum (established in 1950), is a significant institution which treasures, restores and shows to its visitors one of the world's greatest collections of Judaica (collected in 1942 by the Nazis from all over Bohemia and Moravia): ceremonial and household objects, paintings and prints on Jewish themes and the like. The museum also has a valuable collection of Hebrew manuscripts and old prints.

Hundreds of significant personalities who contributed to the field of science, religion, economy and art were born or lived in Prague. Unfortunately, we cannot mention all of them as we did with some smaller towns. Prague is the native town of some famous **rabbis**, e.g. Mordecai Jaffe (about 1530-1612 Poznan), Yesayah ben Abraham Horowitz (1565-1630 Jerusalem), Aaron Simeon Spira-Wedeles (1640-1679 Prague), Zacharias Frankel (1801-1875 Wroclaw); **the philosopher** Hugo Bergmannn (1983-1975 Jerusalem) and the religious thinker Alfred Fuchs (1892-1942 Dachau); **other scientists**, e.g. the historian and lawyer Guido Kisch (1889-1985 Basle), historian Otto Muneles (1894-1967 Prague), the pathologist Samuel von Basch (1837-1908 Vienna), the 1947 Nobel Prize winer for physiology and medicine Gerta Theresa Cori (1896-1957 St. Louis, USA); **politicians.**, e.g. Victor Adler (1852-1918 Vienna), the founding father of the first Jewish magazine in America Isidor Busch (1822-1898 St. Louis, USA), the Synek brothers (Otto, 1900 - executed in 1941 Prague and Viktor, 1903-1942 Mauthausen) - Communist journalists; **painter and graphic artists**, e.g. Emil Orlik (1870-1932 Berlin), Hugo Steiner-Prag (1880-1945 New York), cofounder of the Osma group of artists Fred Feigl (1884-1965 London); **composers**: Ignaz Moscheles (1794-1870 Leipzig), Erwin Schulhoff (1894-1942 Wülzburg, Germany), Jaromír Weinberger (1896-

1967 St. Petersburg, USA), Viktor Ullmann (1898-1944 Auschwitz), Hans (Hanuš) Krása (1899-1944 most probably Auschwitz), Frank Pelleg (1910-1968 Haifa), Petr Skoumal (1936); **conductors**: Vilém Zemánek (1875-1922 Prague), Egon Pollak (1879-1933 Prague), Rudolf Pekárek (1900-1974 Brisbane, Australia), Adolf Heller (1901-1954 Santa Barbara, USA), Hans Walter Süsskind (1913-1980 Berkeley, USA) and **the cameraman** Otto Heller (1895-1970 London); **actors**, e.g. Herbert Lom (1917 - resident in England), Miloš Kopecký (1922) and others.

Prague is the native town of many **writers**, let us mention the most famous: Andreas L. J. Jeitteles, pseud. Justus Frey (1799-1878 Graz), Salomon Kohn (1825-1904 Prague), Julius Zeyer (1841-1901 Prague), Auguste Hauschner 1851-1928 Berlin), Oskar Wiener (1873-1944 Terezín), Emil Faktor, pseud. Jussuff (1876-1942 Lodz), Paul Adler (1878-1946 Prague), Franz Kafka (1883-1924 Kierling, Austria - there is a memorial tablet on his native house on the corner of Maislova and U radnice streets), Pavel Amann (1884-1958 Fairfield, USA), Max Brod (1884-1968 Tel Aviv), Leo Perutz (1884-1957 Bad Ischl, Austria), Egon Erwin Kisch (1885-1948 Prague - there is a memorial tablet on his native house on the corner of Kožná and Melantrichova streets), Alma Johanna König von Ehrenfels (1887-1942 Minsk), Otto Pick (1887-1940 London), František Langer (1888-1965 Prague), Pavel Eisner (1889-1958 Prague), Paul Kornfeld (1889-1942 Lodz), Franz Werfel (1890-1945 Beverly Hills, USA, there is a memorial tablet on his native house in Havlíčkova street No. 11 and in Opletalova street No. 41), Hans Janowitz (1890-1954 New York), Willy Haas, pseud. Caliban (1891-1973 Hamburg), Hans Natonek (1892-1963 Tuscon, USA), Jiří Langer (1894-1943 Tel Aviv), Johannes Urzidil (1896-1970 Rome), Franz C. Weiskopf (1900-1955 Berlin), František R. Kraus (1903-1967 Prague), Peter Lotar (1910-1986 Ennetbaden, Switzerland), Hans G. Adler (1910-1988 London), Jan Martinec

(1915), Ewald Osers (1917 - resides in London), Jiří R. Pick (1925-1983 Prague), Franz Wurm (1926, resides in Zurich), Arnošt Lustig (1926, resides in Washington), Dagmar Hillarová (1928), Ota Pavel (1930-1973 Prague), Ivan Klíma (1931), Karol Sidon (1942).

The well-known chess-player Wilhem Steinitz (1836-1900 New York) was a native of Prague as were the parents of the leading American lawyer and economist Louis D. Brandeis (1856-1941) and the mother of the Viennese composer Arnold Schönberg (1874-1951).

Many famous people, born elsewhere, lived or spent some time of their lives in Prague: e.g. prominent **rabbis** and authors of theological works Yehudah ben Bezalel Liva-Löw (about 1525-1609 Prague), David ben Abraham Oppenheim (1644 Worms - 1736 Prague), Ezechiel ben Jehuda Landau (1713 Opatow - 1793 Prague), Solomo Juda Rapoport (1790 Lemberg - 1867 Prague), Heinrich Brody (1868 Uzhgorod - 1942 Jerusalem). Prague was the temporary home of the Renaissance historian David Gans (1541 Lippstadt - 1613 Prague), the poets Hugo Salus (1866 Česká Lípa - 1929 Prague) and Friedrich Adler (1857 Kosova Hora - 1938 Prague), the painter Max Horb (1882 Mladá Boleslav - 1907 Prague), the conductor Angelo Neumann (1838 Vienna - 1910 Prague), the musicologist Paul Nettl (1889 Vrchlabí - 1972 Bloomington, USA).

The philosopher Martin Buber (1878-1965) lectured in Prague in 1909, 1910 and 1937, the physicist Albert Einstein (1879-1955) was Professor at Prague University in 1911-12 (there is a memorial tablet in Lesnická street No. 7 and Viničná street No. 7). After 1932 Prague became a home for many German Jewish refugees: e.g. the philosopher Ernst Bloch (1885-1977), the writer Hermann Adler (1911), the painter Friedl Dicker-Brandeis (1898 - 1944) and others.

The Jewish Town, from the mid-19th cent. **Josefov** or the so-called Fifth District (Prague V). An extensive ghetto consisting of two different-sized enclaves in the NW part of the district Staré Město, between Staroměstské náměstí (the Old Town Square) and the Vltava river. The smaller part of the ghetto surrounded the Spanish Synagogue (a J. settlement existed here at the turn of the 11th and 12th cent.), the larger part was in the vicinity of the Altneuschul and the other four synagogues (this part originated most probably in the 12th - 13th cent.). The ghetto was separated from the rest of the city by walls and gates. However, it was spreading as new houses and lots were being purchased outside the ghetto boundaries up to the 17th cent. The town witnessed an extensive building program in the Renaissance period, begun by its mayor Mordecai Maisel (1528-1601). In 1792 the ghetto consisted of 274 houses, 10 synagogues and many communal buildings (ritual baths, hospitals, schools, slaughter houses etc.) and many prayer halls.

The Jewish Town was several time damaged by devastating fires (e.g. in 1240, 1336, 1389, 1523, 1689, 1754), bloody pogroms (the worst swept through in 1389), plague epidemics (in 1348-49, 1680, 1713-14). Several times Jews have been temporarily expelled from the city (e.g. in 1543-45, 1557, 1745-48).

In 1636 the ghetto was a densely populated area, the population of the Jewish Town was 7,815 persons (the earliest preserved census), in 1729 the community numbered 12,796 persons (the second largest J. community in Europe after Istanbul). After 1848 most of the J. families moved from the J. Town - Josefov and the former ghetto became a district of the Christian and Jewish poor. The ancient J. T. with its many Renaissance and Baroque houses was pulled down in 1896-1911 and new buildings were erected. A part of the original network of streets, the cemetery (reduced in size), six synagogues and the Town Hall are all that is left of the former Josefov.

The Jewish Town Hall - Maislova street No. 18, corner of Červená street. Built most probably in the 1560s by P. Roder, rebuilt in the Rococo style in 1763 by architect J. Schlesinger. It was extended on the S side in 1908 and another storey was added (the ceremonial hall - restaurant on the ground floor and the congregational meeting room on the third floor). Today it is the seat of the Jewish Religious Congregation and the Federation of Jewish Religious Congregations, the rabbinate, the editorial office and the kosher restaurant.

The Altneuschul or **the Old New Synagogue** in Červená street. It represents the oldest surviving synagogue north of the Alps. Built most probably in the last third of the 13th cent. with a 14th cent. vestibule in the south, annexes used as women's areas in the west (dating from the 16th - 17th cent.) and on the north (from 1723). Damaged by fire in 1689 and 1754. Restorations occurred in 1883 (a purist alteration of the Gothic brick gables), in 1921-26 and in 1957. Composed of a double-naved main room with a bimah in the centre surrounded by a late Gothic wrought-iron grille. A Gothic-Renaissance stone aron ha-kodesh. Chandeliers from the 16th to the 19th cent., a banner of the J. Community from the early 18th cent. A small Gothic portal. The synagogue has no wo-

men's gallery, women attend services in the surrounding annexes with windows. Regular services are held here at present. - North of the synagogue is a small park with a statue representing **Moses** by František Bílek made in 1905 (the present statue is a copy from 1948, the original sculpture was destroyed by the Nazis).

The Pinkas Synagogue in Široká street. Built as a private prayer hall (documentary evidence from the 15th cent.), enlarged in the 1st half of the 16th cent., the Gothic-Renaissance synagogue was completed in 1535. The synagogue was redesigned in the late Renaissance style in the 1st quarter of the 17th cent.(e.g. women's section was built in the S), tasteless modern alterations were carried out in the interior in

1861-62. A Renaissance-Baroque stone aron ha-kodesh, a stone bimah (almemar) surrounded by a Rococo grill from 1798. A ritual bath-house and a well are preserved in the courtyard. Services were held here until World War II. The synagogue was restored in 1950-59. In 1960 the synagogue became a unique memorial to the Jewish victims of the Holocaust - the interior walls were covered with 77,297 names of Jews from Bohemia and Moravia deported by the Nazis to death camps. Since 1968 the synagogue has been under reconstruction; the inscriptions, damaged by humidity, were removed.

The High Synagogue in Červená street. The building was completed in 1568 (master-builder P. Roder). The original entrance was only from the adjacent J. town-hall: the synagogue was used as a meeting place of the J. Town committee. Damaged by fire in 1689. Repaired in the late 17th cent. (a women's nave built), in 1883, 1961, 1977-79 and in 1982. A Renaissance building housing an early Baroque stone aron ha-kodesh from 1691. Ser-

street. Built in 1591 - 92 as a private synagogue of the J. Town's mayor Mordecai Maisel by master-builders J. Wahl and J. Godschmied de Herz. Destroyed by fire in 1689 (rebuilt but reduced in length), damaged by fire again in 1754. Rebuilt in 1862 - 64 and redesigned by architect A. Grotte in the neo-Gothic style in 1893-1905. Services were held there until World War II. The building was repaired in 1963-64 and since 1965 a large exhibition of silver synagogue objects from the collections of the State Jewish Museum is to be found in the synagogue.

The Klaus Synagogue in the street U starého hřbitova. The building was completed in 1694, built on the site of a smaller synagogue and other buildings assigned for adult studies called "klauses". The synagogue was extended in 1883-84 and a women's gallery was

vices were held there until World War II and from 1946 to 1950. Since 1950 it has been a part of the State Jewish Museum and since 1982 an exhibition of synagogue textiles is to be found in the synagogue.

The Maisel Synagogue in Maislova

added on the W side. Restoration was carried out in 1910, 1960 and 1979-84. It is an early Baroque building with a stone aron ha-kodesh dating from 1696. Services were held here until World

War II. In 1942 the synagogue housed a non-public exhibition for the Nazis of objects related to J. customs and J. holidays throughout the year, in 1946 the exhibition was open to the public. In 1984 the State J. Museum installed an exhibition of old J. manuscripts and prints here. A wooden aron ha-kodesh from the synagogue in Podbořanský Rohozec was transferred here and is to be found by the western wall.

The Spanish Synagogue in Dušní street. Built in 1867-8 on the site of the earliest Prague synagogue called **the Altschul.** Built in the so-called Moorish style by architect V. I. Ullmann, interior designed by architect J. Niklas. The interior was decorated in 1882-93 with arabesque ornamentation (architects A. Baum and Bedřich Münzberger). The Moorish and Iberian architectural features gave the synagogue its name. Services were held until World War II. The building was restored in 1958-59. A collection of synagogue textiles was displayed by the State Jewish Museum in the synagogue in 1960 - 82. An exhibition hall was set up on the first floor of the modern annex built in the 1930s (originally a winter prayer hall). The synagogue has been under reconstruction since 1982.

(**The New Synagogue** built in the late 16th cent., twice rebuilt after a fire in 1703 and 1755, pulled down in 1898.)

(**The Gypsy Synagogue [Cikánova synagoga]**, also called **Zigeiner Synagogue,** was built most probably in the early 17th cent., rebuilt after the 1701 fire, redesigned in the 19th cent. and demolished in 1906. The thirteen-year-old Franz Kafka had his Bar Mitzva here in 1896.)

(**The Great Court Synagogue [Velkodvorská** or **Řeznická synagoga]** built after 1626, rebuilt after the 1708 fire, redesigned in the 2nd half of the 19th cent., demolished in 1906.)

The Jubilee Synagogue in Jeruzalémská street (beyond the J. Town). Built by architect W. Stiassny in 1905-6 to replace the three synagogues (The Gypsy S., the Great Court S. and the New S.) which had been demolished

during the urban renewal of Josefov. It is a blend of Moorish and Art-Nouveau style features. Regular services are held here at the present time, Saturday services are held in a small prayer room on the first floor.

The cemetery lies between the streets U starého hřbitova, 17. listopadu and Široká, entrance from U starého hřbitova street. Founded in the 1st half of the 15th cent. (the earliest legible tombstone dates from 1439), burials until 1787. Enlarged several times in course of the 16th and 17th cent., reduced in size in 1903 during the urban renewal of Josefov. Due to the lack of space the existing graves

were covered with earth resulting in many layers burials (in some places there are up to twelve layers of graves). There are about 12,000 tombstones in the cemetery: remarkable gravestones from the late Gothic period up to the Rococo period and several ark-shaped-tombs dating from the 17th and 18th cent. Tombstones of many famous Jews are to be found in the cemetery: let us mention for example the scholar and poet Avigdor Karo (d. 1439), the famous rabbi, philosopher and pre-emi-

nent teacher Yehudah ben Bezalel Löw (about 1525-1609), the astronomer and mathematician David Gans (1541-1613), the atronomer and physician Joseph Delmedigo (1591-1655) and the renowned Rabbi David Oppenheim (1664-1736), a bibliophile whose unique collection of books was purchased by Oxford University.

Near the E front of the Klaus synagogue there is an elevation called Nefele where children who had died before they reached the age of one month were buried; in 1903 remains from the demolished parts of the cemetery were interred here and a three-dimensional tombstone commemorating those buried was erected there. Fragments of tombstones from an older cemetery in Vladislavova street were embedded in the wall near the Nefele elevation (the earliest dates from the mid-14th cent.). - Gradual restoration work has been carried out since 1946. The cemetery is under the administration of the State Jewish Museum and is open to visitors.

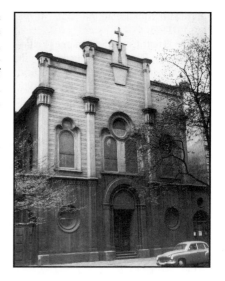

The Ceremonial Hall of the Burial Society is in the street U starého hřbitova. Built in the neo-Romanesque style about 1906-8 by architect J. Gerstel. It has been used as the museum's exhibition space for children's drawings from Terezín.

(**The oldest** known **cemetery** was in the district of Malá Strana on the W bank of the Vltava river, founded most probably in the 11th cent., ceased to exist and no traces of it were left. - **The second cemetery** in the district Nové Město, around today's Vladislavova street, existed in the 13th - 14th cent. and was closed down after 1477. Fragments of its tombstones were transferred in the 19th cent. to the cemetery in Josefov.)

Autonomous J. communities and religious societies with prayer rooms used to exist in other districts and suburbs of Prague:

BRANÍK (6 km S): A J. community with a prayer room existed here in the 18th cent.

BUBNY (2 km NE): A prayer hall existed here from the mid-19th cent. A small **synagogue** from the late 19th cent. used to be in the courtyard of the house No. 25/719 in Heřmanova street, today used as a store-house.

DOLNÍ POČERNICE (11 km E): A prayer room is said to have existed here in the 19th cent.

HORNÍ POČERNICE (a town 15 km ENE, incorporated into Greater Prague in 1974): A religious society with a prayer hall existed here in the 2nd half of the 19th cent.

KARLÍN /Ger. *Karolinenthal*, a town 2 km E, incorporated into Greater Prague in 1920): **A synagogue** was built in the neo-Romanesque style in Vítkova street after 1860, at present it is used by the Hussite Church (interior redesigned). An auxiliary small synagogue was built in the early 20th cent. in the courtyard, at present it is used as a meeting room of the Ecumenical Council.

KOŠÍŘE (a town 4 km SW, incorporated into Greater Prague in 1920): **A synagogue** was built here about 1849, after 1930 it was used as J. orphanage, later converted into a flat.

KUNRATICE (10 km SE): A prayer room, converted into a flat.

LIBEŇ /Ger. *Lieben* (a town 10 km ENE, incorporated into a Greater Prague in 1901): Remains of a J. quarter. **The old synagogue** from about the 16th cent., pulled down before 1900. **The new synagogue**, built in the neo-Romanesque style in 1846-58, in Ludmilina street, is used as a store-house at present. **The old cemetery** from the 16th cent. was liquidated about 1964. **The new cemetery** was founded in 1892, burials until 1975; the grave of the writer Vojtěch Rakous (1862-1935) is to be found here.

LOCHKOV (11 km SSW): The prayer room was converted into a flat.

MICHLE (5 km SSE): **The synagogue** in the street U michelského mlýna was built most probably in the 1st half of the 18th cent., rebuilt in the 2nd half of the 19th cent. and before 1989, at present it is used by the Hussite Church. Several J. tombstones of unknown origin are to be found in front of the synagogue.

SMÍCHOV (a town 3 km SSW, incorporated into Greater Prague in 1920): **The synagogue** in Stroupežnického street was built in 1863, enlarged and rebuilt in the period of Functionalism in 1930-31 by architect L. Ehrmann, at present it is used as a store-house.

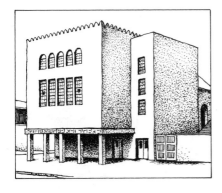

The old cemetery in the street U starého židovského hřbitova was consecrated in the 2nd half of the 18th cent., burials until 1921.
The new cemetery in Liebknechtova street dates from 1903 and is still used. There is a memorial tablet of the Ger-

- Jewish poet Rudolf Fuchs (1890 Poděbrady - 1942 London) there.

STRAŠNICE (5 km ESE): A prayer hall used to exist from the end of the 19th cent. to the mid-20th cent. in the building of the J. old people's home in Vinohradská street.

UHŘÍNĚVES /Ger. *Aurinowes* (a town 14 km SE, incorporated into Greater Prague in 1974): The late Classicist **synagogue** in the street called tř. Přátelství was built in 1848, at present it is used as a launderette. **A cemetery** with tombstones from the early 18th cent. up to World War II.

VINOHRADY /form. *Královské Vinohrady*, Ger. *Königliche Weinberge* (a town 3 km SE, incorporated into Greater Prague in 1920): **The synagogue**, built in 1896-98 and demolished in an air-raid in 1945, used to be the largest synagogue in Prague. The sculptor Otto Gutfreund (1889-1927) was buried in the municipal cemetery in Vinohrady (Vinohradská street) and the journalist and writer Egon Erwin Kisch (1885-1948) rests in the neighbouring urn grove.

VYŠEHRAD (a town 3 km S, incorporated into Greater Prague in 1883): There was no J. community in V. The writers Julius Zeyer (1841-1901) and František Langer (1888-1965) were buried in the famous Vyšehrad cemetery where lie the most famous personalities of the Czech culture.

ZBRASLAV /Ger. Königsaal (a town 13 km SSW, incorporated into Greater Prague in 1974): A prayer hall from the late 19th cent. was converted into a flat.

ŽIŽKOV (a town 3 km ESE, incorporated into Greater Prague in 1920): The large late-19th cent. prayer hall in Seifertova street is used at present by Plymouth Brethren's Church. There are two cemeteries in Žižkov:
The old cemetery in Fibichova street was consecrated in 1680 as a plague burial ground and after 1787 it represented the main Prague J. cemetery. The last burial was in 1890. 180 damaged Torah scrolls deported by the Nazis from the Netherlands were buried in the cemetery in 1948. A greater

part of the cemetery was converted into a park (Mahlerovy sady) in 1960, in 1985-90 a TV transmitter was built there. - The oldest part of the cemetery, the N. part, was restored in 1986. A number of remarkable Baroque and Classicist tombstones. Here lie Chief Rabbi Ezechiel ben Jehuda Landau of Prague (1713-1793), chairman of the rabbinical board Eleazar ben David Flekeles (1754 - 1826), Provincial Chief Rabbi of Moravia Nehemias ben Selig Trebitsch (1779-1842), Chief Rabbi Solomon Judah Löb Rapoport (1790-1867) as well as scientists, physicians, leading Prague industrialists etc.

The new cemetery in the street called Nad vodovodem. Founded in 1890, still used today. The neo-Renaissance ceremonial hall was built at the same time. The urn grove dates from 1933, the Functionalist style ceremonial hall was designed by architect L. Ehrmann. A monument in memory of the victims of the Terezín ghetto was erected in the cemetery above the grave with the ashes of 15,000 victims in 1949; a monument in memory of the sinking of the steamship Patria; a monument in memory of the Nazi victims, dedicated in the cemetery in 1985; a memorial commemorating the inundated Dolní Kralovice J. community; a group of old tombstones transferred here from the Uhříněves cemetery. - Many renowned personalities were buried here, let us mention, e.g. the painter Max Horb (1882-1907), Bohumil Bondy (1832-

1907), sponsor of the Czech-Jewish movement, the writer Franz Kafka (1883 - 1924) and his parents, the poet Jiří Orten (1919-1941), Chief Rabbi Gustav Sicher (1880-1960), the writer Ota Pavel (1930-1973) and many others. There is a memorial tablet of the writer Max Brod (1884-1968) here and a number of remarkable tombstones by leading sculptors and architects.

Prague is an architectural marvel and is said to be one of the most beautiful cities in the world. The historical centre with an abundance of historical monuments has been declared an urban conservation area. Many books on Prague's architecture, art collections and museums have been published for visitors wishing to find out more about the city.

PROSTĚJOV   **94**
(Ger. *Prossnitz*)

District town in Moravia, 200 km ESE of Prague, 48 km NE of Brno. Chartered about 1390.

Jewish families that had been expelled from Olomouc settled in P. most probably about the mid-15th cent. A large J. community existed here by the end of the 16th cent. J. families from Poland and Vienna came to settle here in the 17th cent. From the late-18th cent. to the mid-19th cent. 328 J. families were granted permission to reside in P. The community numbered 1,704 persons of the J. faith (about one quarter of the total population) in 1804, 2,000 in 1857, 1,553 in 1900 and the number dropped to 1,442 in 1930. Over 1,200 persons perished during the Nazi occupation. In 1945 the J. religious congregation was revived and later changed into a synagogue group (active until about 1980).

P. was a well-known centre of J. learning and Talmudic studies and was renowned for its Hebrew printing press. The names of almost 30 rabbis have been recorded since the late 16th cent. In 1785-94 the local yeshiva was led by Rabbi Moses Schreiber, called Hatam Sofer (1762 Frankfort - 1839 Bratislava).

P. is the native town of many significant personalities: let us mention e.g. the founding father of scientific Hebrew bibliography and literary historian Moritz Steinschneider (1816-1907 Berlin), the linguist and bibliographer - Rabbi Nathan Porges (1848-1924 Würzburg) or Moritz Eisler (1823-1902 Opava), a historian of philosophy, and the famous philosopher and founding father of phenomenology Edmund Husserl (1859-1938 Freiburg). It is also the birthplace of synagogue architect Max Fleischer (1841-1905 Vienna), of the composer Ignaz Brüll (1846-1907 Vienna) and the playwright Max Zweig (1892, resident in Israel).

The Jewish quarter - a ghetto - used to be in the SE part of the town's historical core (today's Křížkovského, Demelova and Lutinovova streets), consisting of over 50 houses. Most of the original houses were demolished after World War II. Another ghetto, a much smaller one, consisting of about 18 houses, used to be in the NE part of the town, in Školní street.

(**The first** known **synagogue**, from about 1676, was renewed after the 1698 fire and demolished before 1905.)

The second synagogue (formerly serving as a house of learning - beth ha-midrash) stood by the W side of Demelova street. A Classicist style building from the early 19th cent. Services were held here until World War II. In 1953-64 used by the Orthodox Church, in 1970 it was converted into an exhibition hall.

The third synagogue (The New Synagogue) stood by the E side of Demelova street, entrance from nám. Svatopluka Čecha. Built in the Art Nouveau style in 1904 and orientated towards the south (a rare exception in Czechoslovakia). Services were held here until World War II. The building was considerably modernized in 1947-49 and since 1949 it has been used by the Hussite Church.

The last **prayer room** was established in 1945-46, 150 m SE of the synagogue in the street Sádky No. 2, on the first floor of the J. community house. Services were held here until 1980. Since 1982 the building has been used by the Plymouth Brethren's Church.

(**The first** known **cemetery** with tombstones from the 17th cent. was closed down after 1800.)

(**The second cemetery** was founded about 1801, destroyed by the Nazis in 1943, several tombstones were transferred to the third cemetery.)

The third cemetery lies 2 km S of the synagogues, in Brněnská street, next to the municipal cemetery. Founded in 1908, it is still used at present. Tombstones from the 1st half of the 19th cent. have been transferred here from the older cemetery. A memorial

to the Nazi victims was unveiled in the cemetery in 1950. Tablets with the names of the victims are to be found in the Art Nouveau ceremonial hall.

P. has a 16th cent. Renaissance château, a former Renaissance town hall (today housing a museum) and several churches from the 14th up to the 18th cent. and other places of interest.

A J. labour camp was set up in 1942 in **Hamry**, a small village 10 km W, from where J. were sent to Terezín.

5 km W Plumlovská vodní nádrž, a dam with sporting facilities; 7 km W Plumlov - a small town with an incomplete Renaissance château from the 17th cent.

PŘEROV 95
(Ger. *Prerau*)

District town in Moravia, 225 km ESE of Prague, 65 km NE of Brno. Chartered in 1252.

J. are recorded in P. before the mid-14th cent. In 1564 eight domiciled Jewish families are recorded in the town (the number of undertenants is not known) and 16 domiciled families in 1614. In 1638 the J. community was granted the privilege to build a synagogue, a hospital, a water-supply system for the ritual bathhouse and Jews were allowed to own houses in the town. 66 persons of the J. faith are said to have lived in the town in 1756, 230 persons (8% of the total population) in 1791, 44 J. families (286 persons) were permitted to reside here in 1830, 342 persons in 1848, 622 persons (the maximum) in 1890, 267 in 1930 and 316 in 1938. Only 4 persons of the J. faith returned to P. after the liberation, the J. religious congregation was not revived.

J. families were most probably concentrated from the very beginning in the so-called Židovská ulice (Jewish st.), mentioned as early as 1447 (the W side of today's Žerotínovo náměstí, SE of the château). It was not an enclosed ghetto, J. houses intermingled with Christian houses. 14 houses in J. ownership are recorded in 1724 and 21 J.

houses in 1830. The community suffered serious hardship during the 1774 pogrom and anti-Jewish riots in 1850.

Names of seventeen rabbis have been recorded in Přerov since the 16th cent. Rabbi Salomo Singer officiated in P. from 1883 - 85 and later in Dambach, Alsatia. P. is the native town of the composer and pianist Gideon Klein (1919 - 1945 concentration camp Fürstengrube). Oskar C. Donath (1882 - 1940 Prague), a literary historian and publicist, came from the suburb **Újezdec** (3 km SE).

The synagogue is in the street Čs. armády, on the W edge of former Jewish street. It was built in 1860 on the site of an earlier synagogue, which had been mentioned as early as the 1st half of the 17th cent. and destroyed by fire in 1832. The building without traces of style, is oriented towards the NE. Services were held here until World War II. Since 1950s it has been used by the Orthodox Church.

The cemetery is in Partyzánská street, 1,200 m SE of the synagogue, next to the municipal cemetery. Founded in 1882, burials also after World War II. Several tombstones from the older cemetery were transferred here in 1956. In the 1980s it was reduced in size and the ceremonial hall was pulled down.

(**The older cemetery**, founded in 1585, and closed down about 1888, was removed in 1956.)

P. has a Renaissance château (housing a museum), churches and chapels from the 12th up to the 18th cent., old arcaded houses and other sights.

Mineral water springs near the village Horní Moštěnice, 4 km S.

PŘÍBOR 96
(Ger. *Freiberg*)

Town in Moravia, 270 km ESE of Prague, 11 km NE of the district town Nový Jičín. Chartered as early as the beginning of the 14th cent.

We have no records of early J. settlement. Several J. families, mostly from Poland, lived in P. before 1848.

50 persons of the J. faith lived here in 1848, 157 (the maximum) in 1890, only 48 in 1930. A J. religious society existed in the town in 1888, administered by the Nový Jičín congregation from 1902. After World War II the religious society was not revived.

Příbor is the birthplace of the famous Austrian psychiatrist and founding father of psychoanalysis Sigmund Freud (1856 - 1939 London): **a memorial tablet** is to be found on his native house (Zámečnická No. 117), **a memorial hall** in the local museum (Lidická No. 50) and **a statue** by the sculptor Vincenc Makovský in the park in Jičínská street.

(The last **prayer room** was established on the first floor of the house No. 225 in Čs. armády street. Services were held here until 1938, later converted into a flat.)

(**The cemetery** forms the NE part of the municipal cemetery in Ostravská street, N of the centre. A J. section was established after 1868, all tombstones were removed during the Nazi occupation.)

There are three churches from the 15th up to the 17th cent. in P., Renais-sance and Baroque arcaded houses and a Renaissance town-hall from the 16th cent. The historical centre with its historical monuments has been declared an urban conservation area.

The following J. communities and religious societies used to exist in the vicinity: **Frenštát pod Radhoštěm** /Ger. *Frankstadt* (town 10 km SE, a religious society recorded in the late 19th cent., the birthplace of the Viennese composer Arnošt Kohn-Karsten [1896-1942 Eastern Europe]); **Nový Jičín** /Ger. *Neu-Titschein* (district town 11 km SW, a medieval synagogue and cemetery became extinct after the expulsion of J. inhabitants in 1563, a new synagogue from 1908 today used as archive offices, remains of a cemetery from 1875, destroyed by the Nazis, a memorial to the Nazi victims from 1948, a ceremonial hall used by the Seventh Day Adventists); **Kunín** /Ger. *Kunwald* (11 km W, a prayer room recorded in the 19th cent.); **Sedlnice** (4 km NW, a prayer room recorded in the 19th cent.); **Bílovec** /Ger. *Wagstadt* (town 16 km NW, the house in which a prayer room used to be was demolished in 1945 during an air raid, remains of a cemetery from 1876, destroyed by the Nazis). - In **Suchdol nad Odrou** (14 km WNW) 47 prisoners - victims of a railway transport from a concentration camp - were buried in 1945.

*10 km NNE **Stará Ves nad Ondřejnicí** with a 16th cent. Renaissance château; 6 km ESE **Hukvaldy**, ruins of a castle from the 13th - 17th cent., below the castle a museum of the composer Leoš Janáček (1854-1928); 4 km **Kopřivnice**, Tatra automobile museum; 6 km SSW **Štramberk**, an urban conservation area with popular wooden architecture and a lookout-tower; 11 km SW **Nový Jičín**, an urban conservation area with Renaissance architecture and a museum of hats.*

PŘISTOUPIM 97

Village in Bohemia, 35 km E of Prague, 22 km WNW of the district town Kolín, 2 km SE of Český Brod.

No records of early J. settlement have been preserved. Three J. families lived in P. in 1724 and there was a small prayer room in the village, used also by the vicinity. 8 J. families are recorded in the 1st half of the 19th cent. Most of the houses in J. ownership were concentrated in the N part of the village, near the road to Český Brod. In the mid-19th cent. many more J. families resided in the neighbouring town Český Brod. The J. religious congregation "Český Brod - Přistoupim" numbered 200 persons in 1890. After 1917 a rabbi lived in Č. Brod but the synagogue and cemetery were in Přistoupim. Only 10 persons of the J. faith are recorded in P. in 1930 (74 persons in Č. Brod). After World War II the J. religious congregation was not revived.

The synagogue is 270 m NNW of the Catholic church, in the street leading to Č. Brod. Adjacent are former J. houses. Built about 1842 in the neo-Romanesque style. Services were held

here until World War II. After the liberation it was converted into offices of the local authorities, today used as a library. The stone Ten Commandments have been preserved above the entrance.

The Community House is a one-storey house, 60 m NNE of the synagogue, in the street leading to Č. Brod. It was most probably the seat of the J.

religious congregation from the 18th cent., housing a J. school in the 19th cent. and a **prayer room** before 1842. The building was rebuilt in 1950 and converted into a dwelling house.

The cemetery is 60 m ENE of the synagogue, next to the former Community house. Founded most probably after the first half of the 18th cent. (allegedly in 1785), extended in 1847. Burials (from Č. Brod and vicinity) until World War II. A grave of 8 women prisoners - victims of a railway transport from Auschwitz in January 1945 - is to be found in the cemetery. The cemetery was repaired in the 1970s. Remarkable Baroque and Classicist tombstones.

There is an early Baroque church from the 17th cent. with a belfry from the late 16th cent. in P.

The following J. communities and religious societies with prayer rooms used to be in the vicinity: **Kostelec nad Černými lesy** /form. *Černý Kostelec*, Ger. *Schwarzkosteletz* (town 7 km SSW, a synagogue from the 1st half of the 19th cent., pulled down in the 20th cent.); **Škvorec** (a small town 10 km W, a prayer room recorded in the 19th cent.); **Úvaly** /Ger. *Auwal* (town 11 km WNW, a synagogue built in 1850, pulled down in 1925); **Vykáň** /Ger. *Wikan* (8 km NW, a J. community existed here in the 18th cent.); **Kounice** /Ger. *Kaunitz* (small town 6 km NNW, a synagogue built in 1863, pulled down in the 20th cent.).

2 km NW Český Brod, a town with remnants of a Renaissance gate, a Renaissance church with a wooden belfry and other sights; 6 km SE Lipany - near the village a memorial commemorating the defeat of the Hussites in 1434; 2 km SW Tuchoraz, a Gothic gate of a 15th cent. stronghold; 4 km W Tismice, an extremely well-preserved Romanesque basilica from the late 12th cent.

PUCLICE   98
(Ger. *Putzlitz, Pustlitz*)

Village in Bohemia, 120 km SW of Prague, 14 km NNE of the district town Domažlice.

No records of early J. settlement have been preserved. The J. population numbered 4 families (29 persons) in 1724, 10 J. families living in 8 houses in the 1st half of the 19th cent. J. houses were concentrated in the middle of the village near the synagogue on the S bank of the pond. After the mid-19th cent. more J. families are recorded in the neighbouring small town Staňkov (3 km E): in 1872 there existed a J. religious congregation "Puclice - Staňkov", in 1892 - 93 the seat of the congregation was transferred to Staňkov and services were held only there. From 1931 the Staňkov congregation was administered by the Domažlice J. religious congregation. Only 4 persons of the J. faith lived in P. in 1921 (33 in Staňkov), and 2 persons in P. in 1930.

(**The synagogue** was in the middle of the village, on the W bank of the pond. Built about 1823, services were held here until 1892-93, subsequently converted into a dwelling house and pulled down in 1975.)

The cemetery lies 1 km SW of the village centre, on the edge of a wood. Founded allegedly in 1750. The earliest preserved tombstones date from the early 19th cent., burials (from Staňkov

and vicinity) until World War II. It is a relatively preserved cemetery.

A 15th cent. stronghold is to be found in the village.

The following J. communities and religious societies used to be in the vicinity: **Nedražice** (11 km N, a prayer room recorded in the 19th cent.); **Stod** /Ger. *Staab* (town 13 km NE, a prayer room, converted into a flat, remains of a cemetery from 1906, where 236 prisoners - victims of a railway transport from a concentration camp - found a temporary grave in April 1945); **Staňkov** /form. *Městys Staňkov*, Ger. *Markt Stankau* (town 3 km E, a prayer room, converted into a flat); **Koloveč** /Ger. *Kollautschen* (a small town 10 km SE, a prayer room, converted into a flat); **Osvračín** /Ger. *Wostratschin* (4 km SSE, a prayer room recorded in the 19th cent.); **Kanice** (9 km SSE, a prayer room recorded in the 18th - 19th cent.); **Chotiměř** (5 km S, a prayer room existed there most probably in the 19th cent.); **Horšovský Týn** /Ger. *Bischofteinitz* (town 6 km SW, a prayer hall from 1875 converted into a club. 16 J. prisoners - victims of a death march in April 1945 - are buried in Horš. Týn.

Several châteaux and remarkable churches are to be found in the vicinity; 6 km SW Horšovský Týn - an urban conservation area with a remarkable Renaissance château (interior open to visitors), four churches and noteworthy houses.

RÁBÍ   99

A small town in Bohemia, 105 km SSW of Prague, 27 km ESE of the district town Klatovy. Chartered in 1499.

A J. community is mentioned in R. as early as the 15th cent.; in the late 15th cent. it was allegedly the seat of the district rabbi. Only 3 J. families are recorded in R. in 1654, 7 J. families (42 persons) in 1727, 10 J. families in 8 houses in the 1st half of the 19th cent. The community had a rabbi until 1872, after 1890 the J. religious congregation in R. merged with Horažďovice J. religious congregation. The last J. family left town in 1900.

Jewish houses were concentrated in two groups W of the square: on the S side of the so-called Koňský trh (4 houses, a prayer hall and a school) and W of the J. cemetery (4 houses). The first group of J. houses was built in the late 15th cent. Most of the houses, today rebuilt, have been preserved.

The last **prayer room**, of unknown origin, used to be in the house No. 102. Services were held there until about 1890, after 1897 it was converted into a flat.

The cemetery lies on the NW slope of the castle hill, W of the prayer room. Consecrated before 1724, burials until 1901 or 1911. Simple Baroque and Classicist tombstones. A small Rococo entrance portal in the cemetery's wall.

Extensive ruins of a Gothic castle from the 14th to 15th cent. and two churches (from the 15th and 18th cent.) are to be found in R. Gold was washed in the Otava river in the Middle Ages.

A religious society with a prayer room is said to have existed in the 19th cent. in the village **Mačice** (7 km SE).

1.5 km SE Žichovice, a Renaissance château from the early 17th cent.

RABŠTEJN NAD STŘELOU   100
(Ger. *Rabenstein an der Schnella*)

Small town in Bohemia, 80 km W of Prague, 34 km NNW of the district town Plzeň. Chartered in 1337.

The first three J. families are said to have settled here in the 2nd quarter of the 17th cent. during the Thirty Years' War. Further records of J. settlement date from the mid-19th cent. - mentioning two J. families in R. 15 persons of the J. faith are recorded in R. in 1870, 5 persons in 1917, the last (the only) J. family left in 1938, before the Nazi occupation. We have no records of a J. religious congregation, a prayer hall or a Burial Society in R. The old cemetery was most probably administered by one of the J. religious congregations in the vicinity.

The cemetery lies 270 m SW of the highest point in the town (the post office), near a path leading to the river. We have no records of the origin of the cemetery (the preserved tombstones date from the 18th cent.), burials until the 1930s (mostly from the neighbouring small town Žihle and the vicinity). The older part of the cemetery is elevated, the earth reaches almost to the top of the cemetery wall (many strata of burials), the new part dates from the early 20th cent. A granite portal with the date 1787 above the entrance to the old cemetery was walled up and covered by earth from the inside during the elevating of the terrain. The new part of the cemetery was devastated by the Nazis. There is an information tablet and a map here as the cemetery is a stopping point of a tourist instructional path.

This picturesque small town is probably the smallest town in Central Euro-

pe (about 40 inhabitants). It has many places of interest: remains of a Gothic castle, a Baroque château from the early 18th cent., a Baroque church with a former monastery, old timber framed houses, remains of a fortification wall and a 14th cent. stone bridge.

The following J. communities and religious societies used to exist in the vicinity: **Lubenec** /Ger. *Lubenz* (small town 10 km NNE, a synagogue from 1925, destroyed by the Nazis); **Libyně** /Ger. *Libin* (11 km NNE, a synagogue from 1830-32, pulled down after 1933); **Drahonice** /Ger. *Drahenz* (12 km NNE, a prayer room or synagogue recorded before 1791, a cemetery from about the 16th cent. with tombstones from the 1st half of the 19th cent.); **Petrohrad** /form. *Chlumčany*, Ger. *Klumtschan*, *Petersburg* (14 km NE, a prayer room existed here in the 19th - 20th cent.); **Jesenice** /Ger. *Jechnitz* (small town 14 km NE, a prayer room from the 2nd half of the 19th cent., converted into a flat; a J. section in the municipal cemetery from 1927, several old tombstones from the cemetery near Zderaz have been transferred and installed in the courtyard of the local museum, exhibits commemorating the J. community are to be found in the museum); **Vysoká Libyně** /Ger. *Hochlibin* (11 km ESE, a prayer room existed here in the 19th - 20th cent.); **Nečtiny** /Ger. *Netschetin* (small town 12 km SW, a J. street, a mid-19th-cent. synagogue, devastated by the Nazis; remains of a cemetery from about the 17th cent., destroyed by the Nazis); **Štědrá** /Ger. *Stiedra* (13 km W, a prayer room, converted into a garage); **Brložec** /Ger. *Pürles* (16 km W, a prayer room recorded in the 19th cent.); **Žlutice** /Ger. *Luditz* (town 10 km NW, a synagogue from 1883, converted into a dwelling house); **Budov** /Ger. *Buda* (15 km NW, a synagogue from about the early 19th cent., demolished probably at the beginning of the 20th cent.); **Luka** /Ger. *Luck* (small town 16 km NW, remains of a synagogue from 1842 and a cemetery of unknown origin, destroyed by the Nazis; an orphanage for J. children from Prague used to be in the local small Re-

naissance château in 1905-19); **Chyše** /Ger. *Chiesch* (small town 7 km NNW, remains of a small ghetto, remains of a mid-19th-cent. synagogue, pulled down in 1972, an old cemetery with tombstones from the 17th cent. and a new cemetery from 1883, closed down before 1973). - The mother of the writer Franz Werfel was born in **Žihle** /Ger. *Scheles*, a small town 6 km E. Over 250 prisoners - victims of a railway transport from the Buchenwald concentration camp - were buried here in a mass grave in April 1945.

There is a romantic rocky valley of the Střela river S of R.; 7 km SW Manětín, a town with an 18th cent. Baroque château, housing an art gallery (interior open to visitors).

Village in Bohemia, 85 km SSE of Prague, 13 km SE of the district town Tábor.

At least one J. family must have lived in R. before 1622. Nine J. families are recorded in R. in 1723 and a J. community with a prayer room or a synagogue existed here at that time. The number of J. families increased by the mid-19th cent., thereafter the J. population began to decline. Only 18 persons of the J. faith lived in R. in 1921, 9 persons in 1930. The J. religious congregation merged with the Tábor J. religious congregation after 1921.

The Jewish quarter - a ghetto - on the N edge of the village, 200 m NNE of the château. The ghetto existed as early as the 1st quarter of the 18th cent. A characteristic urban whole with houses surrounding the village green (7 houses in 1727, 10 houses and a synagogue in 1830). The ghetto was separated from the village proper by the château area and the estate. The houses (some of them rebuilt) have been preserved. The school used to be in No. 67.

The synagogue used to be in No. 88, on the N side of the village green, in the ghetto. There are no records of its origin, it stood there before 1830. Services were held there most probably until 1930, in 1935 it was converted into a dwelling house (still inhabited today).

The cemetery is set on a knoll, 500 m NE of the ghetto. Consecrated before 1723, the oldest legible tombstones date from the 1st half of the 18th cent., burials until World War II. Tombstones of the Baroque and Classicist types.

R. has a château from the 16th - 19th cent., a church from the 14th - 18th cent., remains of a fortification wall and other places of interest.

The following J. communities used to exist in the vicinity: **Černovice** /Ger. *Tschernowitz* (small town 8 km E, a synagogue from the mid-19th cent., rebuilt into a dwelling house; a cemetery with tombstones from the late 17th cent.); **Choustník** (small town 4 km S, a synagogue of unknown origin, pulled down about 1911, a J. street). - The minister of social welfare Lev Winter (1876-1935 Prague) was born in the village **Hroby** (2 km N).

4 km SSE **Choustník**, ruins of a Gothic castle with a lookout-tower; 4 km NW **Chýnov**, a small town with the stu-

dio (a memorial hall) of the famous sculptor Fr. Bílek (1872-1941); 6 km N **Chýnovská jeskyně**, a cave among limestone rocks (open to visitors).

RAKOVNÍK 102
(Ger. *Rakonitz*)

District town in Bohemia, 50 km W of Prague. Chartered in 1286.

The earliest record of J. settlement dates from 1441. Isolated J. families lived in R. in the 15th and 16th cent. Three J. families from nearby Senomaty settled here in 1618 - 21 and in the course of the 17th cent. a J. community was probably established (it received official recognition in 1796). The J. population numbered 38 persons of the J. faith in 1690, 7 families in 1724, 14 families after 1830 and about 30 in the mid-19th cent. when R. was the seat of a district rabbi. 329 persons of the J. faith lived in the town in 1900 and only 153 in 1930. The J. religious congregation was not revived after World War II.

R. is the native town of the conductor Robert Brock (1905-1979 Prague) and of the family of the German-J. writer Leo Perutz (1884-1957).

Remains of a small **Jewish quarter**, surrounding the synagogue, are to be found on the N edge of the town's historical core: in the street V brance (e.g. a one-storey timber framed house No. 228) and in Vysoká street. Originally, there were about 10 J. houses in the J. quarter.

The synagogue is in Vysoká No. 232. The former Baroque synagogue originated most probably in 1763-64 with the rebuilding of a house in which a prayer room used to be since 1736. The synagogue is said to have been rebuilt and enlarged in 1792, the prayer hall was enlarged again in 1865 and partly modernized in 1917. The building was damaged by fire in 1920. Its present appearance dates from the last reconstruction in 1927. Services were held here until World War II. (By agreement between the J. religious congregation and the congregation of the

Czechoslovak Church the synagogue was used in the course of the years 1938-41 for Saturday J. services and on Sundays Christian services were held here - a unique instance in the history of Czech J. congregations.) The synagogue was used by the Hussite Church until 1950, plans have been made recently to convert it into a concert hall. A Rococo aron ha-kodesh and a stone portal from 1887 - 88 with a gild psalm

quotation have been preserved. The former women's gallery is used for exhibitions: it is connected with the adjacent building of the former **school and rabbinate**, today housing the Rabas Art Gallery.

The cemetery lies on the SE edge of the town, 1200 m SE of the synagogue, in Fr. Diepolta street, leading to the village Nový Dům. Consecrated in 1635, extended in 1745, 1856 and 1891. The oldest legible tombstone dates from 1656 - 57. The cemetery is still used. A ceremonial hall from the early 20th cent., an urn grove. It is a picturesque cemetery, set on a slope, with remarkable Baroque and Classicist tombstones.

There are three churches from the 14th up to the 16th cent., a town hall from the 16th - 18th cent., two tower gates from the 16th cent., remains of a city wall and other places of interest in the town.

The following J. communities and a religious societies used to exist in the vicinity: **Řevničov** /Ger. *Rentsch, Hohenrentsch* (10 km NE, a prayer room recorded in the 1st third of the 20th cent.); **Nové Strašecí** /Ger. *Neu-Straschitz* (town 13 km NE, a small ghetto from the 18th cent. with a synagogue from 1856-58, today used by the Hussite Church and the Czech Brethren's Protestant Church; a wall of an old mid-17th cent. cemetery, closed down and liquidated after 1952, a new cemetery from 1835); **Všetaty** (6 km SSE, a prayer room existed here in the 17th - 18th cent.); **Slabce** (11 km S, a synagogue from 1867 - 68, pulled down after 1970); **Svinařov** (11 km SSW, a prayer room existed here in the 18th - 19th cent., a cemetery from 1858); **Petrovice** (8 km SW, a prayer room existed here from the 18th until the early 20th cent.); **Šípy** (13 km SW, a prayer room existed here until 1723); **Zdeslav** /Ger. *Deslawen* (14 km SW, a prayer room is said to have existed here in the 19th cent.); **Kůzová** /Ger. *Wallisgrün, Wallisdorf, Heinrichsdorf* (16 km SW, remnants of a timber framed synagogue from 1812, pulled down after 1970); **Strachovice** (18 km SW, a J. community existed here in the 1st half of the 18th cent.); **Kožlany** (town 18 km SW, a J. community existed here until the 18th cent.; a cemetery of unknown origin with tombstones from the 1st quarter of the 18th cent. up to World War II); **Olešná** /Ger. *Woleschna* (4 km NW, a prayer room used to be here in the 18th cent.); **Kolešovice** (small town 8 km NW, a house of prayer from the 19th cent., converted into a flat); **Zderaz** /Ger. *Dereisen* (11 km NW, a synagogue from the 2nd half of the 19th cent., today used as a store-house; a remarkable cemetery allegedly from the 15th cent. [documentary records from the 17th cent.] with preserved tombstones from the 18th cent.); **Děkov** (13 km NW, a prayer room recorded in the 19th-20th cent.); **Kounov** /Ger. *Kaunowa* (12 km NNW, a prayer room recorded in the 19th - 20th cent.). - Until the 1st half of the 17th cent. there used to be a J. cemetery near the village **Nouzov** (6 km W) which may have belonged to a presumed J. community in **Senomaty** (small town 5 km W).

*Many country manors and interesting pieces of architecture are to be found in the vicinity of R. 12 km SE is the well--preserved Gothic castle **Křivoklát** from the 13th - 16th cent. (housing a museum and a picture gallery). The second Czechoslovak president Edvard Beneš (1884-1948) was born in **Kožlany**, a town 18 km SW.*

ROUDNICE NAD LABEM   103
(Ger. *Raudnitz*)

Town in Bohemia, 40 km NNW of Prague, 15 km SE of the district town Litoměřice. Chartered as early as the 13th cent.

The pogrom of 1541 is the earliest documentary record of J. settlements. The J. population numbered 14 families in 1592, 25 (90 persons) in 1631, 218 persons in 1651, one third of the J. population died during the 1713 plague, 101 families (448 persons) are recorded in 1724, 176 families in the mid-19th cent., only 79 families in 1893 and only 166 persons of the J. faith in 1930. The J. religious congregation was not revived after World War II.

The names of rabbis of the R. community have been recorded since 1650. Its rabbis included e.g. the noted scholar Joseph Deutsch (died in 1826 in Roudnice) and Albert Kohn (1811 Tachov - 1870 Roudnice), who introduced the Czech language into J. schools in 1837 and published the Statistical Tables of J. communities in Bohemia in 1852.

R. is the native town of the German-J. writer Seligmann Heller (1831-1890 Vienna) and of the Czech prose writer and playwright Arthur Breisky (1885-1910 New York).

(**The first Jewish quarter** used to be SE of the château. In the last quarter of the 16th cent. it consisted of about 16 to 18 small houses with a synagogue and a cemetery. In 1614 all the J. families had to leave and the quarter was demolished. A Capuchin monastery was built on the site of the J. quarter in 1615 - 28.)

The new Jewish quarter - a ghetto - used to be in today's Havlíčkova street, W of the château and the bridge over the Elbe. Established most probably in 1614 after the demolition of the old J. quarter. Originally, it consisted of 12 houses (bought from the Christians), 28 houses are recorded in 1631 (the same year the ghetto was burnt down by the Saxon army), 51 houses in 1718. The E part of the ghetto (near the Catholic Church) was abolished in 1727 - 28, only 45 houses are recorded in 1785 and 63 in 1840. The ghetto used to be beyond the city wall, separated from the rest of the town by a gate. Houses along the S side of Havlíčkova street (some of them rebuilt today) have been preserved.

(**The first synagogue**, of unknown origin, in the J. quarter SE of the château, ceased to exist after 1613 and no traces are left. - **The second synagogue** on the N side of Havlíčkova street was built in 1619, rebuilt in 1675 (350 seats) and pulled down in the mid-19th cent. during the construction of a railway.)

The third synagogue, by the N side of Havlíčkova street, was built in the neo-Romanesque style in 1852 partly on the site of the second one. Services were held here until World War II. The synagogue was converted into a boarding-house in 1953.

(The first cemetery was most probably on the site of the garden belonging to the Capuchin monastery, SE of the château. The cemetery, of unknown origin, ceased to exist after 1613. Several tombstones had been transferred to the second cemetery, the remaining ones were used as building stones in the 17th cent. Some of the tombstones were found in the 19th cent. and deposited in the municipal museum, closed down after 1956.)

The second cemetery is beyond the W boundary of the former ghetto, 350 m W of the synagogue. Founded about 1613, several times enlarged, burials until about 1890. The earliest preserved tombstone dates from 1611 (transferred here from the first cemetery). Several graves of martyrs - victims of pogroms and feudal despotism - are to be found in the N part of the cemetery. Remarkable Renaissance, Baroque and Classicist tombstones. In 1974 the cemetery was registered as a historical monu-

ment with the Council for the Preservation of the Historical Monuments.

(The third cemetery was founded 1 km W of the second one, beyond the municipal cemetery. Founded about 1890, burials also after World War II. Closed down in 1985. Remains of a Moorish style ceremonial hall which was destroyed by fire.)

There are many interesting historical monuments in the town: an early Baroque château from the 2nd half of the 17th cent. (the former riding school houses an art gallery of modern Czech painting), Gothic structures belonging to the former Augustinian monastery with a 14th cent. church (rebuilt in the Baroque-Gothic in the 17th cent.), a 15th cent. keep, the former Capuchin monastery from the 17th cent. (built on the site of the former J. quarter) and other places of interest.

5 km SE Říp (456 m), a hill with a Romanesque rotunda from the 1st half of the 12th cent., the hill played an important role in Czech mythology, where it is linked with the legends on the arrival of the Czechs to Bohemia; 7 km NW Doksany, a former monastery built in the 13th - 18th cent. with a Romanesque crypt, open to visitors.

Town in Moravia, 200 km SE of Prague, 11 km SW of the district town Vyškov. Developed into a small town in the early 15th cent., became a town in 1967.

J. families settled in R. most probably in the 2nd half of the 15th cent. after their expulsion from the Moravian royal towns. The earliest documentary records of J. settlement date from 1554 and of the existence of J. community from 1593. At least 29 J. families resided here in 1673, the number of J. began to increase in the following years. From the late 18th cent. up to the mid-19th cent. 195 J. families were granted permission to reside in R. 1,039 persons of the J. faith lived here in 1830, 1,148 persons (about 50% of the total population) in 1857, only 199 persons in 1900 (13%) and the number dropped to 31 (1% of the total population) in 1930. The J. religious congregation was not reestablished after World War II.

The names of 20 rabbis of the Rousínov J. community have been recorded since the 17th cent. (some of them came from Frankfurt am M. Lemberg, etc.). Mordecai ben Yesayah, a native of the R., set out on a journey to the Holy Land in 1614 and described it in *Tocaot eretz Israel*. Rousínov is the native town of the German-J. poetess and writer Rosa Barach (1841-1913 Vienna), of the Frankfort Rabbi Nehemias (Nahum) Brüll (1843-1891 Frankfurt am M.), who was famous for his unique collection of books consisting of 10,000 volumes, of the historian and dean of the Prague Faculty of Philosophy Siegfried Reiter (1863-1942 probably in a concentration camp) and of the Viennese painter and illustrator Lisa (Elise) Frankl (1895 - died after 1940, place not known).

An extensive **Jewish quarter** used to be S of the main square. It is said to have spread widely from the 16th cent. to the 2nd half of the 19th cent.: 7 houses about 1600, 35 about 1650, 146 in 1826. J. houses were built north, west and south of the original core (surrounding the synagogue). The wide street, called Trávníky, in the middle of the quarter acquired the character of a square.

All the houses in the W half of the main square were in J. ownership by 1726, surrounding the Catholic church from three sides. This fact is said to have brought Emperor Charles VI to issue an order in 1727 according to which ghettos were to be established in all towns and villages where they had hitherto not existed. (Nevertheless, an enclosed ghetto was not established in R. and J. families were permitted to stay in the houses on the main square.)

The J. quarter suffered damage by fires (e.g. in 1726 and 1825) and pillage. Most houses, today rebuilt, have been preserved.

The synagogue is in the street Trávníky, 100 m SW of the town-hall. The synagogue existed here as early as 1591 and was altered several times (e.g. in the 18th cent. and in 1842), with dominating Classicist style elements. Services were held here until World War II, the interior and furnishing was destroyed during the Nazi occupation. Since 1949 it has been used by the Hussite Church and the Czech Brethren's Protestant Church.

(**The community house** with an auxi-

liary **prayer room** and class rooms was pulled down after 1970.)

The cemetery lies 250 m SE of the synagogue, at the S end of the street Trávníky, entrance from Skálova street. We have no records of its origin, the earliest legible tombstone dates from 1695, burials until World War II. It is a remarkable cemetery with Baroque and Classicist tombstones.

There are a Baroque church and a Baroque town-hall from the 1st half of the 18th cent. in the town.

The following J. communities used to be in the vicinity: **Bučovice** (town 10 km SE, the last synagogue was built in 1853, pulled down in 1966, remnants of a J. quarter, a cemetery with tombstones from the 18th cent.; a small exhibition on the history of the J. community in the municipal museum; Moravian rabbinical synods were held there in the 18th cent.; the birth-place of the pianist and composer Joseph Fischhof [1804-1857 Vienna]); **Slavkov u Brna** /Ger. *Austerlitz* (town 5 km S, remains of a formerly large J. quarter, a synagogue from 1858, today used as a store house; an extensive a cemetery from 1872 with tombstones from the 18th cent. transferred here from an older cemetery; in 1941 a regional ghetto was set up in S. by the Nazis from where

detainees were deported to Terezín in 1942).

10 km SE Bučovice, a town with a noteworthy Renaissance château from the 16th - 17th cent., open to visitors; 5 km S Slavkov u Brna with a noteworthy Baroque château from the 18th cent. housing an art gallery and an exhibition of the Napoleonic Wars.

RYCHNOV NAD KNĚŽNOU   105
(Ger. *Reichenau*)

District town in Bohemia, 130 km E of Prague. Founded as a small town in the 13th cent., chartered as a town in the 2nd half of the 15th cent.

Jews resided here as early as the 1st half of the 16th cent. Five J. families are recorded in R. in 1569, 14 in 1650. (The earliest mention of a J. community dates from 1604, the names of the community's elders have been recorded since 1650 and of rabbis since the early 18th cent.) The J. population numbered 22 families in 1654, 45 in the mid-18th cent., 50 in 1836, 216 persons of the J. faith in 1890 and only 71 persons in 1930. The J. religious congregation was not reestablished after World War II.

The musicologist Jan Löwenbach (1880 - 1972 Glen Falls, USA) and the

Czech-J. writer Karel Poláček (1892 - 1944 Auschwitz) were born here.

The Jewish street - today's Palackého street, leading from the main square to the SE. J. houses were concentrated in this street not later than the beginning of the 17th cent.: 5 houses in 1615, 8 houses in 1690 (8 J. houses and a synagogue was the permitted maximum), 17 in 1755 and only 14 houses (after fires) in 1840. Several houses in J. ownership used to be on the S side of Komenského street. - Most of the houses were destroyed by the 1782 fire and the entire archives of the J. community were destroyed by the 1830 fire. - **The rabbinate and school** used to be on the N side of Palackého street, the year 1780 has been preserved on the gable.

(The old synagogue existed as early as the 1st half or the 17th cent., with 90 numbered seats. It was destroyed by the 1782 fire.)

The present synagogue is in Palackého street, about 30 m N of the street line. Built in 1787, most probably on the site of the old synagogue. It had been damaged by fire in 1830 and remodelled in the Classicist style. Services were held here until World War II, later used as a store house. Plans have been made to convert the building into an exhibition hall commemorating famous Rychnov natives.

The cemetery lies 600 m NW of the square, near the road leading to the village Lokoty. Founded in 1588 (according to other sources in 1616), enlarged in 1695 and also later. The earliest legible tombstones dates from 1690, burials until World War II. The parents of the writer Karel Poláček are buried here. Remarkable Baroque and Rococo tombstones. The cemetery was restored abut 1970. In 1984 the former mortuary was converted into **a memorial of the J. community** which also houses a tablet commemorating the 124 victims of the Nazis from the town and its vicinity and a memorial tablet from the demolished native house of K. Poláček.

The town has a large Baroque château from the 17th to the 18th cent. (open to the public, housing a remarkable picture gallery) and two late Gothic churches.

*6 km NE **Liberk**, a village with a timber framed 17th cent. church, a timber framed belfry and rectory; towards the N is the wooded chain of mountains **Orlické hory** (the highest peak 1,115 m).*

Village in Bohemia, 95 km SSW of Prague, 32 km E of the district town Klatovy.

We have no records of early J. settlement, J. are said to have lived in S. in the 17th cent. Six J. families (27 persons) are recorded in 1724, 12 families in the 1st half of the 19th cent. Only 4 J. families lived here in 1894 and still in 1913. The last J. inhabitant of the village was killed during World War I. (A monument in memory of the war dead was financed by the J. natives resident in the USA.) - The J. religious congregation in S. (allegedly established in the 1st half of the 18th cent.) merged in 1893 with J. religious congregation in Horažďovice.

The Jewish quarter is said to have existed since the early 18th cent. on the N side of the village green, spreading to the N. In the 1st half of the 18th cent. it consisted of 7 J. houses, 10 houses are recorded in 1837. Just a few buildings have been preserved.

(The first synagogue used to be among the J. houses, N of the village green. It was a wooden structure, built most probably in the 18th cent., abolished about 1850 and later pulled down.)

The present synagogue - house No. 58 on the N edge of the village green. A simple Classicist structure, built in 1850, repaired in 1893. In the W part of the building there used to be a classroom, the rabbi's home (on the 1st floor), the slaughter house and the matzah bakery (on the ground floor). Services were held here until 1912, after 1919 used as a barn and granary. Reverential reconstruction works were carried out after 1983: the W part has been converted into a flat, the prayer hall is to be converted into a memorial hall housing an exhibition on the history of the extinct Jewish community.

The cemetery is set in a wood, 1 km N of the village green, W of the road to the village Bezděkov. The cemetery originated in 1723 during the enlargement of an older burial ground (with tombstones from 1668). The earliest preserved legible tombstone dates from the mid-18th cent., the last burial was in 1937. About 170 tombstones have been preserved, mostly Baroque and Classicist types.

A J. religious congregation used to be in the near-by town **Horažďovice** (8 km SSW, the last synagogue was built in the 2nd half of the 19th cent., pulled down in 1980, a J. street, a cemetery from the 1st half of the 19th cent. with tombstones from the 17th cent., transferred here from an older, closed-down cemetery). - **Záboří** (6 km ESE) is the native village of Adolph Joachim Sabath (1866-1952 Bethesda, USA), an American politician, who supported the foundation of the Czechoslovak republic in 1918.

Renaissance and Baroque strongholds, châteaux, manors and interesting ecclesiastic architecture are to be found in the vicinity.

District town in Bohemia, 95 km SSW of Prague. Chartered as early as the beginning of the 14th cent. The southern suburb **Bezděkov** (with Jewish population) became a town in 1869 and was renamed - **Nové Strakonice**. The two towns merged into one in 1920.

The earliest documentary records of J. settlement date from 1499. A J. community existed in Bezděkov most probably in the 17th cent. The community numbered 12 J. families (58 persons) in 1724, a prayer hall existed here in those days. About 25 J. families lived here before the mid-19th cent. The J. population in both towns numbered 95 families in 1878, 326 persons of the J. faith in 1890 and only 169 in 1930. 82 persons were subject to the Nazi racial laws in 1942. The J. religious congregation was not reestablished after World War II.

The production of the famous brimless felt hat, the fez, was maintained and financed by a few J. families of Strakonice. The first factory was founded in 1811 by Wolf Fürth, other fez

factories were founded by L. Gut-freund, I. Stein, M. Weil and M. Zucker.

Strakonice is the birth-place of the physiologist and bio-chemist Otto von Fürth (1867-1938 Vienna), of the director of the Milanese academy of music Ricardo Pick-Mangiagalli (1882-1949 Milan) and of the American writer and journalist Owen Elford (formerly Otto Fürth, born in 1894).

The Jewish quarter used to exist most probably from the 16th cent. in the Bezděkov suburb (Nové Strakonice), E and SE of the castle, along both banks of the Volyňka creek. It consisted of about 20 J. houses before the mid-19th cent. Most of the houses on the E bank of the Volyňka creek, the synagogue and the community house were pulled down in 1970-76.

(The earliest recorded **prayer hall** burnt down in 1741. - **The old synagogue**, which had been built to replace the prayer hall, collapsed in 1858. - **A new synagogue** was built on the site of the old one in 1860, on the E edge of the J. quarter. It was used by the Hussite Church from 1951 and pulled down in 1976.)

The cemetery lies 1,600 m WSW of the castle, S of the road to the village Drachkov. The cemetery existed here most probably about 1700, the earliest legible tombstone dates from 1736, burials also after World War II. It is a well-preserved cemetery with Baroque and Classicist tombstones.

The town has a remarkable castle - formerly a monastery of the Maltese Knights - built in the course of the 13th to the 18th cent. (today housing a museum and exhibition hall), churches from the 13th - 18th cent., old houses and other places of interest.

The following J. communities used to be in the vicinity: **Lažany** /or *Enisovy Lažany* (12 km N, a prayer room recorded in the 19th cent.); **Osek** /Ger. *Wossek* (8 km NE, a synagogue was built in 1817, pulled down in 1980, a J. street, a cemetery from the 1st half of the 19th cent., where Franz Kafka's grandparents were buried, his father was born in Osek).

STRÁŽ   **108**
(Ger. *Neustadtl am Klinger*)

Small town in Bohemia, 125 km WSW of Prague, 17 km SE of the district town Tachov. S. became a small town before 1331.

The first J. families to settle in S. are said to have come from Germany - Jews who had been expelled or fled before pogroms. The earliest records of J. settlement date from 1331, a J. community existed here most probably in the 15th cent. 15 J. families lived in S. in 1580 but only 2 J. families are mentioned in the 1620 census and no Jews are recorded in the 1651 census. We cannot exclude that the J. community ceased to exist after an expulsion (detailed documentary records are not available because the J. community's archives were destroyed by fire in 1876). The synagogue was "revived" in 1664 and 18 J. families (98 persons) are recorded again in 1724, 47 J. families in the 1st half of the 19th cent. 31 persons of the J. faith lived in S. in 1930. The J. religious congregation was not reestablished after World War II as only one single J. survivor returned to S.

The Jewish street leads from the square to the west, towards the cemetery's church. There were about 15 J. houses and a synagogue here in 1838. There was no intact ghetto here, J. houses were scattered among Christian houses. Most of the J. houses have been preserved.

(**The old synagogue** used to stand on the S side of the J. street. According to the earliest preserved documentary records it was "renewed" in 1664. The synagogue was destroyed by fire in 1876. - **A new synagogue** was completed by 1882 on the site of the old one. Services were held there until 1938. It was burnt down by the Nazis in the autumn of 1938 and the remaining walls were pulled down in 1950.)

The cemetery lies 1 km NW of the square. Founded allegedly in 1330, documentary records date from 1450, the last time extended in 1860, burials until the Nazi occupation. It used to rank among cemeteries of utmost historical value with tombstones from the 15th cent. In the old part of the cemetery there used to be special rows of the Kohanim and the Levites. The cemetery suffered serious damage by the Nazis, most of the tombstones have been used as building stones. The oldest preserved tombstone dates from 1579.

There are three churches from the 14th up to the 18th cent. and other historical monuments in S.

The following J. communities and J. religious societies used to exist in the vicinity: **Ošelín** (13 km NNE, a house of prayer recorded in the 18th - 20th cent.); **Svojšín** /Ger. *Schweissing* (14 km NE, a J. community and a house of prayer recorded in the 17th - 19th cent., a cemetery from 1660 with tombstones from the 1st half of the 18th cent. near to the village Ošelín); **Cebiv** /Ger. *Zebau* (23 km NE, a synagogue of unknown origin, converted into a dwelling house); **Stříbro**, /Ger. *Mies* (town 19 km NE, a synagogue from 1879, converted into an administration building; a cemetery from 1900 with a grave of the victims of a death march who died in the spring of 1945); **Butov** /Ger. *Wuttau* (23 km NE, a prayer room existed here about 1700); **Prostiboř** (9 km ESE, remains of a synagogue from the mid-19th cent.; the birthplace of Isak Löw Hofmann von Hofmannsthal [1759-1849 Vienna], Head of the Vienna Jewish Community and great grandfather of the Austrian poet Hugo Hofmann von Hofmannsthal); **Telice** /Ger. *Dölitschen* (11 km ESE, the house in which a prayer room used to be was demolished after 1945, remains of a J. quarter, a cemetery with tombstones from the 2nd half of the 18th cent.); **Bernartice** /Ger. *Pernartitz* (5 km SSE, a J. community recorded in the 19th cent., remains of a J. quarter with remains of a synagogue of unknown origin); **Bělá nad Radbuzou** /Ger. *Weissensulz* (a small town 9 km SSW, a prayer room recorded in the 18th cent.). - An internment J. camp was set up in **Mílov** /Ger. *Mühlloh* (8 km W) in 1941.

5 km N Bor, a town with a Gothic-Renaissance castle with neo-Gothic alterations, churches and chapels dating from the 16th to the 18th cent., remains of a city wall, etc.; 7 km W Přimda, a small town with ruins of a Romanesque castle from the early 12th cent. - the oldest noble stone castle on the territory of Czechoslovakia, below the castle there are remains of an ancient town (e.g. a church from the 14th - 16th cent.), destroyed in an air raid in 1945.

(Ger. *Strassnitz*)

Town in Moravia, 245 km SE of Prague, 14 km ENE of the district town Hodonín. Chartered most probably in the 14th or 15th cent.

A J. community is said to have existed here in the early 15th cent. and to have suffered hardship during the Hussite wars. The earliest documentary records of J. settlement dates from 1490. At least 55 J. families lived in S. in 1669, 84 J. families were permitted to reside in S from the late 18th cent. 569 persons of the J. faith are recorded in 1848, only 323 in 1900 and the number dropped to 194 in 1930. The J. religious congregation was reestablished after World War II but due to a decrease in congregants it merged with the Hodonín J. religious congregation.

The common J. surname Dresnitz has been derived from the old J. name of the town.

The names of nearly 30 rabbis have been recorded since the early 17th cent. The community's rabbis include famous scholars and authors of important theological works. Rabbi Shabtai ben Meir HaKohen, of Mohylev, called Šach (Shah), officiated here in 1650-57 (his grave in the Holešov cemetery has become a place of pilgrimage). Rabbi Moses Schreiber, called Hatam Sofer, from Frankfurt am M. officiated in S. in 1794-98 (visitors from all over the world seek his grave in Bratislava).

S. is the native town of the Viennese painter Margarete Siebenschein (1886 - ?? Israel), of the famous Germanist and Professor at the Charles University Hugo Siebenschein (1889-1970 Prague) and the writer Josef Vinař (1934).

(**The former Jewish settlement** is said to have been in the quarter called Staré Město [The Old Town], on the SW boundary of the town. The quarter was burnt down during the Hussite wars.)

A new **Jewish quarter** was established on the NE boundary of the town (today's Sadová, Bzenecká, Zákoutí, B.

Hrejsové and Kramářská streets). The historical core of the quarter was built most probably in the 15th - 16th cent. 44 inhabited houses and 13 perhaps deserted houses are mentioned in 1669, 56 houses in 1834 and about 80 in the mid-19th cent. It was not an enclosed ghetto, Christian houses were scattered in the J. quarter. Most of the houses, today rebuilt, have been preserved. A modern housing estate was built in the SE part of the former J. quarter in 1970. **The school** and the rabbi's home used to be in Bzenecká No. 33.

The synagogue is in Sadová street, 500 m NNE of the main square. The synagogue, of unknown origin, was rebuilt in the neo-Romanesque style

after 1869 and renewed in 1906. Services were held until World War II. The interior and furnishing were destroyed during the Nazi occupation and the women's NW extension was pulled down. It has been used as a store house but plans have been made to convert the building into a concert hall. The synagogue is surrounded by a cemetery from three sides, which is unusual in our country.

The cemetery lies in Sadová street, on the NE side of the town, next to the park, surrounding the château. It was founded to replace an older closed-down cemetery in the quarter Staré Město: allegedly in the 15th cent., most probably after 1627. The oldest legible

tombstones date from 1647, burials also after World War II. Many remarkable Baroque and Classicist tombstones. The cemetery was repaired in 1986 - 87.

Remains of two 16th cent. Roman type gates survive of the former fortification. The town has a château from the 15th - 19th cent., today housing a museum of folk art, churches from the 15th up to the 18th cent. and other places of interest. Well-known folklore festivals are held in S. every summer.

A religious society used to be in **Velká nad Veličkou** (a small town 15 km E, a prayer room, converted into a flat; a cemetery from the 2nd half of the 19th cent.) and a religious congregation in **Vrbovce** /Hung. *Verbóc* (a small town in Slovakia, 15 km SE, a synagogue used by an agricultural cooperative; a cemetery with tombstones from the 1st half of the 19th cent.).

*3 km SW near the village **Petrov** - a picturesque complex of wine cellars from the 18th - 19th cent., protected as a conservation area (some cellars open to the public); E and SE **Bílé Karpaty** (White Carpathians) a wooded chain of mountains forming a natural border between Moravia and Slovakia (the highest peak - 970 m).*

Town in Bohemia, 115 km SSW of Prague, 24 km SE of the district town Klatovy. Chartered as early as the mid-13th cent.

The earliest documentary records of J. settlement date from 1562. Only isolated J. families must have resided in S. in the 16th cent., no J. population is recorded in the town in 1618. The first J. family to settle again in S. came in 1625 and was followed by other J. families; a prayer room was established in 1659-60. Ten J. families are recorded in the town in 1700, 15 J. families (93 persons) in 1734 and 26 (124 persons) in 1825. By 1860 the J. population considerably increased: 300 persons of the J. faith in 1860 but only 171 persons in 1890 and 112 in 1930. About 10 congregants returned to the town after the liberation but the J. religious congregation was not reestablished after World War II.

J. families played an important role in the foundation of the famous match industry: Bernard Fürth founded a phosphorus match factory in the 1st half of the 19th cent., the two local match factories were managed by the Fürth family from 1903. J. houses in S. were damaged during a pogrom in 1866.

The well-known Prague painter-autodidact Robert Guttmann (1880-1942 Lodz) was born in S.

The Jewish street used to be in today's Vodní street, SW of the square. J. houses were concentrated in the S part of the street since the 17th cent. (10 houses in 1825, 14 in 1837). The street burnt down in 1923 and some of the houses have been replaced by modern buildings.

(**The first synagogue** or prayer hall was established in 1659-60: a wooden structure in a courtyard on the W side of the J. street. Destroyed by fire before 1710. - **The second synagogue** was built in 1709 on the site of the first one. Services were held there until

1859, later it was converted into a dwelling house, damaged by fire in 1923 and pulled down. - **The third synagogue** was built in the neo-Romanesque style in 1857-59 on the E side of the J. street. Services were held until World War II, demolished in 1963-64.)

The old cemetery is in the street Příkopy, 80 m SW of Vodní street, next to the city wall. Founded about 1626, enlarged in the 17th, 18th and 19th cent. The earliest legible tombstone dates from 1708, the last burial was in 1875. It represents a valuable cemetery with Baroque and Classicist tombstones. Repaired in 1987-88.

The new cemetery lies 900 m SW of the old cemetery, near the road to the village Červené Dvorce. Founded most probably in 1876, the last burial was in 1946.

The town has several remarkable churches and chapels from the 14th up to the 18th cent., beautiful Renaissance houses and remains of a city wall. A museum of local glassmaking and match production.

The following J. communities used to be in the vicinity: **Podmokly** (4 km E, a J. quarter; a synagogue, of unknown origin, converted into a flat; an early 18th cent. cemetery); **Petrovice** (6 km WSW, a prayer room existed in the 19th cent.); **Hrádek** /Ger. *Bürgel* (3 km NNW, a prayer room recorded in the 19th - 20th cent.).

The picturesque country surrounding the town is rich in historical monuments (strongholds, châteaux, manors and churches); gold was washed in the Otava river S and N of the town; 2 km W Svatobor, a hill (845 m) with a lookout-tower; towards the south rolls the wooded Šumava mountain range (peaks over 1,000 m), popular with tourists.

SVĚTLÁ NAD SÁZAVOU 111

Town in Bohemia, 80 km SE of Prague, 13 km NW of the district town Havlíčkův Brod. Became a small town in 1562 and a town in 1937.

The first J. family settled in S. most probably in the 17th or the 1st quarter of the 18th cent. One J. family lived in S. in 1721, 4 families in 1787 and 10 in 1802. An autonomous J. religious congregation was established in 1854. The number of J. families increased in the second half of the 19th cent. Only 79 persons of the J. faith (3% of the total population) are recorded in S. in 1930. The J. religious congregation was not revived after World War II.

S. is the native town of the Czech-J. patriotic poet Leopold Kohn (1838-1901 Mimoň) and of the composer Oskar Morawetz (1917 - resident in Canada), author of the composition *The Diary of Anne Frank.*

There was no ghetto in the town, before the mid-19th cent. J. houses were concentrated in the suburb Malá Strana on the S bank of the Sázava river. A prayer room used to be in one of the houses.

The synagogue is in the street Pěšinky No. 15, between the square and the Sázava river, SE of the Catholic church. Opened in 1889, it is an older partly timber-framed building. A prayer hall with a wooden ceiling imitating a vaulted ceiling, a wooden women's gallery. The rabbi's home and a flat for the shammash used to be in the building. Services were held here until World War II. Since 1949 the synagogue has been used by the Hussite church. The original furnishing has been preserved, except for the aron ha-kodesh.

(**The old cemetery** used to be in the suburb Malá Strana, near the road to

Lipnička. Founded in 1742, burials until about 1886. All the tombstones were removed during the Nazi occupation.)

The new cemetery is 500 m N of the square, in Komenského street leading to Horní Bohušice. Adjacent to the municipal cemetery. Burials from 1887 to World War II.

S. has a neo-Baroque château from the late 19th cent. and a Gothic-Renaissance church.

The following J. communities and religious societies used to be in the vicinity: **Lipnice nad Sázavou** (small town 6 km S, a prayer room recorded in the 19th - 20th cent., father of the composer Gustav Mahler was born here); **Zahrádka** (12 km SW, a prayer room existed here from the 19th cent. probably until World War I); **Ledeč nad Sázavou** (town 9 km WNW, a synagogue from 1739, today used as a store house, an early 17th cent. cemetery with valuable Baroque tombstones; the mother of the composer Gustav Mahler was born in this town).

E and W is the charming valley of the Sázava river; 6 km S Lipnice nad Sázavou with a Gothic-Renaissance castle (some parts are open to visitors) and a museum of the writer Jaroslav Hašek (1883-1923), author of The Good Soldier Schweik.

ŠIROKÉ TŘEBČICE   112
(formerly *Rozlezlé Třebčice*, Ger. *Weiten-Trebetitsch*)

Village in Bohemia, 80 km WNW of Prague, 20 km S of the district town Chomutov.

Jews settled here before 1618. 12 J. families (50 persons) lived in the village in 1724, they had a prayer hall or a synagogue. Before the mid-19th cent. the J. population numbered 57 families (about 400 persons, i.e. 60% of the total population). Later the number of J. in the community dropped: 38 families (208 persons) in 1890, only 32 persons in 1900 and 5 in 1930. The J. religious congregation merged with the Podbořany congregation in 1929.

The Jewish quarter took up the entire N part of the village green and spread further north. The former village ghetto, built most probably in the 1st half of the 18th cent., formed the heart of the J. quarter: it represents a noteworthy urban whole consisting of several blocks of houses on the NE side of the village green, divided by narrow streets. The houses were raised by one storey in the 19th cent. About 50% of the houses in the village were inhabited by J. families in 1843. Most of the houses have been preserved.

Remains of the synagogue in the centre of the ghetto, 20 m N of the village green. The synagogue was built in 1848 on the site of **an earlier synagogue** (built most probably in the 18th cent.). Services were held here until about 1929. The upper part of the synagogue was demolished in 1935; only the peripheral walls of the ground floor were left, the entrances in the W front were walled up and the space has been used as a courtyard.

The cemetery is set among fields, 1 km E of the synagogue, on the N sloping bank of a brook. It is said to have been founded in the 15th cent.; it must have existed in the 1st half of the 18th cent. (the rules of the local Burial Society date from 1743-4). Burials until the Nazi occupation. Baroque and Classicist tombstones. Modern tombstones were removed by the Nazis during the war.

A Baroque château from the 1st half of the 18th cent. and a church from the 18th - 19th cent. are to be found in the village.

There used to be many J. communities and religious societies with prayer rooms in the vicinity: **Chomutov** /Ger. *Komotau* (town 20 km N, the synagogue from 1876 was destroyed by the Nazis, remains of a cemetery from 1892; the native town of the German - J. poet Max Fleischer [1880-1941 in a concentration camp] and of the writer and playwright Viktor Fleischer [1882-1951 South Africa]); **Hořenice** /form. *Hořenec*, Ger. *Horschenz* (16 km NNE, a synagogue built in 1839, pulled down

about World War I, a valuable ghetto from the town-planning point of view, remains of a cemetery, destroyed by the Nazis, a grave of the victims of a death march in spring 1945); **Bílence** /Ger. *Bielenz, Billentz* (17 km NNE, remains of a J. quarter, a synagogue from the 1st half of the 19th cent., converted into a house; remains of a cemetery from the 1st half of the 19th cent., destroyed by the Nazis); **Údlice** /Ger. *Eidlitz* (small town 17 km NNE, a synagogue from about 1694, rebuilt in the 18th and 19th cent., pulled down after 1920, minor remains of a 16th cent. J. quarter, an old 16th cent. cemetery, entirely destroyed by the Nazis, remains of a new cemetery from the 2nd half of the 19th cent., destroyed by the Nazis, a grave of the victims of a death transport in 1945); **Jirkov** /Ger. *Görkau* (town 24 km NNE, remains of a small ghetto with a synagogue from about 1865, today used as a store house); **Čeradice** /Ger. *Tscheraditz* (8 km NE, remains of a J. quarter with a small synagogue, converted into a dwelling house; remains of a cemetery from about the 1st half of the 19th cent.); **Libočany** /Ger. *Libotschan, Liebotschan* (10 km NE, a synagogue of unknown origin, pulled down about 1967); **Žatec** /Ger. *Saaz* (town 12 km NE, a synagogue from 1872, today used as store-house; remains of a cemetery from 1869, destroyed by the Nazis; the native town of the linguist Otto Stein [1893 - about 1942 Poland] and of the composer Karel Reiner [1910-1979 Prague]); **Liběšice** /Ger. *Liebeschitz* (16 km E, a synagogue recorded in the 18th - 20th cent., an old cemetery from about the 18th cent., devastated by the Nazis, remains of a new cemetery from 1897, destroyed by the Nazis); **Líčkov** (16 km E., a prayer room recorded in the 19th cent.); **Libořice** (10 km ESE, a prayer room recorded in the 17th - 19th cent.); **Měcholupy** /Ger. *Michelob* (11 km ESE, a small synagogue from 1857, converted into a dwelling house; remains of a cemetery from 1857, devastated by the Nazis); **Želeč** /Ger. *Seltsch* (13 km ESE, a prayer room recorded in the 19th cent., remains of a J. quarter); **Nečemice** (18 km ESE, a prayer room recorded in the 19th - 20th cent.); **Liběšovice** (9 km SE, a prayer room from about the 19th cent., pulled down after World War II); **Letov** /Ger. *Ledau, Letau* (7 km SE, remains of a J. quarter, a synagogue of unknown origin, pulled down in 1874, a cemetery from about the 1st half of the 18th cent. with tombstones from the 1st half of the 19th cent., devastated by the Nazis); **Blšany** /Ger. *Flöhau* (a small town 9 km SE, a prayer room recorded in the 18th - 20th cent.); **Podbořany** /Ger. *Podersam* (town 6 km SSE, remains of a synagogue from 1874, converted into a garage; remains of a cemetery from 1886, destroyed by the Nazis; the birth-place of the German-J. poet and prose writer Max Glaser, pseud. Litumlei [1875-??]); **Kryry** /Ger. *Kriegern* (a small town 12 km SSE, a religious society recorded in the late 19th cent.); **Podbořanský Rohozec** /form. *Německý Rohozec*, Ger. *Deutsch - Rust, Rust* (13 km SW, remains of a J. quarter, a mid-19th cent. cemetery; the birthplace of the traveller to Saudi Arabia Eduard Glaser [1855-1908 Munich]; a synagogue from 1816, demolished in 1957, the aron ha-kodesh from the synagogue has been transferred and installed in the Klaus synagogue in Prague); **Mašťov** /Ger. *Maschau* (a small town 8 km WSW, the last synagogue built in 1830, pulled down after 1960, remains of two J. streets, remains of a cemetery allegedly from the 15th cent., devastated by the Nazis, about 50 tombstones were removed and deposited in the Teplice museum in 1982); **Žďár** /Ger. *Saar* (an extinct village 15 km W, a J. quarter and prayer house recorded in the 18th - 19th cent., houses demolished after 1950); **Kadaň** /Ger. *Kaaden*, (town 12 km NW, a prayer room from 1887 in the bastion of the town's fortifications, converted into a flat; a synagogue from 1890, demolished by the Nazis; a cemetery from 1884, destroyed by the Nazis, remains of a Nazi destroyed J. section from 1924 in the municipal cemetery).

Detention camps for men of mixed marriages used to be in 1944-45 in the villages **Načetín** /Ger. *Natschung* and **Kalek** /Ger. *Kallich* (31 km NNW). In the small town **Březno** /Ger. *Priesen* (13 km NNE) 426 prisoners - victims of a transport from a concentration camp - were buried in the spring of 1945. At least 230 prisoners - victims of a railway transport from a concentration camp - were buried in the village **Kaštice** /Ger. *Kaschitz* (4 km SE) in April 1945.

*Several remarkable manors, strongholds and churches are to be found in the vicinity; 11 km S **Vroutek**, a small town with an extremely well-preserved Romanesque church from the 13th cent.; 3 km SSW **Krásný Dvůr**, a beautiful* *Baroque château (open to visitors) with several Classicist and Romantic style structures in the surrounding large park; the historical centres of **Žatec** (12 km NE) and **Kadaň** (12 km NW) have been declared urban conservation areas.*

ŠVIHOV 113

Small town in Bohemia, 105 km SW of Prague, 10 km N of the district town Klatovy. Š. became a small town most probably in the 14th cent., chartered as a town in 1501.

The earliest documentary record of J. settlement (perhaps an isolated J. family) dates from 1570. Continuous J. settlement began in 1632, a prayer room is recorded in 1670. The J. population numbered 15 J. families (78 persons) in 1724, 17 families in 1846. The number of congregants had dropped and after 1890 the Švihov J. religious congregation merged with the Klatovy J. religious congregation. Only 21 Jews lived in Š. in 1930.

The Jewish street - a ghetto - today's Vrchlického street, N of the square, parallel with its N side. The ghetto is said to have originated in 1736 as a result of a forced exchange of houses between the Jewish and Christian inhabitants. The ghetto consisted of about 16 houses in J. ownership. Several J. families resided outside the ghetto from 1759. The street was destroyed by fire in 1773. Some of the houses, today rebuilt, have been preserved.

(**The old synagogue**, a wooden building of unknown origin, burnt down in 1773. **A new synagogue** was built about 1783, in the Rococo style on the E side of street. Services were held there until World War II. The synagogue was pulled down after 1960.)

The old cemetery is 600 m ESE of the square, near a railway and the road leading to the municipal cemetery (150 m SSE). Consecrated in 1644, enlarged in 1828. The oldest tombstones date from the time of the cemetery's foundation, burials until the 2nd half of the 19th cent., one burial still in 1913.

Remarkable Renaissance and Baroque tombstones.

The new cemetery is 150 m E of the old cemetery, beyond the railway. Founded in 1878, burials until World War II. Tombstones are to be found only in a small part of the cemetery, most of the burial ground has not been used.

There is a remarkable water castle from the 15th - 16th cent. (open to the public) in the town and a church from the 14th - 18th cent.

The following J. communities used to be in the vicinity: **Lužany** (7 km NNE, a prayer house from about the 19th cent., pulled down after 1946); **Přeštice** (town 10 km NNE, a synagogue from 1910, demolished in 1974, a cemetery from the early 20th cent., the native town of Georg Leopold Weisel [1804-1873 Všeruby], a writer who had collected and later published a book of J. legends); **Dolní Lukavice** /Ger. *Unter-Lukawitz* (13 km NNE, a mid-19th cent. synagogue, converted into a dwelling house; a cemetery allegedly from the late 15th cent. with tombstones from the early 18th cent.); **Vlčí** /Ger. *Wölfling* (6 km NE, a synagogue from about the 1st half of the 19th cent.,

today used as a storehouse); **Malinec** (6 km E, a synagogue from about the 1st half of the 19th cent., converted into a dwelling house); **Klatovy** (town 9 km S, a synagogue from 1879, converted into a records office; a cemetery from 1887 with a monument in memory of the victims of the Nazis dedicated in the cemetery in 1989; the native town of Gustav Sicher [1880-1960 Prague], Chief Rabbi of Bohemia and Moravia, of the Czech-J. poet and painter Karel Fleischmann [1897-1944 Birkenau] and the Czech-J. poet František Gottlieb [1903-1974] Prague]); **Merklín** (small town 10 km NW, a synagogue from 1826, converted into a dwelling house; a cemetery with tombstones from the early 18th cent.); **Dnešice** (13 km N, a synagogue from the 1st half of the 19th cent., converted into flats).

There are many places of interest in the surrounding villages (manors, churches); 7 km NNE Lužany, a neo-Renaissance château from the 16th - 19th cent. with a park (open to the public).

TÁBOR   **114**

District town in Bohemia, 75 km SSE of Prague. Founded in 1420, chartered in 1437.

The earliest documentary record dates from 1548 and mentions "Jew of Tábor" but the first J. family is recorded in the town only in 1594 (until that year J. were not permitted to stay in the town overnight). Two J. families are recorded in T. in 1618, 8 families in 1653 (this number was not to be surpassed until the mid-18th cent.). 18 J. families resided in the town in 1769, 32 (according to another source only 20) in 1830. The J. population stood at 212 persons of the J. faith in 1840, 455 in 1884, 311 in 1930 and only 265 in 1933.

The municipal authorities tried to expel Jews from T. several times during the 17th cent. An order to establish a ghetto was issued in 1769 but was not carried out.

A J. community was established in

the 1st half of the 17th cent., the first cantor came to T. about 1686, a rabbi in 1843. The J. religious congregation was revived after World War II but was later changed into a synagogue group (the prayer room was used until 1972).

(**The first prayer room** was established about 1643 in an old house in the square Tržní nám. Services were held there until 1885, later on the house was pulled down. - **The synagogue**, between the streets Hradební and Na parkánech, was built in 1885 in the so-called oriental style. Services were held there until World War II. After the war it had been used as a storehouse and was pulled down in 1977.)

Remains of **an old cemetery** in Korandova street, 270 m SSW of the gate Bechyňská brána. Connected with a neighbouring park (formerly a municipal cemetery). Consecrated in 1634, later enlarged. Burials until the end of the 19th cent. All the tombstones were removed during the Nazi occupation. A monument in memory of Nazi victims was erected here in 1955. The cemetery has been converted into a small park.

(A **new cemetery** was founded in the late 19th cent. in the N part of the town. All the tombstones were removed by the Nazis, the ceremonial hall was demolished and the cemetery converted into a small park.)

The historical centre of T. with a great number of historical monuments has been declared an urban conservation area: remains of a Gothic castle and fortifications with a gate, several churches from the 15th up to the 18th cent., a late Gothic town hall and many outstanding Gothic and Renaissance houses. T. was founded by the Hussites and became a centre of the Hussite movement. The name of the town comes from the hill Tabor near Nazareth. The great lake Jordán on the N side of the town is called after the Biblical river.

The following J. communities used to be in the vicinity: **Prudice** (10 km N, a prayer room existed there in the 18th cent., a cemetery with tombstones from the 18th cent.); **Nemyšl** (11 km NNE, a J. community with a prayer room is said to have existed there in the mid-

19th cent.); **Jistebnice** (a small town 11 km NW, minor remains of a synagogue of unknown origin; a valuable cemetery with tombstones from the mid-17th cent., a stream called Cedron flows through J.); **Střezimíř** (13 km NNW, a prayer room recorded in the 19th - 20th cent.).

*The surrounding countryside is rich in castle ruins, strongholds, châteaux, manors and other places of interest; to the west is the charming romantic valley of the **Lužnice** river.*

TACHOV 115
(Ger. *Tachau*)

District town in Bohemia, 130 km WSW of Prague, 55 km WNW of Pilsen. T. was founded and chartered in the 2nd half of the 13th cent.

Jews are said to have resided in T. as early as the 13th cent. but documentary records mention 5 J. families only in 1552. The J. population numbered 15 J. families in 1605, 17 families (104 persons) in 1724, 266 persons in 1836, 287 persons of the J. faith in 1890 and only 179 in 1930.

A J. community is said to have existed here in the 13th cent., according to other sources it was established (or legally reconstituted) in 1605: the community's statute issued by the municipal council dates from that year. At the end of the 19th cent. the religious congregations in the Tachov vicinity were administered by the Tachov J. religious congregation and their Torah scrolls were brought to the town. The religious congregation was not re-established in T. after World War II.

Rabbi Moses ben Hisdai, allegedly one of the authors of the prayer *Avinu malkenu* is said to have been born in T. sometime in the 13th cent. There was a world famous Talmud Torah school in T. at the turn of the 18th and 19th cent. At that time several rabbis resided in the town, which became the seat of the district rabbinate. T. is the native town of Rabbi Wilhelm Stern, who officiated as rabbi in Liverpool and Copenhagen and of Max Schornstein, Chief Rabbi of Copenhagen.

The Jewish street - now K. H. Borovského street - in the S part of the town's historical centre, between the square and the city wall. There were 4 houses in J. ownership in T. in 1554, 8 in 1608, 12 in the mid-18th cent. and later on over 20 houses in the street. The ghetto suffered serious damage during fires in 1719, 1748, 1818 (most houses rebuilt) and 1911. After last fire most of the former houses were pulled down.

(**The old synagogue** used to be in the J. street, by the city wall. It stood there as early as the beginning of the 17th cent., enlarged after the 1818 fire, pulled down after the 1911 fire. - A **new synagogue** was built in 1911-12 on the site of the old one. Built in the Art Nouveau style after the design of architect Alfred Grotte. Services were held there until 1938. The synagogue was burnt down and demolished by the Nazis.)

(**The first cemetery** is said to have existed as early as the 13th cent. It ceased to exist about the 17th cent. and no traces are left.)

The second cemetery is 450 m ESE of the square, by the crossroad of the roads leading to Velký Rapotín and to Trnová. The cemetery was officially recognized in 1615 (but had been used before), burials until 1933. The cemetery was full of graves with valuable 17th cent. tombstones. Graves of rabbis were situated by the W edge of the cemetery, e.g. the grave of Rabbi Nahum Sofer (died 1815), to which crowds of pilgrims used to flock. The cemetery was devastated by the Nazis, damaged in an exchange of fire in 1950, reduced in size in 1968 (the W part with the graves of rabbis was closed down) and will most probably be completely liquidated. At present the most precious tombstones are being gradually transferred to the cemetery in Mariánské Lázně.

The third cemetery lies 1,500 m SE of the square, near the road to Trnová. Founded in 1933, only 7 tombstones are left. Prisoners of war were buried here during World War II, later a municipal urn grove was established here. - About 600 prisoners - victims of a railway transport from the Buchenwald concentration camp (200 were killed at the local railway station) - were cremated here in April 1945. In 1989 a monument in their memory was erected above the mass grave containing their ashes.

A grave-mound - N of the town, near the road to Ctiboř, above the graves of 232 prisoners and victims of death marches in Western Bohemia. About 108 women from the Auschwitz concentration camp (murdered near Nýrsko) and prisoners from Buchen-

cent.); **Studánka** /Ger. *Schönbrunn* (3 km SW, a prayer room existed here in the 19th cent.); **Lesná** /Ger. *Schönwald* (8 km SW, a house of prayer recorded in the 19th cent.).

Strongholds, châteaux, manors and noteworthy churches are to be found in the surrounding villages.

TEPLICE 116
(formerly *Teplice - Šanov*, Ger. *Teplitz - Schönau*)

District town in Bohemia, 75 km NW of Prague. T. became a small town in 1383, a town in the 15th cent.

The earliest documentary record of J. settlement dates from 1414, a J. community existed here most probably about 1480. The J. population numbered 29 J. families in 1600, 231 persons (about one third of the total population) in 1652, 60 families (320 persons) in 1724. About 550 persons of the J. faith (12% of the total population) in the mid-19th cent., 1,865 persons in 1890 and 3,213 (11%) in 1930.

Only a Reform rite synagogue had been in the town since the 1st half of the 19th cent. but in the early 20th century the number of Orthodox J. began to increase and the first strictly Orthodox prayer hall was established in 1907. And old ritual bath-house, which had fallen into disuse, was renovated in 1923, an Orthodox synagogue was consecrated in 1925 and a private Orthodox Beth ha-Midrash was established in 1934.

The Teplice J. religious congregation was revived after World War II (over 200 congregants) but was changed later to a synagogue group. Its present address: Lípová ul. 25, 415 01 Teplice.

Teplice is the native town of the Vienna painter Otto Herschel (1871 - after 1950, USA), the composer Arthur Willner (1881-1959 London), and of the Czech-J. poet Hanuš Bonn (1913-1941 Mathausen). The writer Arthur Breisky (1885 Roudnice n. L. - 1910 New York) lived in T. in 1905-10.

(The Jewish quarter - a ghetto - SE of the main square, N of the château.

wald and other places were buried here. Relics of victims were being brought here from 1946, the barrow was mounded in 1948 and reconstructed in 1985.

T. has a Baroque château (formerly a Romanesque castle from the 12th cent.), three churches from the 13th - 18th cent., remarkable Gothic houses and large sections of preserved fortifications.

The following J. communities and religious societies used to be in the vicinity: **Tisová** /Ger. *Tissa* (6 km SE, a prayer room existed here in the 19th - 20th cent.); **Částkov** /Ger. *Schossenreith* (5 km SE, a prayer room recorded in the 19th cent.); **Nové Sedliště** /Ger. *Neu-Zedlisch* (8 km SSE, a synagogue allegedly built in 1786-88, pulled down after 1917, remains of a J. quarter, a cemetery with tombstones from the early 18th cent.); **Labuť** /Ger. *Labanth* (10 km SSE, a synagogue or prayer room recorded in the 19th cent.); **Dlouhý Újezd** /Ger. *Langendörflas* (3 km SSW, a synagogue recorded in the 18th - 19th cent., remains of a ghetto, a cemetery from the 18th cent.); **Pořejov** /Ger. *Purschau* (an extinct village, 7 km SSW, a synagogue from the mid-19th cent., demolished together with the whole village after 1970, a cemetery with tombstones from the mid-18th

The quarter had been developing from the 16th cent., in 1620 it consisted of 11 houses and over 50 houses are recorded in three streets in the mid-19th cent. The ghetto was demolished after World War II. - J. curative baths existed outside the ghetto as early as the 18th cent. and a J. hospital was built beyond the ghetto's boundaries in 1831.)

(**The old synagogue** used to be on the S edge of the ghetto. Recorded in the 16th cent., rebuilt several times after fires. Observing the Reform rite since the 1830s, services until 1882. In 1925 it became an Orthodox rite synagogue. Orthodox services were held there until 1938. The synagogue was demolished after World War II. - **A new synagogue** was built in 1880-82 after the design of architect Wilhelm Stiassny, combining the neo-Renaissance and Moorish styles. Built between Chelčického and Hálkova streets, E of the main square. Services were held there until 1938 [blown up by the Nazis]).

The present **prayer hall** is 800 m E of the main square, in Lípová No. 25. Established in 1945. The building houses a smaller winter prayer room, a meeting room, a community hall, and a cantor's home.

(**The first cemetery** used to be on the site of the present theatre in the street U divadla. Founded not later than 1480, burials until 1669, later on ceased to exist. Three tombstones from the 16th and 17th cent. were transferred to the second cemetery. - **The second cemetery** used to be E of the main square, between Jungmannova and Chelčického streets, S of the Czech Brethren's Protestant church. Consecrated about 1669, burials most probably until 1862. The cemetery with its remarkable Renaissance and Baroque tombstones was completely destroyed by the Nazis.)

The third cemetery is 700 m NW of the main square, in the street called Hřbitovní, entrance from the street Křižíkova. It forms the S part of the complex of municipal cemeteries. Founded in 1862. It was not damaged by the Nazis and is still used today. Children's graves by the NE wall, Soviet soldiers buried by the SW wall in 1945.

About 50 old tombstones were removed from the J. cemetery in Mašťov

and transferred to the Regional Museum in 1982.

Ruins of a castle from the 15th - 16th cent., a château from the 15th - 18th cent. (housing a museum), a 16th cent. church and many Classicist style buildings are to be found in the town. T. is a well-known spa with curative thermal springs.

The following J. communities and J. religious societies used to exist in the vicinity: **Soběbruhy** /Ger. *Soborten* (3 km NE, formerly a village with mostly J. population, a synagogue built around the beginning of the 18th cent., pulled down before 1958, a cemetery from probably from 1669 with valuable tombstones from the 17th cent.); **Sezemice** /Ger. *Sensomitz* (6 km SE, a J. community and a prayer room are said to have existed here in the mid-19th cent.); **Křemýž** /Ger. *Kremusch* (4 km S, an early 19th cent. prayer room, converted into a flat); **Bílina** (town 10 km SSW, a late 19th cent. synagogue, converted into a dwelling house, remains of a cemetery from 1891, devastated by the Nazis); **Duchcov** /Ger. *Dux* (town 7 km SW, a prayer room recorded from the early 20th cent. until 1938, Rudolf Popper [1873 Vienna - 1967], a painter of the Ústí region, died here); **Most** /Ger. *Brüx* (town 18 km SW, a synagogue from 1872-73, destroyed by the Nazis, a cemetery from 1878, the Most community's Rabbi Gotthard Deutsch was associated professor at the Hebrew Union College in Cincinnati [USA] in 1892-1921, M. is the native town of the German-J. poet Oskar Neumann [1894-1981 Ber Tuvia, Israel]); **Hořany** /Ger. *Hareth* (an extinct village 22 km SW, a synagogue from about 1817, rebuilt into a private house, demolished together with the whole village in 1972); **Líšnice** (24 km SW, a small 19th cent. synagogue, converted into a dwelling house). - The writer Bernard Kosiner (1903-1939 Prague) was born in **Hora Svaté Kateřiny**, a small town 26 km WSW. A mass grave of 313 prisoners - victims of a death march of April 1945 from an unidentified concentration camp - is to be found near the town **Krupka** /Ger.

Graupen, 4 km NE. 206 prisoners - victims of a railway transport from a concentration camp - were buried in April 1945 in **Třebušice** /Ger. *Triebschitz*, an extinct village 20 km NW.

5 km NE **Krupka**, a town with ruins of a Gothic castle, several churches from the 13th up to the 18th cent. and other sights; 7 km SW **Duchcov**, a town with a Baroque château (rich collections and an exhibition on the life of Giacomo Casanova); 9 km WSW **Osek** with noteworthy architecture of a former monastery from the 13th - 18th cent. and ruins of a Gothic castle; to the W and N spreads the mountain range **Krušné hory** (the highest peaks over 800 m).

TEREZÍN   117
(Ger. *Theresienstadt*)

Town in Bohemia, 50 km NNW of Prague, 3 km SSE of the district town Litoměřice. T. was founded as a fortress in 1780, chartered in 1782.

We have no documentary records of early J. settlement in T. In the mid-19th cent. 3 J. families resided in the town, a religious society (most probably with a prayer room) existed here towards the end of the century. 103 persons of the J. faith are recorded in T. in 1921, 98 in 1930. The majority were J. soldiers of the local garrison. Over 100 J. refugees from the parts of Bohemia that had been annexed by Germany settled in T. in 1938.

In **the municipal cemetery**, 1 km S of the square, there is a Jewish section with graves of J. prisoners of war from the Russian army and of Galician refugees from World War I. Tombstones of the late Classicist and Art Nouveau styles.

In 1941 the Nazis selected Terezín to be converted into a ghetto. In November 1941 the first transport of J. men from Prague arrived at T. In 1942 the inhabitants of Terezín were forced to move out, with the exception of J. families, and by the end of 1942 56,717 persons subject to the Nazi racial laws were interned in the overcrowded ghetto. (Until then the town's population stood at 7,000.)

By the year 1945 152,000 prisoners of 53 nationalities from most parts of Europe (including 75,000 Czechoslovak citizens) passed through Terezín. 87,000 people were deported from here to the Nazi extermination camps, 34,000 people died in Terezín. 30,000 deportees (including 8,500 Czechoslovak citizens) survived the war in Terezín. About 3,000 Czechoslovak citizens returned from Nazi extermination camps after the liberation. - A great number of J. prisoners were tortured to death or executed in the Small Fortress prison outside the ghetto.

In spite of the harsh living conditions in the ghetto the inmates managed to organize basic health care and social welfare, cultural and secret educational activities and to hold services (including Catholic and Protestant services). There were at least seven makeshift prayer rooms in the ghetto with Torah scrolls and ceremonial objects. In the beginning each prayer room had its own rabbi and cantor (of the many rabbis only four survived untill the end of 1944).

Hundreds of remarkable personalities from various parts of Europe passed through the Terezín ghetto - rabbis, politicians, scientists, artists. The ghetto gave rise to many works of art - poetry, music, drawings and paintings. The State Jewish Museum treasures a great collection of poetic and pictorial works of the children of Terezín (the great majority of these children died in extermination camps).

Many remarkable personalities perished in the Terezín ghetto. Let us mention here e.g. the German Rabbi Leopold Lukasch (the prize for humanity and tolerance, awarded annually by the Tübingen University, bears his name), the German sculptor Arnold Zadikow, the writer and organizer of the Czech - Jewish movement Eduard Lederer - Leda, Prague painters Richard Pollak - Karlín and Adolf Wiesner...

A great number of books, studies, documents and memoirs dealing with the Terezín ghetto have been published. Life in the ghetto has been depicted in prose and drama (e.g. Josef Bor: *The Terezín Requiem*, Jiří R. Pick: *A Born Loser with a Yellow Cap*) and films (e.g. *Butterflies Do Not Fly Here*, *Long Way*, *Transport from Paradise*). The Museum of the Ghetto is to be founded in 1991.

Memorial tablets are to be found on some buildings in the town, e.g. on No. 84 on the W side of the square (a Hebrew inscription has been preserved in the attic of a former prayer room), No. 215 on the E side of the square (the Terezín inmates rehearsed Verdi's *Requiem* and Smetana's *The Bartered*

Bride in the cellar), at the end of Nádražní street, 200 m S of the square (near a siding, in memory of transports to and from Terezín).

Two **mortuaries** (Jewish and Christian), 300 m S of the square, near the road leading to Bohušovice nad Ohří. Pious alterations were carried out after the liberation.

The ghetto's cemetery - 800 m S of the square, next to the municipal cemetery. The first burial in 1941, the last in October 1942 (the dead were later on cremated). The total of about 13,000 people were buried here in 11,250 individual and 217 mass graves. A mass grave of 16 men, executed in 1942, in the W part of the cemetery. - In 1975 the cemetery was altered - symbolic tombstones and a granite memorial in the shape of a menorah were erected. Individual tombstones bearing the names of those buried were transferred to the W part of the cemetery. The former cemetery of prisoners of war from the period of World War I forms a part of the cemetery (a Russian Orthodox memorial and a row of Muslim tombstones in the SW part).

The crematorium, in the centre of the cemetery, was built in 1942 and about 30,000 people were cremated there (up to 90 cremations a day). Part of the ashes in cardboard urns were interred, urns were also interred in Prague after the liberation. In 1944 the Nazis ordered to empty 22,000 urns into the nearby river Ohře. The interior of the crematorium is open to the public (a small exhibition has been installed there).

A symbolic **Lane of Nations** in the SE part of the cemetery. Granite blocks, bearing the names of all the countries whose citizens were imprisoned in Terezín.

A memorial in memory of the victims was erected in 1955 in the E part of the cemetery, bearing a Czech and Hebrew text in memory of the victims from sixteen European countries.

A tumulus and a small memorial are to be found 900 m N of the square, on the bank of the river Ohře where 22,000 urns with ashes of the ghetto's

inmates were emptied in 1944.

*The former garrison town has an extensive, well-preserved Baroque fortification system with two preserved gates. Simple Classicist houses and an early 19th cent. Classicist church. - **The Small Fortress**, 700 m E, served as a prison of the Gestapo in 1940-45 (35,000 prisoners passed through the prison). Interiors open to the public (today housing an exhibition). **A National Cemetery** was laid out in front of the Small Fortress where the remains of 26,000 prisoners were laid to rest. - Terezín and the Small Fortress have been declared a National Cultural Monument.*

The following J. communities used to exist in the vicinity: **Třebušín** /Ger. *Triebsch* (10 km NNE, a prayer room existed here in the 18th cent.); **Úštěk** /Ger. *Auscha* (town 15 km NE, remains of a small J. street, an unused tower-like synagogue from 1794, a cemetery with valuable tombstones from the 2nd half of the 16th cent.); **Vlastislav** /Ger. *Watislaw* (13 km WSW, a prayer room existed here in the 18th cent.); **Lovosice** /Ger. *Lobositz* (town 6 km W, a synagogue from 1762, destroyed by the Nazis; a J. quarter demolished after World War II, an old cemetery allegedly from the 17th cent., removed in 1956, remains of a new cemetery from about 1872, a ceremonial hall, used today by the municipal cemetery); **Milešov** (14 km WNW, a house of prayer recorded in the 19th - 20th cent.); **Litoměřice** /Ger. *Leitmeritz* (town 3 km NNW, a memorial tablet with a Hebrew inscription is to be found on the rear facade of the house which was built on the site of a medieval synagogue [Velká dominikánská street No. 102/22]; a medieval cemetery, closed down after 1541; a synagogue from 1883 or 1893, destroyed in an air raid in 1945, a small J. section from 1876 in the municipal cemetery; during World War II a branch of the Flossenbürg concentration camp and a crematorium used to be in L. to where inmates of the Terezín ghetto were sent to work - victims have been buried in the National Cemetery in Terezín); - Near the village **Horní** or **Dolní Chobolice** /Ger. *Koblitz* (10 km NE) a cemetery of unknown origin is said to have been until the 16th - 17th cent. (a J. community is not recorded here), some of the tombstones were allegedly transferred to the Úštěk cemetery. A cemetery from 1800 with tombstones from the 1st half of the 19th cent. (a J. community is not recorded here) is to be found near the village **Čížkovice** (8 km SW) - the cemetery was mainly used by the Milešov J. community and the Terezín garrison.

3 km NNW Litoměřice, an urban conservation area with a 14th-cent. castle, several churches from the 13th - 18th cent., a Gothic-Renaissance town hall and many other sights; 4 km NW Radobýl, a hill (399 m) offering a splendid view of the surrounding countryside.

TOVAČOV   118
(Ger. *Tobitschau*)

Town in Moravia, 215 km ESE of Prague, 12 km WSW of the district town Přerov. T. became a small town in the 14th cent., a town in the 15th cent.

We do not know whether J. families settled in T. in the 15th cent. (after the expulsion from Olomouc) or in the 16th cent. The earliest preserved documentary record of J. settlement dates from 1549, a J. community existed in T. most probably in the 16th cent. 25 J. families were granted permission to reside in the town from the 18th to the mid- 19th cent. 244 persons of the J. faith (the maximum) are recorded in 1869, 133 in 1900 and only 52 in 1930. In 1937 the Tovačov J. religious congregation merged with the Kojetín J. religious congregation. No J. citizens returned to the town after World War II.

The Viennese poetess and writer Sidonia Grünwald (1859-1907 Karlovy Vary) and the composer, violinist and violist Hugo Kauder (1888-1972 Bussum, the Netherlands) were born in T.

The ghetto used to exist from the 16th cent. in today's Denisova street and its neighbourhood (between the square and the NW city wall). The ghetto consisted of about 30 to 33 houses. Most of the houses, today rebuilt, have been preserved. **The school and rabbinate** used to be in No. 330.

(**A synagogue**, of unknown origin, used to stand on the S side of Denisova street. It was rebuilt or altered in the neo-Romanesque style in the 19th cent. Services were held there until World War II. Demolished in 1956.)

(**The old cemetery** used to be at the W end of Denisova street, on the site of today's department store. The cemetery, of unknown origin, was demolished most probably after the mid-17th

cent. Two tombstones were transferred to the new cemetery.)

The new cemetery is 300 m SW of the square, entrance from Švermova street. Founded most probably after the mid-17th cent., burials until 1941. Remarkable Renaissance and Baroque tombstones. A ceremonial hall from the 19th cent. with the coat-of-arms of the Guttmann family. Two tombstones from 1614 and 1615 were transferred here from the old cemetery and embedded in the cemetery's wall N of the ceremonial hall.

There are a water château from the 14th - 16th cent. (open to the public), an 18th cent. Baroque church and other sights in the town. A monument in memory of a tank battle that took place here the last days of World War II.

TŘEBÍČ 119

District town in Moravia, 140 km SE of Prague, 52 km W of Brno. Chartered in 1335.

The earliest reliable documentary record of J. settlement dates from 1433. A J. community existed here as early as the 16th cent. From the 18th cent. to the mid-19th cent. 260 J. families were permitted to reside in the town, the Třebíč J. community was one of the largest J. communities in Moravia. The J. population in T. numbered 1,770 persons of the J. faith (59% of the total population) in 1799, 1,612 (20%) in 1848, the number dropped to 663 in 1900 and to 300 in 1930. The J. religious congregation was re-established in T. after World War II but abolished soon after due to a considerable decrease in members.

Moriz Habrofsky (1822-1849 Germany), head of the student's revolutionary committee in Vienna and participant in the 1848 revolution, was a Třebíč native as were the Teplice rabbi and editor of the journal *Jüdische Chronik* Adolf Kurrein (1846-1919 Teplice) and the historian and Communist journalist Kurt Beer, pseud. Konrad (1908 - executed in 1941, Dresden) - there is a **memorial tablet** on his native house in Blahoslavova street.

The common J. surname Trebitsch has been derived from the German name of the town.

An extensive **Jewish quarter** - a ghetto - N of the city centre, separated by the Jihlava river. It consisted of two main streets with many narrow crosswise streets and two synagogues. 18 J. houses are recorded in 1556, 110 two-storey houses before the mid-19th cent., later on the number of houses increased. - The exact time of the ghetto's foundation is not known but its

construction had to adhere to building plans issued by the lordship in the 2nd half of the 16th cent. The easternmost part of the J. quarter (including a hospital and a slaughter-house) was demolished at the end of the 19th cent. - The Třebíč ghetto is a remarkable example of town-planning and ranks among the best-preserved ghettos in Europe. Renaissance and Baroque style details have survived in several houses. The J. quarter is to be restored in the near future.

The old synagogue on the square Tiché nám., on the W side of the J.

quarter, was built in 1639-42 (according to another source at the outset of the 18th cent. on the site of **an earlier wooden synagogue**). In 1757 the lordship issued an order to lower the synagogue to the hight of the surrounding houses. The synagogue was damaged by fires in 1759, 1821 and 1856. In the 19th cent. the building was twice redesigned (in the neo-Gothic style in 1880) and enlarged. Services until World War II. Since 1954 it has been used by the Hussite Church (interior modernized).

The new synagogue is in Blahoslavova street, in the E part of the J. quarter. According to one source it was built in the early 17th cent., according to another in 1737 on the site of **an earlier wooden synagogue** of unknown origin (destroyed by a fire in 1724). It was renovated in 1845, a W women's section was added in 1881. Service until World War I, thereafter the synagogue fell into disuse. The synagogue was to be converted into a J. museum after World War II. Recently plans have been made to convert it into a concert and exhibition hall. The interior is valuted with a stucco decorated ceiling.

(**The old cemetery** used to be close to the château, the origin of the cemetery is not known. Closed down in the 17th cent., no traces have been left.)

The new cemetery is set on a slope above the Týnský brook, 400 m NE of the old synagogue, entrance from the street Hrádek. Founded in the 1st half of the 17th cent., several times enlarged, still used. About 11,000 burials,

about 3,000 tombstones (the earliest tombstone dates from 1625). It is a remarkable cemetery with Renaissance, Baroque and Classicist tombstones. A monument in memory of the Nazi victims was dedicated in the cemetery in 1957. The ceremonial hall dates from 1903. The whole cemetery was restored in 1983-87.

Třebíč has a Renaissance-Baroque château, rebuilt from a formerly Romanesque-Gothic monastery, with an outstanding 13th cent. basilica (the château houses a collection of Christmas cribs and an exhibition of vanished art handicraft), churches from the 13th up to the 17th cent., Renaissance and Baroque houses, a wind-mill and other interesting sights.

A J. community used to be in **Moravské Budějovice** /Ger. *Mährisch-Budwitz* (town 17 km SSW, a medieval cemetery, vanished in the 18th cent. , a synagogue from 1910, used as a storehouse; a cemetery from 1908; the birthplace of the composer Ralph Benatzky [1884-1957 Zürich]).

*Gothic strongholds, castle ruins, châteaux, manors and other places of interest are to be found in the surrounding countryside. 9 km NNE **Hroznatín**, a village with a museum in the native* *house of the Czechoslovak president Ludvík Svoboda (1895-1979), commander of the Czechoslovak army corps in the Soviet Union during World War II.*

TŘEŠŤ
(Ger. *Triesch*)

120

Town in Moravia, 115 km SE of Prague, 14 km SW of the district town Jihlava. T. became a small town most probably in the 13th cent., a town in 1901.

We cannot exclude that Jewish families (expelled from Jihlava) began to settle in T. as early as in the 1st half of the 15th cent. but the earliest documentary records of J. settlement date from the 1st half of the 17th cent. Fourteen J. families are recorded in the small town in 1679, a J. community may have existed here in those days. In the course of the 18th cent. the number of J. considerably increased: 102 J. families were permitted to reside in the town from the late 18th cent. (in fact more families lived in T. at that time). 750 persons of the J. faith are recorded in 1830, 621 (14% of the total population) in 1848, only 169 in 1900 and the number dropped to 64 in 1930. The rabbinic post has remained unfilled since 1922. The J. religious congregation was not reestablished after World War II.

In the 18th cent. the J. community in T. had several rabbis-authors of theological works. Rabbi Wolf ben Löw Lichtenstadt (died in 1827), author of *Kedushat Israel*, was born in T. There was a yeshiva in T. until 1848.

The Jewish quarter formed the NW part of the town's centre (today's) square called nám. Svobody together

with Leninova street and the narrow streets running to the W). The ghetto was established not later than the 2nd half of the 17th cent. and was sealed off from the rest of the town by a wall with gates. In 1837 the ghetto consisted of 77 houses. The entire J. quarter burnt down in 1824. Many houses, today rebuilt, have been preserved.

The synagogue used to be in the S part of the former ghetto (W of the main square), in today's nám. Svobody. The synagogue originated probably by the rebuilding of an older synagogue which had been destroyed by the 1824 fire or it was newly built in 1825. A Classicist front with an arcade (the only arcaded synagogue in Czechoslovakia), a vaulted hall with a stucco ceiling. Services were held there until World War II, since 1959 it has been used by the Hussite Church.

The cemetery lies 1,500 m SSW of the synagogue, near the road to the village Hodice. Founded most probably in the 17th cent., enlarged in 1736 and in the 2nd half of the 19th cent., burials until World War II. The earliest legible tombstone dates from 1705. A valuable cemetery with Baroque and Classicist tombstones. Repaired in 1981.

There are a Renaissance château and two Gothic-Renaissance churches in T.

There are many lakes in the wooded countryside surrounding Třešť; 6 km SW Roštejn, a Gothic-Renaissance castle (open to the public) with a tower offering a wide view of the surrounding countryside.

TUČAPY 121

Village in Bohemia, 95 km SSE of Prague, 17 km SE of the district town Tábor.

There exists no documentary record of early J. settlement in T., a J. community was established here about 1697. The J. population numbered 12 families in 1723, about 30 before the mid-19th cent. and only 17 persons of the J. faith in 1921 (the entire J. religious congregation numbered 21 persons), 11 persons in 1930. In 1921 the J. congregation merged with the Soběslav J. religious congregation.

The conductor of the Czech Philharmonic Karel Ančerl (1908-73 Toronto, Canada) was born in T.

The Jewish quarter consisted of two parts separated by a pond (today drained), the same as the J. quarter in the neighbouring Myslkovice. A synagogue used to be in the N quarter (in the street leading to the village Dvorce), **a school** in No. 64 and **the rabbinate** in No. 65 (9 houses in 1830). The S quarter (today's street called Na nouzi, W of the road leading to the village Dírná) consisted of 13 houses and a hospital. The houses in both quarters, today rebuilt, have been preserved.

(The old **prayer room**, recorded in the late 17th cent., used to be probably on the first floor of the school in No. 64. It was closed down after the construction of the synagogue.)

The synagogue, in the N quarter, SW of the village centre, was built about the 1st half of the 19th cent. Services were held there until about World War I. Converted into a gymnasium in 1934, after 1950 rebuilt and modernized. The NW front with an entrance portal has been preserved.

The cemetery is at the W end of the S quarter, 300 m S of the synagogue, W of the lake Smíchov. Founded about 1713, the oldest legible tombstone dates from 1737, burials until about World War II. It is a well-preserved cemetery with Baroque and Classicist tombstones. Many old tombstones have been embedded in the cemetery wall.

The village has an 18th cent. Baroque church and a château of unknown origin, rebuilt in the late 19th cent.

The following J. communities and religious societies used to be in the vicinity: **Deštná** /Ger. *Deschna* (a small town 9 km ESE, a prayer room is said to have existed here from the 19th cent. until 1920); **Dvorce** (1 km SE, a prayer room is said to have existed here in the mid-19th cent.).

Town in Bohemia, 75 km NE of Prague, 12 km WSW of the district town Semily. Founded and chartered in the mid-13th cent.

The earliest documentary record of J. settlement dates from 1527, a J. community with a prayer room is said to have existed here at that time. There was no ghetto here in those days, 16 houses in J. ownership were scattered throughout the whole town. 45 J. families (about 300 persons) allegedly resided in the town in the mid-19th cent. but only 28 families (104 persons of the J. faith) in 1930. The J. religious congregation had been reestablished after World War II but was changed to a synagogue group in 1950, which ceased to exist later on. The rabbinic post has remained unfilled since 1916.

The Jewish quarter used to be in Krajířova street and its neighbourhood (250 m W of the square, 250 m E of the bridge over the Jizera river). It is said to have been established in the 1st quarter of the 18th cent., J. families were most probably forced to move here. It consisted of 21 houses in the mid-19th cent. Some of the houses, today rebuilt, have been preserved.

(**The first** known **synagogue** was a wooden structure in the centre of the town, S of the town-hall. Allegedly destroyed by fire in 1643. - **The second synagogue**, also wooden, was built in 1647, burnt down in 1707.)

The third synagogue is in Krajířova street, inside a block of houses. The synagogue was built about 1719 and redesigned later. Services were held there until World War II, later on the synagogue was used as a store-house. A simple Baroque structure, the interior furnishing has not been preserved.

(**The first cemetery** is said to have

been in the centre of the town, SW of the square. Abolished most probably in the 1st quarter of the 18th cent., no traces have been left.)

The second cemetery is in the street Pionýrů, 400 m S of the synagogue. Founded about 1720, enlarged for the last time in the 2nd half of the 19th cent., burials also after World War II. The earliest legible tombstones date from the late 17th cent. (allegedly transferred here from the old cemetery). Valuable Baroque and Classicist tombstones.

There are several remarkable churches from the 14th - 19th cent. in the town. On the N boundary of the town there is the Hrubý Rohozec château from the 13th - 19th cent., housing an exhibition on the development of fashion and collections of furniture. T. is a centre for the refinement of precious stones (The Bohemian Paradise Museum - collections of local precious stones and jewellery).

The writer Ivan Olbracht (1882-1952 Prague) is a native of **Semily**, a town 12 km ENE.

2 km NNE Dolánky (an ethnographic museum in a timber-framed farm house); N, NE and S spreads a romantic sandstone rock region with castle ruins, popular with tourists; S of the town Český ráj (The Bohemian Paradise), a charming region with remarkable sandstone rock formations.

UHERSKÝ BROD   123
(Ger. *Ungarisch-Brod*)

Town in Moravia, 260 km SE of Prague, 14 km ESE of the district town Uherské Hradiště. Chartered in 1272.

The earliest documentary record of J. settlement dates from 1470. J. families were not permitted to reside in the town until the mid-16th cent., with the exception of the suburban areas. Five J. families resided in the walled town in 1595, there were about 40 houses in J. ownership in the town about 1671. 438 J. died during the 1683 plague and about 100 J. were massacred from the Kuruczs (Hungarian peasant crusaders) in the same year. 241 families (936 persons) are recorded in U. B. in 1745, 160 J. families were permitted to reside in the town later (the number was probably surpassed). The J. population numbered 827 persons of the J. faith (34% of the total population) in 1843, 1,068 (the maximum, 26% of the total population) in 1857, 825 (16%) in 1900 and only 493 (8% of the total population) in 1930. - The J. religious congregation was reestablished after World War II and changed into a synagogue group in 1950 (active till about 1980).

The Uherský Brod J. community was one of the largest in Moravia. In the 18th - 19th cent. many J. left the overcrowded ghetto and founded a number of J. communities in Slovakia. The well-known Jewish surname Brod has most probably been derived from the town's name.

The names of more than 20 rabbis of the U. B. community have been recorded since the 1st half of the 17th cent. The community's rabbis came from Vienna, Frankfurt a.M., Cracow, Hungary and included authors of significant theological and historical works. Let us mention, for example, the noted Rabbi Moritz Jung (1859 Tiszaeszlár, Hungary - 1921 London), pioneer of modern J. education, who founded a J. high school in U. B. in 1901 and a yeshiva in 1910. From 1912 he was Chief Rabbi of the federation of 68 English J. communities in London.

U. B. is the native town of Rabbi Mose Samuel Zuckermandel (1836 - 1917 Wroclaw), a noted scholar and editor of ancient Judaic works: the Tosefta, the Baraita etc. and the birth place of the German-J. writer and playwright Eduard Nascher - Naschée (1853-1926 Vienna).

(The former **Jewish settlement** with a synagogue and a school used to be outside the walled town, in the suburb SE of the town's centre. It existed as early as in the 16th cent. and suffered serious damage by the Kuruczs [Hungarian peasant crusaders] in 1683. By the end of the 17th cent. the Jews came to live to the ghetto in the town proper.)

Remains of **a Jewish quarter** - a

ghetto - in the SE part of the walled town, E of the street called Bratří Lužů. J. families began to settle here in the mid-16th cent. The ghetto consisted of over 40 houses in the 2nd half of the 17th cent. and 107 houses in several streets in the 1st half of the 19th cent. The J. quarter had been demolished after World War II and later on a modern housing estate was built on its site. Several former houses by the city wall have been preserved and so was the J. school in Jirchářská street No. 823.

(**The old synagogue**, of unknown origin, in the former J. settlement in the SE suburb, was demolished in the early 18th cent.)

(**A new synagogue**, was built in the ghetto in 1717 or 1767 after the model of a synagogue in Amsterdam. It was burnt down by the Czech fascists in 1941 and thereafter pulled down.)

(**An Orthodox prayer room** was established about 1872 after a division in the J. religious congregation. The prayer room was closed down in 1894 and the house pulled down after World War II.)

Remains of the **old cemetery** are to be found on the mound in front of the S city wall, E of the railway station. The origin of the cemetery is not known, burials until about 1870, devastated during the Nazi occupation. The remaining tombstones were transferred to the new cemetery after World War II. Visible fragments of broken and sunken tombstones.

The new cemetery is on the E edge of the town, in the street leading to Těšov, 700 m NE of the old cemetery. The cemetery was founded in 1870 and in still used today. About 80 Baroque and Classicist tombstones were transferred here from the old cemetery and set in the W part of the cemetery. In the large ceremonial hall there is a memorial tablet in memory of about 600 victims of the Nazis from the town and its vicinity.

The town has three churches from the 17th - 18th cent., remains of a city wall with a gate, Renaissance and Baroque houses and other sights. Museum of J. A. Comenius, a renowned scholar and reformer (1592-1670).

The following J. communities used to be in the vicinity: **Uherské Hradiště** /Ger. *Ungarisch-Hradisch* (town 14 km WNW., a medieval cemetery and synagogue, became extinct after 1514, a synagogue from 1875, redesigned in the Art Nouveau style in 1904, today used as a municipal library; a memorial was erected on the site of the former cemetery from 1879, which has been devastated by the Nazis). A religious society existed in **Napajedla** (town 18 km NW, a synagogue from the 2nd half of the 19th cent., converted into a dwelling house). A prayer room used to be in **Luhačovice** (a spa 10 km NE) from the late 19th cent. till World War II, services were held there only in the spa's summer season. - **Drslavice** (4 km NW) is the native village of Adolph Jellinek (1820 - 1893 Vienna), a rabbi and author of theological works and of his brother Hermann Jellinek (1822 - executed in 1848, Vienna), an anti-Habsburg journalist and participant in the 1948 revolution.

Characteristic folk architecture and customs survived in the villages W and S of the town; to the SE spreads the wooded mountain range Bílé Karpaty (White Carpathians), the highest peak 970 m.

ÚSOV   124
(Ger. *Mährisch-Aussee*)

Small town in Moravia, 185 km ESE of Prague, 18 km S of the district town Šumperk. Ú. became a small town in the 1st half of the 14th cent., a town in the 18th cent.

The earliest documentary record of J. settlement dates from 1564: 7 J. families resided in Ú. at that time. A J. community with a rabbi existed here as early as the beginning of the 17th cent. Many Jews were killed during the foray of the Swedish army in 1643. The community numbered about 10 J. families in 1657, 59 in 1753, 110 J. families were permitted to reside here from the late 18th cent. In 1830 its population stood at 656 persons of the J. faith, the number dropped to 101 in 1900 and 20 in 1930 but Ú. was the seat of the J. religious congregation for the whole district. Only one single man survived the Nazi occupation. The J. religious congregation was not reestablished after World War II.

Rabbi Moritz Duschak (1815 Třešť - 1890 Vienna), author of many historical works, officiated as rabbi in Ú. before 1856. The German-J. poet and journalist Vlastimil Artur Polák was born in Ú. (1914-1990 Olomouc).

The Jewish quarter - a ghetto - used to be in the NW part of the small town. The ghetto's historical core, founded after 1589, is set on a knoll between the street leading to the village Police and the street to Klopina. It consisted of 9 houses in 1600, 19 in 1667, 28 in 1753 and 45 two-storey houses in the mid-19th cent. Most of the houses have been preserved, the former ghetto represents a noteworthy whole from the town-planning point of view.

(**The first** known **synagogue** was destroyed by the Thirty Years' War. - **The second synagogue** was built before 1689. In 1722, following a conflict with a Catholic priest, the court decided that the synagogue be demolished.)

The third synagogue, in the centre of the Jewish quarter, was built in 1784 in the Baroque-Classicist style, on the site of the second one. Services were held there until 1938, in the same year the Nazis burnt the interior furnishing and the valuable archives of the J. religious congregation. The building was renovated after World War II to be used by the Czech Brethren's Protestant Church.

(**The old cemetery** is said to have existed as early the 15th cent. Devastated by the Swedish army in 1643, subsequently ceased to exist, no traces of it are left.)

The present cemetery, on the NW boundary of the J. quarter, is said to have been founded about 1645. Enlarged in the 1st half of the 19th cent., burials until World War II. During the Nazi occupation the cemetery was used as a shooting range; the oldest tombstones from the 17th cent. were destroyed, modern tombstones were removed. The earliest preserved tombstone dates from 1745. In spite of the severe damage caused by the Nazis it represents a valuable cemetery with noteworthy Baroque and Classicist tombstones.

The town has a castle from the 13th - 17th cent., housing a museum of hunting and forestry, a Baroque church, a 17th cent. pilgrimage chapel and other places of interest.

The following J. communities and religious societies used to exist in the vicinity: **Rýmařov** /Ger. *Römerstadt* (town 23 km NE, a religious society recorded at the end of the 19th cent.); **Uničov** /Ger. *Mährisch-Neustadt* (town 8 km ESE, a J. community allegedly existed here before the expulsion of Jews in 1454, a religious society in the late 19th cent.); **Šumperk** /Ger. *Mährisch-Schönberg* (town 18 km N, a prayer house probably from the late 19th cent., converted into offices; remains of

a cemetery from 1911). - **Šumvald** (9 km NE) is the native village of the traveller - Orientalist Siegfried Langer (1857-1882 Yemen). **Janušov** /Ger. *Johnsdorf* (part of the town Rýmařov, 23 km NE) is the birth-place of the Impressionist painter Eugen Jettel (1845-1901 Veli Lošinj, Yugoslavia). **Zábřeh** /Ger. *Hohenstadt* (13 km NW) is the native town of the German-J. painter, sculptress and poetess of the Terezín ghetto Gertrud Groag (1889-1979 Haifa). **Hanušovice** /Ger. *Hannsdorf* (32 km NNW) is the native village of the composer and founder of the *Canadian Music Journal* Arnold Walter (1902-1973 Toronto). A concentration camp for J. women, a branch of the Gross Rosen camp, used to be in the village in 1941-44.

Towards the north - Hrubý Jeseník, a chain of mountains (the highest peak - 1,491 m) with protected virgin forest areas, popular with tourists; 16 km NE Sovinec, a well-preserved castle from the 14th - 17th cent.; 8 km ESE Uničov, a town with many historical monuments from the 14th to the 18th cent.

ÚSTÍ NAD LABEM 125
(Ger. *Aussig*)

District town in Bohemia, 70 km NNW of Prague. Chartered most probably as early as the 13th cent.

Isolated J. families resided in the town presumedly in the 16th cent., later on J. were not permitted to reside in Ú. Jews began to resettle in the town after 1848: 30 J. families are recorded in 1880, 95 in 1893, 985 persons of the J. faith (2% of the total population) in 1930. A religious society and the first prayer room was established in 1863. The religious society became a J. religious congregation in 1869 and from 1888 the congregants had their own rabbi.

The J. religious congregation was reestablished after World War II and still exists today. It administers J. religious congregations in the North Bohemian region. Present address: ŽNO,

Moskevská ul. 26, 400 01 Ústí nad Labem.

Ú. is the native town of the painter and graphic artist Ernst Neuschul - Norland (1895-1968 London), who portrayed the first two Czechoslovak presidents. The painter Rudolf Popper (1873 Vienna - 1967 Duchcov) spent 30 years in the town and was buried in the municipal cemetery in the Ústí suburb Střekov. Ignaz Petschek (1857 Kolín - 1934 Ústí n. L.) settled in the town and acted as coal merchant for the domestic and export trade, owning the North Bohemian lignite mines.

(The synagogue was built in 1880 in Malá hradební street on the site of a building which used to house a prayer room. Services were held there until 1938, the interior furnishing was destroyed by the Nazis and the building demolished. A modern market has been built on its site.)

The present prayer room is in Moskevská street No. 26. Established in 1945, damaged by an unknown offender in 1946 and in 1947 (the Torah scroll was stolen). A memorial tablet in memory of the victims of the Nazis was placed here in 1953.

(The first cemetery was founded on the corner of Palachova and Sadová streets in 1866, closed down in 1893, liquidated about 1930. Today it forms the S part of the park.)

(The second cemetery was founded in 1892 as a part of the municipal communal cemetery, between Kekulova and Okružní streets. Another J. section was established in 1924. The cemetery was damaged during the Nazi occupation. Burials also after World War II. The entire municipal cemetery was closed down in 1980, a factory was built on its site. - Today the J. religious congregation uses the cemetery in **Teplice**.)

The town suffered severe damage in an air raid in 1945. A Gothic church from the 14th - 16th cent. with a leaning tower (deflection 186 cm - during the air raid) and an 18th cent. monasterial church have survived the air raid. There is a Gothic castle from the 14th - 16th cent. (open to the public) in the suburb **Střekov**. *A Renaissance château and a valuable Renaissance church from the 16th - 17th cent. are to be found in the suburb* **Krásné Březno**.

12 km ESE **Zubrnice**, *a village with an open-air museum of North Bohemian popular architecture; 6 km SW* **Stadice**, *a village with a monument commemorating Přemysl Oráč, the legendary founder of the Bohemian dynasty of the Premyslids; 7 km NW* **Chlumec** *and* **Varvažov**, *villages with monuments in memory of the defeat of Napoleon's army in 1813.*

VAMBERK 126

Town in Bohemia, 130 km E of Prague, 5 km SSE of the district town Rychnov nad Kněžnou. Founded and chartered most probably in the 14th cent.

The earliest documentary record of J. settlement dates from 1682. Only one J. family lived in V. in 1723, two families in the mid-18th cent., one family in 1826, 9 persons of the J. faith (the maximum) in the mid-19th cent. and only 3 in 1930. - A very small community with a prayer room is said to have existed in V. (allegedly in the

17th cent.), whose members had been expelled from the town and found refuge in the nearby Doudleby n. O. However, there exist no documentary records of its early history.

The cemetery is 700 m N of the square. It is said to have been founded before 1673, the cemetery is recorded in 1688, enlarged in 1753 and 1806. The oldest preserved tombstone dates from 1700, burials until World War II (from the J. religious congregation Kostelec n. O. - Doudleby n. O.). A valuable cemetery with Baroque and Classicist tombstones.

There are two churches from the turn of the 17th and 18th cent. in V. and a museum of Bohemian lace-making.

*5 km SE **Litice**, a well-preserved Gothic castle; 4 km SSE **Potštejn**, a small town with a Baroque château and extensive ruins of a Gothic-Renaissance castle; 2 km SW **Doudleby nad Orlicí**, a Renaissance château housing an exhibition of West European and Bohemian lace-making.*

VELKÁ BUKOVINA   127
(Ger. *Gross-Bok*,
Gross-Bocken)

Village in Bohemia, 115 km ENE of Prague, 13 km W of the district town Náchod.

There exists no documentary record of early J. settlement. According to one source a J. community was established here at the turn of the 17th and 18th cent., according to another one it was established after 1793 following the arrival of J. families who had been expelled from Poland. The Theresian land-register from the mid-18th cent. does not mention any Jews in the village. 18 J. families are recorded in the 1st half of the 19th cent., in 1872 the J. religious congregation had 49 tax-paying members and a school. The J. religious congregation merged with the Dvůr Králové J. religious congregation about 1900. Only two persons of the J. faith lived in V. B. in 1930.

The Jewish lane used to be in the S part of the village, parallel (westwards)

with the road to Střeziměřice. Built as a compact ghetto about the 18th cent. or about the year 1800. In 1840 it consisted of 10 houses, a synagogue and a ritual bathhouse. Most of the small houses, some of them timber-framed, have survived untouched. It represents an extremely well-preserved, intact rural ghetto.

The remains of a synagogue on the E side of the J. lane. Built in the Classicist style in 1829, services were held there until about 1906, demolished before 1910. Only the peripheral walls of the ground floor with two granite portals (with quotations from the Old Testament) have survived. The inner space has been used as a small yard.

The cemetery is set among fields, 750 m N of the J. lane. Founded most probably in the 18th cent. (according to the earliest preserved tombstones), enlarged in the 2nd half of the 19th cent., burials presumedly until the late 19th cent. Remarkable Baroque and Classicist tombstones.

The following J. communities and religious societies used to exist in the vicinity: **Úpice** /Ger. *Eipel* (town 11 km NNE, a prayer room recorded in the 1st third of the 20th cent., a group of J. graves in the municipal cemetery); **Meziměstí** /Ger. *Halbstadt* (28 km NE, a prayer room recorded before 1938); **Broumov** /Ger. *Braunau* (town 30 km NE, a prayer room recorded in the 1st third of the 20th cent.); **Náchod** (town 13 km E, a synagogue allegedly from the 16th cent., rebuilt in the 18th and 19th cent., demolished in 1964; remains of a J. street - a ghetto, an old cemetery from the 16th cent., destroyed by the Nazis, a new cemetery from 1925 with a monument in memory of the Nazi victims; a post-war prayer room, converted into a flat); **Česká Skalice** /Ger. *Böhmisch-Skalitz* (town 6 km ESE, a J. community existed here from the 17th cent. until 1705); **Jaroměř** /Ger. *Jermer* (town 7 km SSW, a 19th-cent. prayer room, converted into a flat; a J. section in the municipal cemetery; the native town of the art historian and director of the State Jewish Museum Hana Franksteinová - Volavková [1904-1985 Prague]; the adjoining town **Josefov** /Ger. *Josefstadt* is the birth-place of Wilhelm Winternitz [1881-1906 Vienna], the founding father of hydropathy); **Dvůr Králové nad Labem** /Ger. *Königinhof* (town 10 km W, a synagogue from 1890, demolished after 1949, remains of a cemetery from the 2nd half of the 19th cent., liquidated after 1957; the birth-place of the famous sculptor Otto Gutfreund [1889-1917 Prague]); **Hostinné** /Ger. *Arnau* (town 20 km NW, a prayer room is said to have existed here at the turn of the 19th and 20th cent.; remains of a cemetery from 1884, devastated by the Nazis, liquidated after 1958); **Vrchlabí** /Ger. *Hohenelbe* (town 31 km NW, a prayer room existed here in the 1st third of the 20th cent., an early-20th cent. cemetery, destroyed by the Nazis; the native town of the musicologist Paul Nettl [1889-1972 Bloomington, USA]); **Trutnov** /Ger. *Trautenau* (town 16 km NNW, a synagogue from 1885, destroyed by the Nazis; a rebuilt mortuary - the last surviving part of the cemetery from 1870, destroyed by the Nazis; a grave of 41 J. girls from the concentration camp in Poříčí in the municipal cemetery; the post-war prayer room has been converted into a flat).

A labour camp for J. women (a branch of the Gross Rosen concentr. camp) existed in 1942-45 in **Poříčí** /Ger. *Parschnitz* (17 km N), the victims were buried in the Trutnov cemetery. The Poříčí camp had several branches in the vicinity: **Bohuslavice nad Úpou** /Ger. *Baussnitz* (14 km N); **Hostinné**

/Ger. *Arnau* (20 km NW); **Hořejší Vrchlabí** /Ger. *Ober-Hohenelbe* (33 km NW) **Horní Staré Město** /Ger. *Ober-Altstadt* (19 km NNW); **Temný Důl** /Ger. *Dunkelthal* (28 km NNW); **Voletiny** /Ger. *Wolta* (18 km N); **Libeč** /Ger. *Gabersdorf* (20 km N); **Bernartice** /Ger. *Bernsdorf* (24 km N, a monument in memory of the victims in the local cemetery); **Žacléř** /Ger. *Schatzlar* (25 km N). - A monument by the grave of 145 victims of the dead march from the Gross Rosen concentration camp in February 1945 has been erected near **Choustníkovo Hradiště** /Ger. *Gradlitz* (5 km W).

Hronov (16 km ENE) is the native town of the Czech-J. writer Egon Hostovský (1908-1973 Montclair, USA) and the painter and graphic artist Friedl Dicker - Brandeis (1898 Vienna - 1944 Auschwitz) lived here in 1938-42. - In **Broumov** (30 km NE) and **Náchod** (13 km E) reception camps were set up in 1946 where J. refugees from Poland were given temporary shelter (32,000 people passed through the camps).

13 km E Náchod, a town with a Renaissance-Baroque château with an art gallery, open to the public; 6 km ESE Česká Skalice with a museum of print textile and a great dam Rozkoš (water sports facilities); 8 km S Josefov, a garrison town built in 1780-89, with preserved fortifications (an urban conservation area); 5 km SW Kuks with a Baroque hospital from the 18th cent. (an apothecary with Baroque furnishing, open to the public, a row of Baroque allegorical sculptures in front of the hospital).

VELKÉ MEZIŘÍČÍ   **128**
(Ger. *Gross-Meseritsch*)

Town in Moravia, 135 km SE of Prague, 24 km SSE of the district town Žďár nad Sázavou. Chartered in the 14th cent.

There exist no documentary records of early J. settlement (archives of the J. community were destroyed during the fire of the ghetto in the 19th cent.). A J. community existed here most probably as early as the 1st half of the 16th cent. At least 22 J. families lived in V. M. in 1679, 888 persons of the J. faith (26% of the total population) in 1790, 1,116 persons (the maximum) in 1857, the number dropped to 289 persons in 1900 and to 76 in 1930. The J. religious congregation was not reestablished after World War II.

The V. M. community's rabbis included many famous authors of theological works. The earliest recorded rabbi was Efraim Kohen (born in Vilno - died in 1678, Pest). In the year of the Revolution of 1848 an Israelite National Guard was organized (over 100 men) in V. M.

The Jewish street - a ghetto - today's Dalimilova street, on the NE boundary of the town's centre, formerly beyond the city wall. J. houses stood here most probably as early as the 1st half of the 16th cent. Only 10 J. houses were inhabited after the Thirty Years' War in 1657, 23 in 1679, over 30 in the 18th cent. (at that time the ghetto was enclosed on both sides by walls and gates), 58 houses are recorded in the 1st half of the 19th cent. The J. street was damaged by fires several times (e.g. in 1823 and 1854). The former one-storey houses, some of them rebuilt today, have been preserved.

(**The small synagogue,** of unknown origin, used to stand between the two surviving synagogues. It is said to have been the earliest synagogue in V. M. Used as a winter prayer hall until World War II, demolished 1962.)

The old synagogue (called **the Old-New Synagogue**) - on the SE edge of the ghetto, on the bank of the Oslava

river. A Gothic-Renaissance synagogue, from about the early 16th cent., later remodelled. Late Gothic windows in the E front, a remarkable Classicist portal in the W front. Services were held here until 1867, later on the building was converted into a store-house and a shop.

The new synagogue is SE of the old synagogue. It is a red brick neo-Gothic building from 1867, built by architect Augustin Prokop. Services were held here until World War II, today used as a store-house. Plans have been made to rebuild and convert the synagogue into a theatre.

The cemetery is set on a slope beyond the Oslava river, 200 m NE of the synagogues. The origin of the cemetery is not known, the earliest legible tombstone dates from 1677, burials until World War II. A great number of remarkable Baroque and Classicist tombstones. The neo-Romanesque ceremonial hall and the wall were repaired in 1984-86.

The town has a château from the 13th - 18th cent., housing a museum, Gothic churches, a Renaissance townhall and burghers' houses, remains of a city wall with a gate and other sights. A 77 m high motorway bridge (the highest bridge in Czechoslovakia).

The following J. societies used to be in the vicinity: **Žďár nad Sázavou** /Ger. *Saar Stadt* (town 24 km NNW, a religious society recorded in the late 19th cent.); **Nové Město na Moravě** /Ger. *Neustadt* (town 22 km NNE, a religious society recorded in the late 19th cent.; the native town of the American philosopher Ernest Nagel [1901]); **Velká Bíteš** /Ger. *Gross-Bitesch, Heinrichs* (town 16 km SE, a religious society recorded in the late 19th cent.). - The well-known architect Otto Eisler (1893-1968 Brno) was born in the town **Bystřice nad Pernštejnem** (25 km NE).

VELKÝ PĚČÍN 129
(Ger. *Gross-Pantschen*)

Village in Moravia, 125 km SE of Prague, 32 km E of the district town Jindřichův Hradec.

The cemetery lies 1,500 m NW of the village centre, 1,300 m SSW of the village Myslůvka. The cemetery, of unknown origin, is set in a forest, 200 m E of the road Myslůvka - Kostelní Vydří. The earliest legible tombstone dates from 1655, burials until 1879 (a new cemetery founded in Telč). Remarkable Baroque and Classicist tomb-

stones. The cemetery was damaged during the Nazi occupation.

(There was no J. community in V. P. The cemetery belonged to the Telč J. community, which was established about the 1st half of the 17th cent.)

The following J. communities and religious societies used to exist in the vicinity: **Telč** (town 6 km N, a synagogue of unknown origin, damaged by fire in 1885 and pulled down; a small J. street; a new synagogue from 1904, converted into offices; a cemetery from 1879 with a ceremonial hall, today used by the Seventh Day Adventists); **Dačice** (town 4 km S, a prayer room recorded in the 2nd half of the 19th cent.); **Dolní Bolíkov** /Ger. *Wölking* (11 km SW, a synagogue of unknown origin, pulled down in 1899-1900, a J. quarter, a late 18th cent. cemetery, the grave of Heinrich Mayer [1835-1905], founder of the *Neues Wiener Tagblatt*); **Slavonice** /Ger. *Zlabings* (town 15 km SW, a synagogue from 1895, converted into flats); **Staré Město pod Landštejnem** /Ger. *Altstadt* (a small town 18 km SW, a wooden synagogue of unknown origin, burnt down in 1830, a new synagogue built in the 1st half of the 19th cent., demolished about 1955, remains of a J. quarter; a cemetery from about the early 17th cent. with tombstones from the 1st half of the 18th cent., seriously damaged by the Nazis); **Markvarec** /Ger. *Markwarding* (10 km WSW, a J. quarter; ruins of a synagogue from 1786; a cemetery with tombstones from the 18th cent.); **Olšany** /Ger. *Wolschan* (14 km WNW, a timber framed synagogue of unknown origin, burnt down in 1928, remains of a J. quarter; a cemetery with tombstones from the 18th cent.).

6 km N Telč, the historical centre with a great number of historical monuments has been declared an urban conservation area: a Gothic-Renaissance castle (open to the public) and many remarkable buildings from the 13th up to the 18th cent.; 4 km S Dačice, a town with a Renaissance castle and an Empire château (the latter open to the public).

VĚTRNÝ JENÍKOV 130
(Ger. *Windig-Jenikau*)

Small town in Bohemia, 100 km SE of Prague, 11 km NW of the district town Jihlava. Became a small town in the early 17th cent.

There exist hardly any documentary records of the local J. community. The earliest record dates from 1724: 9 J. families (44 persons) are mentioned here that year, maintaining a prayer room from 1716. In the mid-18th cent. 8 J. families lived in V. J., 11 families in the 1st half of the 19th cent. Only 4 J. families are recorded in 1870, 2 persons of the J. faith in 1921 and in 1930 there was no J. population in V. J. - The J. religious congregation most probably merged with the Úsobí J. religious congregation in the 2nd half of the 19th cent.

The cemetery, of unknown origin, is set 1,100 m SSW of the square, near Dolní mlýn. The earliest preserved tombstone dates from 1700, burials until about the late 19th cent. It is a remarkable cemetery with Baroque and Classicist tombstones.

There are a Baroque château from the 17th - 19th cent. and an 18th cent. Baroque church in V. J.

The nearest J. community was in **Úsobí** /Ger. *Pollerskirchen* (a small town 5 km NNE, a small J. quarter; a synagogue from about the 18th cent., converted into a dwelling house).

Town in Bohemia, 105 km S of Prague, 24 km ESE of the district town Strakonice. V. became a small town in 1336, a town in 1547.

The earliest documentary record of J. settlement dates from 1500 (2 J. families). Jews had been expelled in 1541 but began to resettle in V. again during the Thirty Years' War: 2 J. families lived here in 1638, a prayer room is recorded in 1724, 8 J. families (52 persons) in 1746, 22 J. families in 1852 and the number of J. population continued to grow until the end of the century. In 1836 V. became the seat of the Regional Rabbi. In 1930 the J. population in V. numbered 114 persons of the J. faith. The J. religious congregation was not reestablished after World War II.

From about the 18th cent. J. houses were concentrated in today's Družstevní street, between the square and the town's E wall. It was not a ghetto in the proper sense of the word, as most of the population were Christians.

(**The first** small **synagogue** was built in 1744 between the house No. 152 and the city wall. Services were held there until the mid-19th cent., later on the synagogue either merged with the house No. 152 or was pulled down.)

The new synagogue, in today's Družstevní street, was built between 1837-52 right next to the old one. A simple Classicist building. Services were held there until World War II, since 1956 it has been used as a municipal museum. - A **J. school** used to be behind the synagogue, by the former city wall.

There is **a monument** in memory of the victims of the Nazis in the municipal park.

The cemetery is set on the edge of a forest, 3 km WSW of the square, 700 m SW of the Pražák settlement. Consecrated in 1840, the earliest legible tombstone dates from 1848, burials until World War II.

The town has a Gothic-Renaissance church from the 15th - 16th cent., remains of a city wall, several Renaissance houses and other sights.

The following J. communities and religious societies used to be in the vicinity: **Protivín** (town 6 km NNE, a wooden prayer hall of unknown origin, burnt down in 1857, the house in which a prayer room used to be from the late 19th cent. was pulled down in 1968; remains of a cemetery from 1878); **Dříteň** /Ger. *Zirnau* (12 km E, a prayer room from the 19th cent. which has fallen into disuse); **Sedlec** /Ger. *Selz* (11 km SE, a prayer room from the 19th cent., converted into a flat); **Čichtice** (8 km SW, a J. street, a prayer room from about the 18th cent., converted into a flat; a cemetery with tombstones from the mid-18th cent.).

*4 km SSE **Libějovice**, a village with a Renaissance château from the 14th - 15th cent.; 5 km S **Lomec**, a noteworthy Baroque pilgrim church from the 17th - 18th cent.; 10 km S **Kratochvíle**, a Renaissance château from the 16th cent., housing a museum of animated film.*

Village in Bohemia, 24 km N of Prague, 10 km SW of the district town Mělník.

There exist no documentary records of early J. settlement in V. Two J. families lived in V. in 1724, one family (other 7 families in the neighbourhood) in the mid-18th cent., about 4 families in the mid-19th cent. There was no J. population in the village at the outset of the 20th cent. - A J. community was established here about 1800. The community had 70 tax-paying members and a school in 1872. In 1893 it merged with the Postřižín J. religious congregation.

Remains of a synagogue are to be found on the E side of the village green, in a yard behind the house No.-25. Built in a simple Classicist style in 1808-14, enlarged in 1834. Regular ser-

vices held there until 1893, thereafter the synagogue fell into disuse. Since then it has been falling into disrepair (the synagogue's parochets were transferred to the museum in Kralupy nad Vltavou in 1938). The peripheral walls of the synagogue have survived, the inner space has been used as a yard.

(There was no cemetery in V., the community buried its dead in the cemetery at **Spomyšl**.)

The following J. communities and religious societies used to be in the vicinity: **Obříství** (7 km E, a prayer room existed here in the mid-19th cent.); **Klecany** (13 km SSE, a prayer room is said to have existed here in the 19th cent.); a prayer room allegedly existed in the 19th cent. also in the village **Přemyšlení** (14 km SSE) or **Brnky** (15 km SSE); **Postřižín** (7 km S, a small mid-19th cent. synagogue, converted into a flat; an early 19th cent. cemetery); **Horní Beřkovice** /Ger. *Ober-Berschkowitz* (6 km NNW, a prayer room recorded in the 18th - 19th cent.). Near the village **Spomyšl** (4 km NNW) is a cemetery, allegedly from the 17th cent. with legible tombstones from the 1st half of the 18th cent., which belonged to the Horní Beřkovice community and later on to the Vojkovice J. community. - A large group of the J. prisoners (54 of them died later in concentration camps) was working in 1942-43 at the country estate of Reinhard Heydrich in **Panenské Břežany** /Ger. *Jungfern-Breschan* (a village 10 km SE).

*4 km SW **Veltrusy**, a small town with a Baroque château from the 18th cent. (open to the public) with several Classicist and Romantic style small temples, pavillions and other architecture scattered in the surrounding large park.*

VOLYNĚ 133
(Ger. *Wolin*)

Town in Bohemia, 110 km SSW of Prague, 10 km S of the district town Strakonice. Founded and chartered in 1299.

The earliest preserved documentary record of J. settlement in V. dates from the late 15th cent. Permanent J. settlement began in 1521 (one J. family), 8 J. families are recorded in 1570 and in 1654, 17 J. families (92 persons) in 1724, 23 in the mid-19th cent. 51 persons of the J. faith are recorded in 1930, 55 persons subject to the Nazi racial laws in 1942. The religious congregation was not reestablished after World War II, only 2 persons of the J. faith survived the war.

J. families lived in the W suburb called Hradčany from the 16th cent. and later on they were forced to settle in a newly established ghetto.

The Jewish street - a ghetto - today's Žižkova street, in the E part of the town (adjoining the square Dolní nám. from the S). It was built in the 17th or 18th cent. and consisted of about 12 houses. The ghetto was accessible from the square Dolní nám. until the 19th cent. Some of the houses, today rebuilt,

have been preserved. - (A smaller cluster of J. houses used to be SSW of the ghetto, in the street leading to the village Nišovice.)

The synagogue in Žižkova street was built in 1838 - 40 on the site of **an earlier synagogue** (built at the same time as the ghetto). The interior was remodelled about 1890. Services were held here until World War II, after 1946 the synagogue was converted into a cinema. A Classicist style building with a relief decorated gable above the E front. A Classicist aron ha-kodesh has been preserved and is kept today in the municipal museum.

The cemetery is in the street U vodojemu, 350 m NW of the main square (the town hall). Founded most probably in the 17th cent., the earliest legible tombstone dates from 1689. Extended in 1870 for the last time, repaired in 1912, burials until World War II. A remarkable, well-preserved cemetery with Renaissance, Baroque and Classicist tombstones. - (**An earlier cemetery** is said to have existed in V. but no traces of the cemetery are left.)

V. has a late Gothic stronghold (housing a museum), two churches from the 14th - 16th cent., a Renaissance town--hall and other sights.

The following J. communities used to exist in the vicinity: **Hoštice** (3 km

NE, a synagogue of unknown origin, pulled down about 1903 - 04, a cemetery from the 1st half of the 18th cent.); **Němčice** (7 km WNW, a prayer room existed here in the 19th cent.). A prayer room existed in the village **Čestice** (6 km W) in the 19th cent.

*4 km WNW **Doubravice u Volyně**, a village with a Gothic tower stronghold; Renaissance and Baroque châteaux and manors are to be found in the surrounding villages.*

VSETÍN   134

District town in Moravia, 265 km ESE of Prague, 60 km SSW of Ostrava. V. became a small town in the early 14th cent., a town in 1852.

The earliest preserved documentary record of J. settlement in V. dates to the year 1669 in which the lordship guaranteed the J. among others "untroubled celebration of services". Several J. families must have lived in the town at that time. There exist no documentary records from the 18th cent. All the J. families, except one, were expelled in 1823. After 1848 the number of J. in V. began to increase again, the J. community was revived and a prayer room was established. 36 persons of the J. faith are recorded in 1848, 111 in 1880, 165 (the maximum) in 1900. - In 1890 the autonomous J. religious congregation changed to a J. religious society, administered by the Hranice J. religious congregation. 101 persons of the J. faith are recorded in 1930, 67 persons are said to have perished during the Nazi occupation. - A J. religious congregation Valašské Meziříčí - Vsetín was established in 1945. Its seat was in Vsetín, services were held in a private house. Soon after, the religious congregation changed to a synagogue group, which no longer exists. The last Vsetín citizen of the J. faith died in 1988.

Erich Kulka (born 1911), historian of the Holocaust and the Jewish resistance, is a native of Vsetín.

(**The synagogue**, built in 1897, was burnt down by the Nazis in 1939 and consequently demolished. Services were held there until World War II.)

The cemetery is next to the municipal communal cemetery, on a knoll NW of the château. Founded in 1888, burials until World War II. The ceremonial hall was converted into a prayer hall of the Seventh Day Adventists in 1945, since 1972 it has been used by the Hussite Church, whose members take care of the cemetery.

V. has a Renaissance château (today remodelled), housing a museum, three churches from the 17th - 19th cent. and other sights.

The following J. communities and religious societies existed in the vicinity: **Valašské Meziříčí** /Ger. *Wallachisch-Meseritsch* (town 14 km N, a military cemetery with a J. section from the period of World War I closed down in 1971-2; the native town of the Israeli diplomat and historian Haim Yahil [1905-1974]). Remains of a cemetery from 1871 in the adjacent small town **Krásno nad Bečvou**, the ceremonial hall is used by the municipal communal cemetery, a synagogue from 1867, pulled down after 1960. **Rožnov pod Radhoštěm** /Ger. *Rosenau* (town 16 km NE, the former seasonal spa prayer rooms have been converted into flats and a municipal library, remains of a cemetery with tombstones from the 2nd half of the 19th cent. were liquidated about 1988); **Nový Hrozenkov** /form. *Nová Dědina*, Ger. *Rosinkau, Neu-Traubendorf* (small town 14 km E, a prayer room existed here from the 19th cent. until World War I); **Velké Karlovice** /Ger. *Gross-Karlowitz* (20 km E, a temporary prayer room recorded here in the 1st third of the 20th cent., a cemetery from 1887); **Halenkov** (10 km ESE, a prayer room recorded in the 1st third of the 20th cent.); **Vizovice** (town 16 km SW, a synagogue from the late 19th cent., converted into a dwelling house).

*The surrounding mountainous and wooded country is very popular with tourists; to the N and E spreads the chain of mountains **Moravskoslezské Beskydy** (the highest peak - 1,323 m), to the W **Hostýnské vrchy** (865 m) and*

Vizovická vrchovina (753 m); timber-framed popular houses have been preserved in many surrounding villages.

VYŠKOV   135
(Germ. *Wischau*)

District town in Moravia, 205 km SE of Prague, 30 km NE of Brno. Became a small town in the 2nd half of the 13th cent., a town in the 2nd half of the 14th cent.

One J. family settled in V. most probably as early as the 1st half of the 14th cent. Two or three J. families lived there before 1465, the town was without J. inhabitants in 1465. No documentary records of J. settlement in the 16th - 18th cent. have been preserved (Jews are said to have lived in V. during the Thirty Years' War in the 1st half of the 17th cent.). 10 persons of the J. faith are recorded in 1848, 89 in 1869, 263 (the maximum) in 1890 but only 44 in 1930. A J. religious society was established most probably after 1860 (administered by the Ivanovice na Hané J. religious congregation), in 1891 it became an autonomous J. religious congregation but was not reestablished after World War II.

The synagogue is on the S side of the square nám. 1. máje (the main square). Built in the neo-Romanesque style in 1885. Services were held there until 1929 (the number of congregants considerably dropped and thus services were held in a small prayer room in a different house). The synagogue had been used as a municipal museum in 1931-54, and in 1957 the interior was redesigned to serve as a prayer hall of the Hussite Church.

The cemetery is 1,500 m E of the synagogue, in Kroměřížská street (leading to the village Hoštice). Founded in the late 19th cent., burials until World War II. There are just a few graves in the cemetery, most of the cemetery's ground has been converted into a garden. The ceremonial hall has been converted into a dwelling house.

V. has a Renaissance-Baroque château from the 16th - 17th cent., two churches from the 16th - 18th cent., a town hall with a Renaissance tower and other sights. The town suffered serious damage towards the end of World War II.

A J. community used to be in **Ivanovice na Hané** /Ger. *Eiwanowitz* (a small town 7 km NE, remains of a formerly extensive J. quarter, a Classicist synagogue, converted into a prayer house of the Hussite Church; a cemetery of unknown origin with tombstones from the early 17th cent.; the native town of Gustav Karpeles [1848-1909 Nauheim], a historian who has contributed to the study of J. literature).

ZNOJMO   136
(Ger. *Znaim*)

District town in Moravia, near the Austrian frontier, 180 km SE of Prague, 55 km SW of Brno. Founded and chartered in 1226.

A J. community existed in Z. most probably as early as the mid-13th cent., a J. street (today's Veselá street in the W part of the town's historical core) is recorded in the 1st half of the 14th cent. Jews were expelled from Z. in 1454 and not permitted to reside in the town until 1848. 19 persons of the J. faith are recorded in Z. again in 1848, 357 in 1869, 749 (the maximum) in 1921 and 675 (2% of the total population) in 1930. 665 members of the Znojmo J. religious congregation perished during the Holocaust. - A modern religious society was established in

1865 and became an autonomous J. religious congregation in 1876. The J. religious congregation was reestablished after World War II (the prayer room used to be in Velká Michalská street) and later on became a synagogue group (no longer exists).

Jewish families contributed to the foundation of the Znojmo canning industry (J. Wertheimer, S. M. Zeisl and others). - The famous sculptor Hugo Lederer (1871-1940 Berlin) was born in Z. as was the engineer Siegmund Strauss (1875-1942 New York) who together with R. Lieben constructed the high-mu tube in 1907.

(**The medieval synagogue**, of unknown origin, was converted into a Christian chapel in 1455. The building had also been used as a malt-house and was converted into a dwelling house later on. No traces of the synagogue are left today. - **A new synagogue** was built in 1888 in the so-called Moorish style. The synagogue was in the square nám. Svobody, services were held there until 1938 when it was burnt down by the Nazis, pulled down two years later.)

(**The medieval cemetery**, of unknown origin, used to be beyond the walled town, S of the square nám. Svobody, between the street Na valech and the city walls. It ceased to exist after the expulsion of J. from the town. Tombstones from the 13th and 14th cent. were found on the site of the former cemetery in 1804 and 1929. Two of them have been embedded in the walls of houses No. 9 and 13 in the street Na valech. The remaining tombstones are kept in the local South Moravian Museum: the tombstone allegedly from the year 1256 is the earliest preserved J. tombstone in Czechoslovakia.)

The new cemetery is 2 km N of the old cemetery, near the parting of roads to Prímětice and Únanov. Founded in 1868, burials until World War II. Remains found on the site of the old cemetery were buried here in 1869 (the grave with an obelisk). The ceremonial hall was demolished by the Nazis. The cemetery is going to be reduced in size and the most valuable tombstones are going to be transferred into the remaining part of the cemetery.

Z. has a Baroque château (housing a museum), a 12th cent. Romanesque rotunda with wall paitings depicting Přemyslid rulers, several remarkable ecclesiastic buildings, a Renaissance town-hall, Gothic, Renaissance and Baroque houses etc. The historical centre of the town has been declared a protected urban area.

6 km NW near the road to Moravské Budějovice is a monument commemorating the end of World War II in Europe; 3 km N Prímětice, a village with a model of the first lightning-conductor and a museum of its inventor Prokop Diviš (1696-1765); 13 km SE Slup, a village with a Renaissance water mill, housing a museum of the miller's trade.

ŽAMBERK 137
(Ger. *Senftenberg*)

Town in Bohemia, 145 km E of Prague, 13 km NNE of the district town Ústí nad Orlicí. Chartered in the 14th cent.

A J. community is said to have existed here in the early 17th cent. but the earliest documentary record of J. settlement dates from the mid-17th cent. 8 J. families are recorded in Ž. in 1723, 24 in 1811 and about 30 after the mid-19th cent. The number of J. began to decline on the late 19th cent. (the last rabbi left the town in 1911) and only about 31 persons of the J. faith lived here in 1930. Only 5 persons of the J. faith survived the Nazi occupation. The J. religious congregation was not reestablished after World War II.

Ž. was the childhood home of the famous painter Max Horb (1882 Mladá Boleslav - 1907 Prague), member of the modern artists' group Osma.

The Jewish quarter - a ghetto - NW of the square, E and SE of the bridge over the Orlice river. The ghetto consisted of the W part of the street Českých bratří and the N part of Hluboká street. J. families settled here as early as the 17th cent. The ghetto consisted of 9 houses in J. ownership in the late

18th cent. and 12 in 1805. The J. quarter was several times destroyed by fire (e.g. in 1810 and 1833). Some of the houses, today rebuilt, have been preserved.

The synagogue is in the street Českých bratří. Built about 1810-11, remodelled in 1860, 1883 and 1930. Services were held there until World War II, since 1947 it has been used by the Hussite Church. The building was remodelled in 1950-54: the stairs leading to the women's gallery were removed, a tower was added, etc. At present the former synagogue is used as a prayer house by four different Christian churches. There is a show case in the interior commemorating the extinct J. community.

The cemetery is next to the municipal museum, 400 m SW of the synagogue, by the street Československé armády. Founded most probably in the 17th cent., the earliest preserved tombstone dates from 1731. Extended in the 2nd half of the 19th cent. and in 1932, burials until World War II. The modern ceremonial hall dates from 1932.

The cemetery was demolished during the Nazi occupation, the surviving tombstones were erected after the liberation. Remarkable Baroque and Classicist tombstones.

There is a château from the 16th -

17th cent. surrounded by a large park in Ž.

A J. community used to be in **Rokytnice v Orlických horách** /Ger. *Rokitnitz im Adlergebirge* (town 8 km N, a wooden synagogue from the 18th cent. was destroyed by fire in 1861; a new synagogue built in 1868, rebuilt after 1920 and converted into a private house, pulled down after World War II; a J. street, an early 18th cent. cemetery, devastated by the Nazis; the Ger.-J. writer Moritz Reich [1831-1857] was born in R. and is buried here, too).

A labour camp for J. women, a branch of the concentration camp Gross Rosen, was set up in 1944 in the village **Bílá Voda** /Ger. *Weiswasser*, 20 km ESE (the victims were buried in the local cemetery). - **Lanškroun** /Ger. *Landskron*, 21 km SE, is the birthplace of Leo Herrmann (1889-1951 Tel Aviv), editor of the Prague weekly *Selbstwehr* and organizer of various J. unions. - 29 prisoners - victims of a railway transport from Auschwitz - were buried in January 1945 in the village **Dlouhá Třebová** (16 km S) and in **Parník** (19 km S). Victims of a transport from Auschwitz were buried in January 1945 in the town **Ústí nad Orlicí** /Ger. *Wildenschwert* (13 km SSW). It is the native town of the satirist and libretist Fritz Beda-Löhner (1883-1942 Auschwitz), author of the lyrics of the song *Buchenwaldlied*.

6 km E Pastviny, a dam in the valley of the Orlice river (water sports faciities); 6 km SE Letohrad, a town with a Renaissance-Baroque château and other sights.

SLOVAKIA

There existed several hundred Jewish communities and about 700 Jewish cemeteries on the territory of the present Slovak Republic. Jews settled in Slovakia as early as in the times of the Roman empire and Jewish communities were recorded as early as the 13th cent. The J. population in Slovakia numbered 136,737 persons of the J. faith in 1930. Jews played an important role in the liberation of Slovakia fighting against fascism and Nazism - about 10 percent of the members of partisan groups were Jews, and 12 percent of the partisans killed during the war were Jews.

Synagogues, former yeshivot, cemeteries with remarkable tombstones and a number of other Jewish historical monuments have survived in many Slovak town and villages. Among the most significant pieces of architecture rank some synagogues built in the 20th cent., e.g. the synagogue in Trenčín (built in 1911, architects Fuchs and Migrai), in Lučenec (built in 1925, architect L. Baumhorn), in Košice (two synagogues built in 1927, architects L. Kozma and L. Oelschläger) and Žilina (1933-34, architect P. Behrens).

Many significant personalities came from Slovakia, let us mention, e.g. the traveller-Orientalist and philologist Armin Vámbéry (1832 Dunajská Streda - 1913 Budapest), the founder of the prominent Berlin publishing-house Samuel Fischer (1859 Liptovský Mikuláš - 1934 Berlin), President of the World Union of J. Women Rebecca Bettelheim-Kohut (1864 Košice - 1951 New York), Chief Rabbi of the British Commonwealth of Nations Josef Hermann Hertz (1872 Zemplínska Široká - 1946 London), the pianist and founder of the Tel Aviv Academy of Music Leo Kestenberg (1882 Ružomberok - 1962 Tel Aviv), the well-known painter Jacob Bauernfreund-Bornfriend (1904 Zborov - 1976 London), the poet and prose-writer Hermann Adler (1921 Sládkovičovo), the leading Israeli artist Shraga Weill (1918 Nitra), the composer Štěpán Lucký (1919 Žilina) and the film director Juraj Herz (1934 Kež marok). The ancestors of the German poet Heinrich Heine came from Slovakia.

This brief guide concentrates on Bohemia and Moravia, therefore we cannot offer foreign visitors a full survey of Jewish historical monuments in Slovakia. Nevertheless, we would like to include at least Bratislava, the capital of the Slovak Republic, to hint at some of the riches of historical monuments in Slovakia and the rich history of the Slovak Jewish communities.

BRATISLAVA   **138**
(formerly *Prešporek*,
Ger. *Pressburg*,
Hung. *Pozsony*)

The capital of the Slovak Republic, 290 km SE of Prague, near the frontier with Austria and Hungary.

Roman troops were stationed as early as the 2nd cent. A.D. on the site of today's Bratislava castle and the Devín Castle. The Bratislava Castle is mentioned in the 9th cent. and the trading settlement round the castle was walled most probably in the mid-13th cent. and chartered in the 13th cent. Capital and coronation town of the Hungarian Kingdom from 1536-1783.

The first mention of J. settlement dates from the 2nd half of the 13th cent. - at that time there existed a J. community with a rabbi. The Bratislava J. community is said to have numbered about 800 persons of the J. faith in the 14th cent. J. had to move their homes and synagogue several times during the 14th and 15th centuries. The Bratislava Jews were also expelled from the town several times: e.g. in 1360-68 and in 1526. In the 1st half of the 16th cent. J. families found refuge in Podhradie (suburb between the castle and the walled town). Over 120 J. families (772 persons) lived here in 1736, 8 synagogues and prayer rooms are recorded in 1830. J. were permitted to resettle in the town proper only in the mid-19th cent.

A second J. religious congregation was established in 1872, observing the Reform rite (the majority of the Bratislava congregants followed the Orthodox rite). 6,368 persons of the J. faith (10% of the total population) are recorded in B. in 1900, 12,852 (9%) in 1927. In those days the Orthodox J. religious congregation maintained 17 synagogues and prayer rooms, 11 houses of learning (Beth Midrash) and 6 schools while the Reform J. religious congregation maintained only 2 synagogues and 2 schools. About 15,000 persons subject to the Nazi racial laws lived in the town in 1941.

Bratislava is the seat of the J. Religious Congregation and of the Central Union of Jewish Religious Congregations in Slovakia. Its present **address**: Šmeralova ul. 21, 814 47 Bratislava. The address of the kosher restaurant: Zámocká ul. 978/49.

For several centuries Bratislava was a significant centre of Talmudic studies and of J. education. There was a yeshivah in the town as early as 1700. A new yeshivah was founded after 1806, which became one of the most famous Orthodox institutions for Jewish learning in Europe. It existed until World War II and was revived for a short period of time after the war. Its tradition has been resumed by the so-called Pressburger Yeshivah in Jerusalem.

Among the most famous rabbi belonged Moses ben Samuel Schreiber, the Hatam Sofer (1762 Frankfurt a.M. - 1839 Bratislava), active in B. from 1806, the founder of the yeshivah and the first school for J. girls and author of theological works.

The number of Jews from Bratislava who attained prominence in culture, science, religion and economy was high: let us mention, e.g. Samuel Rosenblatt (1902), a rabbi and Orientalist in Baltimore, USA; Leopold Dukes (1810-1891 London), a historian of medieval Hebrew literature; Maurice Loewy (1833-1907 Paris), an astronomer and member of the French Academy; the German-J. writers Marie Frischhauf-Pappenheim (1882-1966 Vienna) and Bruno Frei (1897); the actress Gisela Werbisek-Werbezirk (1875-1956 Hollywood); the film producer Arnold Pressburger (1885-1951 Hamburg) and film directors Erich Charell (1894-1974 Zug, Switzerland) and Ján Kadár (1918-1979 Los Angeles); the sculptor and ceramist Arthur John Fleischmann (1896-??); the painter Adolf Frankl (1903-1983), known for his paintings with motifs from Auschwitz; the architect Ernest Leslie Fuchs-Fooks (1906, resides in Australia); the founder of J. agricultural settlements and organizer of religious life in Palestine Akiva Josef Schlesinger (1837-1922 Palestine); the Israeli expert in international law, Professor Yehuda Zvi Blum (1931); the Israeli historian, Professor Josef Dan (1935). Bratislava is the native town of the father of the Austrian composer Arnold Schönberg.

The famous singer Josef Rosenblatt (1880 Bila Cerkev, the Ukraine - 1933 Tel Aviv) was active as a cantor in B. It was also the childhood home of the Austrian literary critic and humourist Moritz Gottlieb Saphir (1895 Lovas Berényi - 1958 Baden, Austria). The German-J. poet Oskar Neumann (1894 Most - 1981 Ber Tuvia, Israel) lived in B. for many years and the famous Czech painter Alfred Justitz (1879 Nová Cerekev - 1934) died in B.

(**The Jewish street** used to be in today's Staromestská street, in the former suburb Podhradie between the city wall and the castle. J. families settled there in the 16th cent. after their expulsion from the town's centre. It was not an enclosed ghetto. The original houses from the 17th - 18th cent. burnt down in the fires of 1811 and 1913. The houses were demolished with the exception of minor remnants after World War II.)

(Little evidence is left of **the medieval synagogues** in the centre of the town. They used to be on the site of today's Uršulínska and Nedbalova streets in the 13th - 16th cent. The earliest known synagogue was demolished after 1334 by the pope's order, another synagogue was built in 1368 or 1399. The last synagogue in the centre of the town must have been abandoned after the expulsion of the J. in 1526. No traces are left of the above mentioned buildings.)

(A **Baroque synagogue** was built on a slope by the J. street in 1716, extended in the 2nd half of the 18th cent. and demolished after the fire of 1796. **Another synagogue**, of unknown origin, on the W side of the J. street, burnt down in 1913.)

(A **great Orthodox synagogue** was built in the so-called Oriental style by architect I. Feigler in Zámocká street in 1862-63. Destroyed during the war in 1945, remains of the building were pulled down after 1980. The synagogue's aron ha-kodesh has been transferred to a yeshivah in Jerusalem.)

The new Orthodox synagogue was built in Heydukova street in 1923 by architect A.Szalatnai-Slatinský. It is a noteworthy modern structure with Oriental style elements and a traditional interior. Services are still held in the synagogue today.

(A **Reform synagogue** used to be on the former square Rybné nám., W of Paulínyho street, on the site of today's car-park. Built in 1893-94 in the so-called Oriental style by architect D. Milch. Services were held there until the 1950's, demolished during the construction of a near-by bridge.)

(Another **synagogue** with a winter prayer hall used to be after 1945 in Klariská No. 5.)

(The location of **the medieval cemetery** of unknown origin has not yet been determined.)

A rabbinical mausoleum on nábrežie Ludvíka Svobodu, WSW of the castle, by the tram tunnel. It is the remains of

an extensive **cemetery** presumedly from the 2nd half of the 17th cent., used until 1846. The cemetery was elevated in 1810 and again in 1825 (graves in three layers, a total of about 6,000 burials). The cemetery was liquidated in 1942 - 45 during the construction of the tunnel: most of the graves were exhumed, the remains of those buried in the cemetery and the tombstones were transferred to the new Orthodox cemetery. A small part of the cemetery with the graves of rabbis was left and roofed over by concrete, creating an underground mausoleum (the surrounding ground was elevated by about 4 m). There are about 23 graves and 64 tombstones in the mausoleum. Pilgrims from all over the world flock to the grave of Rabbi Hatam Sofer (with a copy of the original tombstone).

The Orthodox cemetery is in Žižkova street, 200 m NW of the mausoleum. Founded in 1846, enlarged in 1869 and 1926, still used today. The total of about 7,000 graves. There are two mass graves with the remains transferred here from the older cemetery. Hundreds of tombstones from the 17th - 19th cent. were also transferred here from the older cemetery. A Functionalist style ceremonial hall with a memo-

rial tablet in memory of 15,000 victims of the Nazis.

The neologist cemetery of the Re-

form J. religious congregation was consecrated in the 2nd half of the 19th cent. in Žižkova street, 500 m WNW of the mausoleum and is still used today. The ceremonial hall dates from the late 19th cent.

Autonomous J. communities used to exist in several suburbs:

DEVÍN /Hung. *Dévény*, Ger. *Theben* (originally a small town 9 km WNW, a J. community existed there most probably after 1525);

DEVÍNSKA NOVÁ VES /Hung. *Dévényújfalu*, Ger. *Theben-Neudorf* (12 km NW, no traces are left of the prayer hall and cemetery from about the 19th cent.);

RAČA /form. *Račistorf*, Hung. *Récse*, Ger. *Ratzersdorf* (originally a small town 8 km NE, a J. community existed there most probably from the 16th until the 20th cent., minor remains of a cemetery of unknown origin in the communal cemetery);

RUSOVCE /Hung. *Oroszvár*, Ger. *Karlburg* (originally a small town 11 km SSE, a synagogue from about the 18th cent. pulled down about the 1st half of the 20th cent., a cemetery of unknown origin with tombstones from the 1st half of the 18th cent. liquidated after 1960).

A small labour camp for about 70 J. prisoners was set up during World War II in **Devínska Nová Ves** (12 km NW). A labour camp for about 1,600 J. men from Hungary was set up in 1944 in the suburb **Petržalka** /Hung. *Ligetfalu*, Ger. *Engerau* (2 km S). The Nazis shot 496 prisoners in March 1945, the victims were buried in the local cemetery in Nábrežná street: 50 identified men in individual graves, the others were buried in two mass graves. A monument in memory of the victims was dedicated in the cemetery in 1958.

B. has many historical monuments - e.g. the Bratislava Castle (the main structure dates from the 12th - 15th cent., subsequently rebuilt, the interior houses a museum), a municipal gate from the 14th - 17th cent., a Gothic town-hall, many churches (the earliest from the 13th cent.), Renaissance and Baroque palaces and houses. The town's

historical centre with the B. castle has been declared an urban conservation area. - Ruins of a Gothic castle from the 13th - 15th cent. with the ground plan of a Roman military station from the early 2nd cent. are to be found in the adjoining suburb **Devín.** *Interesting monuments are to be found also in other suburbs.*

The following J. communities used to exist in the nearest vicinity: **Stupava** /Hung. *Stomfa*, Ger. *Stampfen* (a small town 15 km NNW, a synagogue, of unknown origin, was pulled down in the 19th cent., a new synagogue was built in 1803, converted into a storehouse; a cemetery of unknown origin with tombstones from the 1st half of the 17th cent.); **Jur pri Bratislave** /form. *Svätý Jur*, Hung. *Szentgyörgy*, Ger. *Sankt-Georgen* (a town 14 km NE, the first cemetery from about the 1st half of the 18th cent. was liquidated in the first half of the 19th cent., the second cemetery from the 1st half of the 19th cent. was liquidated after 1960; a synagogue presumedly from the late 18th cent., today part of a private house). A J. detention camp used to be near Jur pri Bratislave in 1941-44 through which about 3,000 persons had passed before they were sent to concentration camps.

Explanation of terms

Almemar - or **the bimah** - a raised platform in the centre of the synagogue from which the officiant reads from the Torah scrolls.

Aron ha-kodesh - the shrine or decorated cabinet in which the Torah scrolls are kept. It represents the most significant point in the synagogue or prayer room, situated by the eastern wall.

Bar Mitzve - the ceremony in which a thirteen-year-old Jewish boy reaches the status of a man and becomes a full-fledged member of the Jewish religious congregation. During the ceremony the boy reads from the Torah scrolls for the first time.

Bimah - see almemar.

Cantor - or **chazen** - a preceptor, or "master of prayer", directing prayers before the aron ha-kodesh.

Jewish community - a historical term used for a religious community. From the Middle ages until the 19th century the J. community, besides having jurisdiction over religious matters, enjoyed autonomy in its administrative, economic and legal affairs. From about the mid-19th century J. communities focus mainly on religious matters and we begin to speak about J. religious congregations.

Jewish religious congregation - a religious community, maintaining its own synagogue or prayer hall with a cantor or occasionally also with a rabbi. The term is used for the period beginning from about the second half of the 19th century. Until World War II some J. religious congregations administered different small religious societies in the vicinity. At present synagogue groups in Bohemia and Moravia are part of the J. religious congregation.

Parochet - a decorated curtain which hangs before the aron ha-kodesh.

Religious society - or **prayer society** is a historical term used for a small Jewish religious community maintaining its own prayer room, occasionally with a cantor, established in a place where there was no Jewish religious congregation and administered by one of the J. religious congregations in the district. Religious societies existed in the Czech lands approximately from the mid-19th century until World War II; a synagogue group is its present analogue.

Synagogue group - a small Jewish religious community with its own prayer room, occasionally with a cantor, established in a place where there is no Jewish religious congregation and administered by a J. religious congregation in the vicinity. The term synagogue group was introduced in the Czech Republic after World War II.

Tomb - orohel - a tomb in the shape of a sarcophagus or resembling a little house, usually consisting of several stone slabs.

Torah - a Hebrew handwritten parchment transcript of the Five Books of Moses. The Torah scrolls are the most significant liturgical object in every synagogue or prayer room.

Yeshiva - a college for Talmudic study, with most students receiving a rabbinical degree.

Endnotes

For lack of space it is impossible to list all the sources which helped me to gather the information for this guide. A large amount of information has been taken from the following two principal history anthologies edited by Dr. Hugo Gold - *Die Juden und Judengemeinden Mährens in Vergangenheit und Gegenwart* (published in 1929) and *Die Juden und Judengemeinden Böhmens in Vergangenheit und Gegenwart* (published in 1934) and from several hundreds of regional and local history works. Only after I had completed the manuscript of this guide did I get the opportunity to become acquainted with the *Encyclopaedia Judaica* (published in 1971) since this Israeli encyclopaedia was until 1989 on the so-called list of prohibited literature in our country. For this reason only a minor amount of information could be later included in the text of the guide.

Among other important and helpful sources of information are numerous records kept in the State Central Archives in Prague and in the State Regional Archives in Brno, records assembled by the State Jewish Museum in Prague during the research project in the 50's and 60's and various collections of photographs and maps. Throughout the past years I have also visited most places included in the guide and carried out my personal research.

This book could not have been possibly concluded successfully without the help of several hundreds of individuals: local chroniclers, local town councillors, curators of regional museums and archivists, members of different religious groups, many local historians, witnesses and people who gave personal accounts. I wish to express my gratitude and thank them all for their understanding and willing help.

In spite of my efforts to present precise and objective information, readers may find some facts which are no longer up-to-date or may require more detail. Therefore I would welcome and greatly appreciate all possible comments and disclosure of new facts.

Prague, January 1990

Jiří Fiedler

INDEX OF PLACES

The index of places refers only to places linked with Jewish history. German names of places are given only if their written form is different from the present Czech name of the place: i.e. German versions of names with similar pronunciation and spelling e.g. Boskowitz (Boskovice) are not given. Capital letters refer to one of the 138 main entries, small letters refer to other places mentioned in the guide.

215

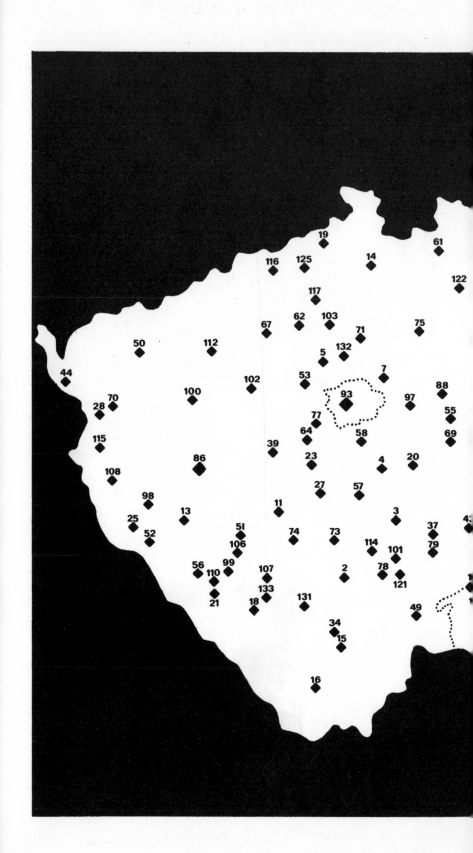